Downward spiral

Manchester University Press

'With a forensic eye and an abundance of jaw-dropping detail, John Bowers paints a picture of the pit into which British public life sank during the age of Boris Johnson. But this is about more than the moral indecencies of one individual. Bowers makes a compelling case that it is the system itself that needs an overhaul, so that no future prime minister can trample on basic standards with such impunity.'

Jonathan Freedland, *Guardian* columnist

'A forensic, scathing dissection of the multiple weaknesses of our democratic order that successive Tory governments exploited shamelessly. This is a must-read and an indispensable manual for those who would reform a political system whose ethical foundations have fallen so low.'

Will Hutton, author of *How Good We Can Be*

'The eminent KC John Bowers believes that our constitutional architecture is no longer fit for purpose. *Downward spiral* is a devastating analysis of the breakdown of ethical standards in public life. He proposes wide-ranging reforms to restore trust in our institutions. This is a book that should be read by every concerned citizen.'

Sir Vernon Bogdanor, Professor of Government, King's College London

'This sadly much-needed book tells a shocking tale of the undermining of parliament, the civil service, ethical codes and good governance. It also sets out an agenda for reinstating integrity and standards in public life. It should be a go-to text for anyone who cares about restoring government's ethical behaviour.'

Baroness Hayter

'With too many cheques and not enough balances in the system, it's time for a new ethical settlement. John Bowers identifies the depths to which our public standards have sunk and suggests a way forwards. Essential reading, especially for those in power or who aspire to power.'

Baroness Royall

'John Bowers has written a very timely book that exposes the damage being done to society by a ruling class that governs without recourse to standards in public life. *Downward spiral* is a wake-up call to all those who care about the future of a fair and accountable political system.'

Robert Verkaik, author of *Posh Boys: How English Public Schools Ruin Britain*

'John Bowers has written a measured, comprehensive and utterly devastating account of the Johnson government's degradation of British public life. Everyone who wishes to restore honour and integrity to the way we are governed should read this outstanding account of how we entered a spiral of decline – and how we can clamber out of it.'

Sir Ivor Crewe, author of *The Blunders of Our Governments*

Downward spiral

Collapsing public standards and how to restore them

John Bowers

Manchester University Press

The right of John Bowers to be identified as the author of this work has been asserted in accordance with the Copyright, Designs and Patents Act 1988.

Published by Manchester University Press
Oxford Road, Manchester, M13 9PL

www.manchesteruniversitypress.co.uk

British Library Cataloguing-in-Publication Data
A catalogue record for this book is available from the British Library

ISBN 978 1 526 16749 1 *hardback*

First published 2024

The publisher has no responsibility for the persistence or accuracy of URLs for any external or third-party internet websites referred to in this book, and does not guarantee that any content on such websites is, or will remain, accurate or appropriate.

Typeset by R. J. Footring Ltd, Derby, UK
Printed in Great Britain by Bell & Bain Ltd, Glasgow

The game of politics certainly does not assure the high moral fibre of people who reach the top.

Professor Yehezkel Dror

Contents

Part III. Cross-cutting issues

Part IV. Conclusion

Prologue

The late Queen's Platinum Jubilee celebration took place on 3 June 2022. It was a magnificent event, held at St Paul's Cathedral. Boris Johnson, in his last weeks as Prime Minister, took to the podium to read a passage chosen for him by unnamed Palace officials. It was surely no coincidence that he was asked to focus on Philippians 4 of the New Testament. 'Whatever is true', Johnson intoned, 'whatever is noble, whatever is right, whatever is pure ... think about such things'.

We can infer that this passage was chosen precisely because Johnson did *not* think about such things. His period in Number 10 was, I will argue, the most corrupt and/or immoral we have seen in the UK since that of Lloyd George, a Prime Minister with a lucrative side-line selling peerages (see Chapter 2). Johnson has often been compared to the 'Welsh wizard', another politician with a very colourful private life.

The paradox is that the voting public knew Johnson did not think much about 'whatever is true' even at the time he won his outstanding eighty-seat majority in 2019. The tide turned only when people began to think that, as one focus group contributor put it, Johnson used to 'lie *for* us', now he 'lies *to* us'. This was referring to 'partygate', the series of COVID rule-breaking events that led to Johnson becoming the first holder of the office of Prime Minister to receive a police penalty. His successor but one, Rishi Sunak, would become the second.

In her James MacTaggart Memorial Lecture,[1] the former BBC *Newsnight* presenter Emily Maitlis rightly described constitutional norms as having been 'trashed' during this period. But when Johnson appeared at his final Prime Minister's Questions on 20 July 2022, he refused to accept blame or apologise for demeaning standards in public life[2] but, rather, said that he thought the rules of the game had changed partway through. Ominously, he signed off with 'hasta la vista baby', channelling Arnold Schwarzenegger in *Terminator 2*.

No one who believes that high standards of conduct are integral to good government should wish to see a second coming of his premiership. During his administration ethics went into a downward spiral.

In this book I ask whether there has been, in recent years, an overall decline in public standards in Britain that is likely to last. Answering this requires a careful assessment of the character and record of Alexander Boris de Pfeffel Johnson. More than anyone else in living memory, he stands accused of bringing the office of Prime Minister into disrepute. This is a serious matter, because the Prime Minister plays a central role in preserving constitutional niceties. He or she should be the person who ensures that others follow the proper standards and generally 'behave'.[3] Crucially, many of these standards are not written down, but are embedded in an implicit understanding of how holders of high office are expected to conduct themselves. One is left wondering with Annette Dittert, the London bureau chief of ARD German TV, whether 'future generations are going to wonder how a shameless PM with only a passing acquaintance with the truth got away with it so easily in one of the world's oldest democracies'.[4]

But this book is not just about Johnson. The decline did not start with him and arguably the spiral has continued since his departure. This is a good time to look at how we police ethics in public life, at who does that policing and what needs to change. During his journey to Downing Street, Johnson revelled in trampling on conventions, but once there the job description required that he be their guardian. I will consider how these conventions work (or do not work) later in the book.

Another part of our constitutional checks and balances that has been undermined in this period is the independence of a civil service that can speak truth to power.[5] One of the less savoury behaviours of the Johnson government – and its brief 'continuation' under Liz Truss – was the (mis)treatment of civil servants, including several Permanent Secretaries. As the former Lord Chancellor Charlie Falconer, a Labour peer, told me:

> Government should not give any impression that ethics are optional for governing. What keeps government ethical is having a bureaucracy that is permanent and essentially honest. That is why it was so distressing to see Permanent Secretaries being terminated.[6]

Worse, there were threats to the rule of law itself during the Johnson premiership, such as the many equivocations over the Northern Ireland Protocol, a binding international treaty. There were attempts to prorogue Parliament and a bid to overturn the House of Commons Committee on Standards' verdict on Owen Paterson.

I realised I needed to write this book when Johnson refused to accept the findings of the Independent Adviser on Ministers' Interests, Sir Alex Allan. Allan determined that Priti Patel, the Home Secretary, had acted in breach of the Ministerial Code by bullying her officials, but after sitting on the damning report for months the Prime Minister took no action against her. Allan resigned and was not replaced for several months. His successor, Lord Geidt, left by the same door after an uncomfortable and even humiliating tenure of office.[7] As a lawyer I found this outrageous, although it is not strictly a matter of law.

So I want to ask: Is there something wrong with our institutions that enabled this particular Prime Minister to rise to the top – or was he an aberration? Did Johnson merely reveal weaknesses in the rules that the 'good chaps'[8] who preceded him tended to obscure? Do we need ethical watchdogs which bark louder? Can we move on secure in the knowledge that ethical standards have now finally reasserted themselves, given that, over the course of his administration, some fifty ministers resigned over various outrages 'up with which they could no longer put' (to paraphrase Churchill)?

Regarding the last question, there are already signs that the answer is 'no'. On taking office in October 2022, Rishi Sunak said he would put integrity at the heart of his commencement speech outside 10 Downing Street, but his list of mistakes soon expanded to include appointing or retaining Nadhim Zahawi, Gavin Williamson and Dominic Raab, and supporting Richard Sharp for many months as he sought to cling on as Chair of the BBC, all of which are covered in this book. Further, it appears that the Future Fund, the Covid start-up fund set up by Rishi Sunak when he was Chancellor, invested almost £2 million in firms linked to Akshata Murty, who is Mrs Sunak, including a luxury underwear business called Heist Studios.[9] This was not declared in the Parliamentary Register of Interests.

The Sunak government's single response to various reports calling for change to the system of ethical regulation – those of the Committee for Standards in Public Life, the Public Administration and Constitutional Affairs Committee and Boardman's report on the firm Greensill Capital – entitled *Strengthening Ethics and Integrity in Central Government*, appeared on 20 July 2023. It was two years late and offered little by way of change. There is to be no statutory embedding of the ethics regulators and little reform of the revolving door or lobbying. There is promised to be a contractual duty for civil servants to obey rules on jobs after they leave and ministers will have to sign up to a deed of undertaking to do the same. Non-executive directors of government departments will also come within the public appointments structure. This is too little too late.

More broadly, the questions I ask are: Are there too few balances and too many cheques (often from foreign interests)? Are the guard rails designed to prevent a slide downwards robust and resilient? Most importantly: What is to be done? A relevant question was formulated succinctly by the Bishop of Oxford in a Parliamentary debate on standards in public life:

> How do we intentionally grow a community of diverse public servants who are ethically formed and equipped, and have the inner capacity to be honest, open, objective, accountable and selfless?[10]

My thesis is that we are witnessing an ongoing downward spiral in public standards that could unhinge the British state.[11] There has been an atmospheric pollution of our public life because of moral failure. This book will try to explain how we got here and what we need to do to reinstate public trust.

Part I

Setting the scene

Chapter 1

Introduction: falling standards (and masonry)

Not many people realise that the Houses of Parliament constitute a Royal Palace. It is a house of grandeur and mystique, a grade I listed building, located within a UNESCO world heritage site. Built in the middle of the nineteenth century in the Perpendicular Gothic style, popular during the fifteenth century, the Palace of Westminster has high vaulted ceilings and tiled floors following designs by Charles Barry and Augustus Pugin. Westminster Hall, within its curtilage, was the site of Simon de Montfort's first Parliament in 1265.

Since October 2012, Parliament has been debating plans for the extensive restoration of this building. Much work needs to be done to return the edifice to its former glory. There has been talk of temporarily relocating the workplace of Parliamentarians to Birmingham, York or Manchester to allow for reconstruction. Even Hull was at one time proposed, although this was perhaps put forward in jest (I say this as a Grimsby boy). Despite numerous reports and endless debates, however, MPs are yet to come close to agreement on what is to happen.

This impasse has resulted in actual physical danger lurking in this Palace. In April 2018, a football-sized chunk of masonry broke away from a stone angel on Parliament's Victoria Tower and plummeted 230 feet to the ground. In October 2017, an MP's car windscreen was smashed when a piece of masonry fell. There have been many reports about dodgy electrics.

Something similar has happened to our constitutional ethical architecture. It has wonderful grandeur in design, but is no longer fit for purpose, and politicians cannot agree on a way forward on this either. In the meantime, big chunks are falling off the constitutional firmament. Trust, the foundation of government in a liberal democracy, is in decline, and real damage is being inflicted. Cynicism about the political process has become rampant. Moral authority has dissipated.

What happens when the safety mechanisms have gone and the guard rails have rusted?[1] This is a question of conventions, culture and expectations. Ethical behaviour should come naturally to those serving the public. Conflicts of interest and, even more so, actual corruption obviously corrode trust in politics. Cronyism and special favours can slide too easily into authoritarianism and contempt for the rule of law.

When that essential trust breaks down, government is in grave danger of decay. Democracy really works only if citizens are satisfied that the political process is legitimate and that public servants operate on the basis of integrity. As Clement Attlee said, 'a leader has got to be trusted. When men start distrusting him, he stops being a leader.'[2] The very rule of law is in jeopardy if standards of public life – that is, the behaviour of the politicians we need to trust – slip. Without accountability on the part of those individuals, we are left with a system that is no longer responsive to the public whom it is designed to serve.[3] Integrity should act as a lubricant for political systems. It means that those who govern are not mendacious, that they are not trying to harm the interests of the voters whom they serve, and that they are not actively attempting to conceal information.[4]

Of course, there never was a golden time when absolutely everyone abided by rules that were crystal clear and known by all public servants, whether they were personally good or otherwise,[5] as can be seen in the next chapter, where I offer a brief history of standards in British public life. As long as there has been a government there have been government scandals. However, the University of Sussex's Centre for the Study of Corruption, founded in 2011, concluded that Johnson's government was more corrupt than any UK Government since the Second World War and that 'there has been an absolute failure of integrity at No 10 which has consequences for democracy'.[6] Transparency International counted 120 incidents between 2015 and 2020 when ministers, MPs or Lords fell short of expected standards, significantly more than in other periods.[7] During the later stages of the Johnson government, hardly a day went by without some ethical problem; there was a veritable tsunami of scandals. Some blew over quickly, as the relentless twenty-four-hour news cycle moved on to something else, but others lingered in the public consciousness. And this gathering storm swept from one area to another.

Perception may be as important as reality here. The overwhelming majority of the public *think* standards have declined, and that in itself has an impact on political life. In terms of trust, MPs have entered an unseemly competition with estate agents and journalists for bottom place in the regularly published overall charts of who can be trusted in the minds of the public.[8] Some 41% of people questioned in an opinion poll taken in July 2021 rated ministers' standards of conduct as quite low or very low, compared with 24% of respondents who viewed standards as quite high or very high, a net score of –17. MPs ranked very low, with only 20% taking a positive view and 44% a negative view, a net score of –24.[9]

The British Social Attitudes Survey for 2021 shows trust in government at a record low: 15% trust the government all or most of the time while 79% think the way we are governed is in need of 'a lot or great deal' of improvement.[10] There is a deeply felt frustration that there is no real accountability to the voting public, whatever the formal processes are. Ethical concerns are at the heart of this.

The cynicism arising from lack of trust threatens to have long-term real-world consequences. It feeds into the decline in the public's propensity to vote,[11] the low level of understanding of politics, and the increasing disengagement from the political process, especially among the young. The Hansard Society's *Audit of Political Engagement 10* (2019) begins:

> opinions of the system of governing are at their lowest point in 15 years – worse now than in the aftermath of the MPs' expenses scandal which broke in 2009. The public are pessimistic about the country's problems and their solution, with sizeable numbers willing to entertain radical political changes as a result.[12]

As another measure, a Gallup poll in 1944 found that 35% of voters thought that politicians were in public life for themselves, while in November 2021 this had risen to 63%. Overall, 43% of the public think standards of conduct today are worse than five to ten years ago, with 19% saying that standards are higher and 37% saying they are the same.[13] Some 66% of the British public agree that MPs and ministers are too easily influenced by the rich and powerful.[14]

This impairs Britain's standing abroad, as Rishi Sunak acknowledged when interviewed during the G20 summit in Bali in November 2022.[15] When the credit rating agency Moody's downgraded the UK in October 2020, it referred to 'the weakening of the UK's institutions and governance'.

As Sir John Major said in a keynote speech, 'where governments fall short, candour is the best means of shoring up support. But that candour must be freely offered – not dragged out under the searchlight of inquiries'.[16] Indeed, according to the academic researchers Jonathan Rose and Paul Heywood, the higher the level of integrity within a state, the better the 'outcomes' of that state – in terms of health, wealth and well-being.[17]

Ethical infrastructure in the Johnson period

There were, of course, many factors at work from 2019 to 2022, besides the personality of the Prime Minister and his erratic and sometimes immoral leadership. Those three years were a tumultuous time, and there was increased anger and vitriol in our political discourse, injected by the divisiveness of having gone since 2010 through four general elections and three referendums, as well as the long-running deadlock over Brexit and the challenges of the COVID-19 pandemic. It was a time of rising populism.

But there were also deeper structural issues, including a feeling that the best and brightest no longer go into politics and that there are few 'big beasts' in the Cabinet. Johnson was not interested in surrounding himself with major figures. The veteran journalist Michael Crick told me that Johnson 'has tall poppy syndrome and does not want to be overshadowed in Cabinet; until Nadine Dorries was appointed no one was older than fifty-eight'. The *Guardian* columnist Rafael Behr put it colourfully, saying Johnson 'turned the Cabinet into a kennel of nodding dogs'.[18]

The former Chair of the Committee on Standards in Public Life, Lord Evans of Weardale, summarised the situation to me thus:

> Undeniably, we have had a bumpy few years. We have had a Prime Minister with a conceptual discomfort with regulation who emphasised direct accountability with electors and a suspicion of unelected intermediate bodies. The political context of the referendum vote and the 2019 election meant that there was a tribe who saw themselves as set against the established way of doing things.[19]

Johnson set the worst possible example in a system that works only if politicians act like 'good chaps'. That is the theory behind our constitutional conventions, with the Prime Minister acting as the guardian of so many of these conventions of our constitution. I will explore this system in more detail in Chapter 14. In the final days of Johnson's premiership, Sir Chris Bryant, Chair of the Commons Committee on Standards, told me that 'The Prime Minister sets a terrible example on ethics and this percolates downwards'.[20]

The guardians

The decline in public standards is happening despite the existence of a complex, reasonably well-staffed and wide-ranging web of committees and structures that act as guardians. There is a confusing patchwork of such bodies. In Part II I will review in particular the work of the Committee on Standards in Public Life (CSPL), the National Audit Office (NAO), the Advisory Committee on Business Appointments (ACOBA), the Commissioner for Public Appointments, the Civil Service Commission, the Independent Adviser on Ministers' Interests, the Electoral Commission, the House of Lords Appointments Commission (HoLAC) and the Registrar of Consultant Lobbyists. I assess their performance and offer a score out of ten. There are others broadly within this curtilage, such as the Independent Parliamentary Standards Authority (IPSA), the Parliamentary Commissioner for Standards, the Commons Public Administration and Constitutional Affairs Committee (PACAC), the House of Lords Privileges Committee and the Boundary Commissions, but they are beyond the scope of the book.

These separate referees of democracy, which we can call an 'integrity branch' of constitutional governance ('a Fifth Estate'), could be brought under one overarching body, though it is not clear whether that would be wise. Some bodies are empowered to launch investigations and sanction breaches while others are merely advisory. There is overlap between them, and some lack sufficient independence, let alone the resources necessary for carrying out their role. But others, for instance the NAO, work well.

Fortunately for me, there is a readily available set of standards by which to make my assessment. This was provided by the Nolan Committee (formally, the Committee on Standards in Public Life, CSPL), set up by John Major in 1994.[21] The Nolan Principles, also known as the Seven Principles of Public Life, ought to suffuse the life blood of public bodies from the lowest to the highest.[22] Baroness Manningham-Buller, former Director General of MI5, told me that she can recite them by heart. Despite significant societal and political change, these Principles still apply to anyone who works as a public office-holder nationally and locally, and to all who are appointed to work in the civil service, local government, police, courts and probation services, non-departmental public bodies (NDPBs), and in the health, education, social and care services. They also extend to other sectors that deliver public services. They provide a set of ethical gold standards and still resonate today. The primary criticism directed against them is that they do not cover equality of treatment.

The Nolan Report laid down three 'common threads' for ensuring that the Principles were properly understood and followed – codes of conduct, independent scrutiny, and guidance and education. Lord Nolan was clear that the necessary guidance and education on ethical standards should encompass training and in particular an induction.[23] They can still be found (as slightly amended) in many other operational documents, such as the Ministerial

Code and in both the House of Commons and the House of Lords Codes of Conduct.

The Principles are worth setting out in full:

1. Selflessness
Holders of public office should act solely in terms of the public interest.

2. Integrity
Holders of public office must avoid placing themselves under any obligation to people or organisations that might try inappropriately to influence them in their work. They should not act or take decisions in order to gain financial or other material benefits for themselves, their family, or their friends. They must declare and resolve any interests and relationships.

3. Objectivity
Holders of public office must act and take decisions impartially, fairly and on merit, using the best evidence and without discrimination or bias.

4. Accountability
Holders of public office are accountable to the public for their decisions and actions and must submit themselves to the scrutiny necessary to ensure this.

5. Openness
Holders of public office should act and take decisions in an open and transparent manner. Information should not be withheld from the public unless there are clear and lawful reasons for so doing.

6. Honesty
Holders of public office should be truthful.

7. Leadership
Holders of public office should exhibit these principles in their own behaviour and treat others with respect. They should actively promote and robustly support the principles and challenge poor behaviour wherever it occurs.[24]

These Principles are not law or constitutional conventions, although they have achieved a quasi-constitutional status. Lord Evans of Weardale explained that they were designed to be a high-level statement 'of the overall direction in adhering to standards', and were not to be enforced as such.[25] Their role is to stand behind the rules and assist in their interpretation.

Dr Claire Foster-Gilbert, Director of the Westminster Abbey Institute, has observed:

> It is much harder to be clear about principles. I mean, a rule is something that you keep or break, whereas a principle is something you aspire to. If we take the Nolan Principles, I can assure you that I have been selfish, I have not practised selflessness all the time, and I am sure that I have been dishonest in some way or other and not been open, and so forth, but I would hope that I would try to be those things. So, you simply can't apply principles in the same way that you can apply rules.[26]

Crucially, despite the continued functioning of select ethical bodies, one of the features of the decline we are witnessing is the progressive undermining of watchdogs designed to protect good standards. The voices of experienced experts and independent advisers like Lord Bew on House of Lords appointments and Sir Alex Allan and Lord Geidt as the Independent Adviser on Ministers' Interests have been ignored and/or rejected (although it could be argued that their voices did contribute to the climate that ultimately brought about Johnson's downfall). Supposedly independent bodies and those designed to oversee standards are packed by Conservative members or supporters or those with close links to the party. Further, public appointments are increasingly made on narrow party political lines rather than on merit.

Of course, there has been corruption at the highest level and rule bending over several millennia. Numerous politicians have failed to resist the temptations presented in public life. Ministers have regularly had to resign, and there have been many sleaze fests, such as cash for questions and the MPs' expenses scandal,[27] which have rocked public confidence, sometimes in the political class as a whole. I will return to these themes – but first, a sense of history.

Chapter 2

A brief history of standards in public life

Corruption has always existed in British politics, and it has not been confined to one party. It has taken many forms, from breaches of written or unwritten codes for ministers, MPs and political parties to outright criminality. The same themes keep reappearing, and sometimes the proposed solutions have been applied too hastily. It generally requires a crisis to create a reaction,[1] but unfortunately that means the reaction is often knee-jerk.

Three hundred years in a few hundred words

Broadly speaking, the journey over the centuries has been from the blatant to the subtle, as high-profile scandals have prompted new regulations and monitoring bodies. King James I was quite overt: he created the title of baronet and sold it for £1,500 a time to raise money for his war in Ireland.[2] During Charles II's reign, influence pedlars positioned themselves on the very stairs of the House of Commons. These early lobbyists would slip parcels of guineas under MPs' dinner plates during banquets.[3] In 1695 the Speaker of the House of Commons, John Trevor, was expelled for taking a bribe of 1,000 guineas from the City of London in connection with the Orphans Bill.[4]

Robert Walpole, often dubbed Britain's first Prime Minister, was habitually corrupt. In 1712, he was accused of venality in the matter of two forage contracts for Scotland. Impeached by the House of Commons and found guilty by the House of Lords, he was expelled from Parliament and imprisoned in the Tower of London for six months. Nonetheless, following his release, he was re-elected as MP for King's Lynn.

There were significant reforms in the mid-nineteenth century, prompted partly by the elite's fear of mass revolt but also by the strong Protestant ethics in vogue at the time. However, they had their limits. Many aspects of corruption were demonstrated by the Marconi scandal, which started just before the

First World War and drew in Liberal ministers such as the Attorney General, Rufus Isaacs, and the Chancellor of the Exchequer, David Lloyd George. The English Marconi Company was negotiating a contract with the UK government for the supply of telegraph stations linking various parts of the British Empire. Ministers used their inside knowledge to make significant profits. Shares had been offered to the ministers by Godfrey Isaacs, the brother of the Attorney General, who was the joint managing director of English Marconi and a director of the related American company. This offer was made at a price which was lower than that at which they were to be made available to the public. It was eventually established that no minister had actually trafficked in English Marconi shares, but the minority report of the inquiry into the affair said that the ministers had conducted themselves in a manner which was inconsistent with 'the highest traditions of public life'.[5]

As a Prime Minister, Lloyd George was described by Stanley Baldwin, his Conservative rival, as 'a real corrupter of public life'.[6] One notorious feature of his premiership was the credible allegation that honours and titles were being sold for cash. The Prevention of Corruption Act 1916 was passed to make such delinquent actions easier to prove, while also extending the range of public bodies covered.[7] The Honours (Prevention of Abuses) Act 1925 followed, tightening the rules further.[8]

When Lloyd George left office, he apparently had amassed a fortune of £1.5 million (equivalent to about £50 million now). Yet, as we will often see in the book, it did not take long for the system to correct itself. Stanley Baldwin, his next-but-one successor, was known for his decency, decorum and fundamental honesty; he was the ultimate 'good chap'. Beyond the two Acts there had been no institutional change, but the change of leadership sufficed, and the familiar system of checks and balances was kicked back into shape.

With the unimpeachable Clement Attlee at the helm, the 1945–1951 Labour government was generally scandal free; nonetheless, there were a few incidents of note.[9] In 1947, Sydney Stanley (who would now be termed a consultant lobbyist) was found to have traded on his political connections to solicit money from businesspeople seeking to circumvent post-war trading restrictions.[10] Two years later, John Belcher, the Parliamentary Under-Secretary at the Board of Trade, resigned as a minister and MP after it was revealed he had accepted gifts from dubious businesspeople.

Harold Macmillan's government enjoyed a massive majority, but even so it struggled to recover from its most salacious scandal, which was sexual rather than financial. In 1963, the Minister for War, John Profumo, was exposed for having an affair with a woman who was involved at the same time with a Soviet military attaché. Profumo resigned when he was shown to have lied to Parliament. It was Harold Wilson who led the relentless attack on the Macmillan government over this. Macmillan went as Prime Minister soon after, ostensibly on the grounds of illness, although he lived for several decades afterwards.

Wilson's government itself suffered from several episodes of sleaze, prompting him to set up the Royal Commission on Standards in Public Life. Under the chairmanship of Lord Salmon, it focused on conflicts of interest and the risk of corruption.[11] The most serious and memorable issue came, however, in 1976, at the end of Wilson's second premiership, when a series of unsuitable persons were ennobled on what became known as the 'lavender list' because it was apparently written on lavender-coloured paper. This was put together by Wilson's long-term political adviser Marcia Falkender, who herself became a peer. This was a clear case of chumocracy in action,[12] and it would be replicated decades later by Boris Johnson, whose outgoing Honours List included several unsuitable characters, some of whom were vetoed by the House of Lords Appointments Commission.

The Poulson scandal was a cross-party corruption affair mainly involving local government. It erupted in the early 1970s under the Heath government and ensnared many Labour and Conservative politicians, including the very senior Conservative figure and former Chancellor of the Exchequer Reginald Maudling and, to a lesser degree, Anthony Crosland, the Labour philosopher and MP for Great Grimsby, who was eventually to become the Foreign Secretary.[13] John Poulson was an architect based in the north of England who once boasted that he had the biggest practice in Europe, but who gained it by bribing his way into many lucrative government contracts.[14] His partners in these crimes were T. Dan Smith, the Labour leader of Newcastle City Council, who was sentenced to six years' imprisonment on counts of corruption, and Andrew Cunningham (father of Jack, a minister under Jim Callaghan), who was handed a five-year sentence, reduced to three on appeal. When Poulson was declared bankrupt, a revealing trove of 27,000 documents was presented at his bankruptcy hearing. These showed a welter of corruption involving local government, councillors and MPs, including Albert Roberts and John Cordle,[15] Labour and Conservative respectively.[16]

The Major government: arms to Iraq and cash for questions

The eleven years of Margaret Thatcher's government were generally scandal free, leaving John Major with a hard act to follow. He was considered a reliable figure, and pushed a wide-ranging agenda of so-called 'back to basics' in an attempt to reassert what some described as 'Victorian values'. But this ran adrift following the exposure of affairs by ministers and sundry other scandals.[17] First there was the arms-to-Iraq affair, in which it was revealed that the government had endorsed sales of British-made armaments to the regime of Saddam Hussein. Around the same time, Jonathan Aitken, a former Cabinet minister, was found to have lied about payments from an arms dealer and about who had paid his bill at the Ritz Hotel in Paris. Aitken fabricated evidence in a libel claim he brought against the *Guardian*[18] and was apparently willing for his daughter to give false testimony. In a third major scandal, David Mellor, the Culture Minister, resigned over his links with a Palestinian official, following an affair with Antonia de Sancha that, according to the press, apparently involved sex in a Chelsea FC shirt.

But one scandal in particular would have a lasting influence on the scrutiny of standards in British public life. It led to the establishment of a new committee and a set of principles for holders of public office. It began in October 1994, when the *Guardian* alleged that a well-connected Parliamentary lobbyist, Ian Greer,[19] had bribed two Tory MPs to ask questions in Parliament and to perform other lobbying tasks on behalf of the majority-owner of the Harrods department store, Mohamed Al-Fayed.[20] The Fayed brothers had spent no less than £615 million purchasing the upmarket shop, and questions were raised as to how they had acquired so much wealth after only a short time in business. The *Guardian* accused Greer of paying the MPs Neil Hamilton and Tim Smith (the latter in a clutch of brown envelopes) to table Parliamentary questions on his behalf for the sum of £2,000 per question. They took up Al-Fayed's concern that an investigation would be started into how he acquired the most famous store in the UK. Significantly, Hamilton failed to disclose this loot in the House of Commons Register of Members' Financial Interests. It also emerged that the well-connected Greer retained on his payroll no less than three officers (all Conservative backbenchers) of the Commons Trade and Industry Select Committee.[21]

Smith resigned as an MP immediately after admitting to having accepted payments from Al-Fayed himself. Hamilton and Greer, however, issued libel writs in the High Court against the *Guardian*. Six weeks later, in December 1994, Mohamed Al-Fayed alleged that he had paid Hamilton directly, in addition to the original allegations that Greer was the paymaster to Hamilton. Hamilton denied this new allegation. Sir Gordon Downey, a former senior civil servant, carried out a specific investigation. In a 900-page report, released in early July 1997, he cleared Greer, Hamilton and Smith of the *Guardian's* original allegations, while simultaneously arguing that the testimony of three Fayed employees amounted to 'compelling evidence' that they had processed cash payments to Hamilton. Despite this, there were to be no repercussions.

The Nolan Report: 'an ethical workshop'

By now, it was clear there was a need to take a wider look at standards in public life. In October 1994, Major called in the senior law lord Lord Nolan to investigate the 'standards of conduct of all public office-holders'. Major described it as 'an ethical workshop', and in his autobiography he expresses pride in having set it up.[22] Major's announcement included the assertion that 'This country has an international reputation for the integrity and honour of its public institutions', a theme to which he would return twenty-eight years later, in a speech at the Institute for Government in 2022 that offered a significant rebuke to the then Prime Minister, Boris Johnson.[23]

Nolan's task was to oversee a committee to 'examine current concerns about standards of conduct of all holders of public office, including arrangements relating to financial and commercial activities'. He was then 'to make recommendations as to any changes in present arrangements which might be required'. The resulting report set the gold standard for morality in public life, and its strong legacy continues to this day, although under Johnson it was more honoured in the breach than in the observance.[24]

The first Nolan Report considered standards in the House of Commons, central government (ministers and civil servants) and non-departmental public bodies (NDPBs). The Committee received some 2,000 letters and written submissions. A hundred witnesses gave 'live' evidence to the Nolan Committee. Professor Ivor Crewe, the influential political scientist, presented his research, which showed that 77% of the British public thought that MPs cared more about special interests than about ordinary people; only 28% thought that MPs lived up to a moral code.[25]

The report's elegantly written pages, dating from a time before the cacophony that is social media was even thought of, make for a soothing read.[26] It is difficult to imagine later governments setting up such a body as Nolan or indeed any truly independent inquiry on governance or ethics. Even if they did so, the likelihood of a consensus being found on these matters between politicians of different hues is remote; public debate is far more polarised today.[27]

Nolan's general and balanced judgement was that 'the great majority of men and women in public life are honest and hard-working and observe high ethical standards', which is still probably true. Most importantly, in the long-term, the report led to the creation of an independent system for regulating public appointments (now under strain)[28] and to the establishment of the Parliamentary Commissioner for Standards, among other initiatives which were supported by all parties. The report stressed the need for independent scrutiny and monitoring as a common theme to be prized across the many issues considered.[29] Importantly, it also said that those in senior positions must set an unimpeachable example and should follow the Seven Principles of selflessness, integrity, objectivity, accountability, openness, honesty and leadership.[30] The Committee's primary finding was that MPs should not be available for financial hire; they should be banned from selling lobbying services or accepting money to ask Parliamentary questions. At the time, 30% of MPs held consultancies of some sort. The Committee recommended that paid work as general multi-client Parliamentary consultants should be restricted, as it was inconsistent with their public duties.

This Nolan Committee has continued in existence ever since as the Committee on Standards in Public Life (CSPL), with similarly wide terms of reference to 'examine current concerns about standards of conduct of all holders of public office'.[31] There have, however, been several attempts to abolish it or limit its powers, as is shown in Chapter 9.

In many respects, the CSPL is still looking at much the same problems it did when first established, in an ethical equivalent of Groundhog Day. In 2021 the Committee reviewed what was then most relevant in terms of ethics in the public sphere and concluded that the basic building blocks for promoting high standards remain much as they had been identified in the Committee's first *Standards Matter* report:

- a set of broadly expressed values which everyone can understand;
- codes of practice elaborating on what the Seven Nolan Principles mean in the particular circumstances of an organisation;
- effective internal processes to embed a culture of high standards and leader-ship by example;
- proportionate, risk-based external scrutiny.[32]

Nolan and post-ministerial jobs

The original report also restricted ministers taking roles after leaving office for a period of up to two years, unless an advisory committee had approved it. The Advisory Committee on Business Appointments (ACOBA) had already been set up some decades before under Harold Wilson (albeit under a different name), but had dealt only with senior civil servants.

The Nolan Committee's guidance on jobs for former ministers was, however, specific: it was, they thought, in the overall public interest that there should be as much interchange as possible between the private and public sectors,[33] but in particular cases there should be restrictions because 'Ministers have the opportunity whilst in Government to take decisions which may favour or disadvantage outside bodes including individual firms'.[34]

As to the question of second jobs for MPs, which has remained contentious since, the Nolan Committee accepted the views of Tony Newton, the then Conservative Leader of the House of Commons, who gave evidence to it. He expressed the belief that the holding of second jobs by MPs was of benefit for the public. The argument was that no one would gain by having MPs cut off from the experience of the contacts they had outside politics. We will consider this refrain, which is still heard, among Conservative MPs in particular, in Chapter 12.

Nolan and public appointments

Nolan opined that public appointments should be decided on merit but ministers should also take into account the diversity of the boards to which the appointments were being made, to ensure that there was a balance of skills and backgrounds on each of them. This referred to appointments to NDPBs and NHS bodies.[35]

The government told Nolan that it was 'committed to the principle that selection for public appointments should be made on merit by the well-informed choice of individuals who through their qualifications, experience or qualities match the needs of the public body and the post in question'.[36] This need to balance merit with decision making by ministers who will have a strong political agenda (and who are ultimately accountable to Parliament) is very much part of today's discourse.

Tony Blair and Gordon Brown

With this guidance provided by Nolan, there were high hopes for a stronger ethical regime in the era of New Labour. Tony Blair seemed to be a new type of politician. He was younger and appeared cleaner cut, and he was initially a firm favourite of the media, including normally Conservative-supporting newspapers. He appeared classless, with a hint of an estuary accent, although he had actually attended Fettes, often referred to as Scotland's version of Eton. The Labour Party manifesto for the 1997 general election was even entitled *New Labour: Because Britain Deserves Better*, and the theme tune incessantly played during the campaign was the pop classic 'Things can only get better'. The key section on standards in the Labour manifesto was bravely, if foolhardily, entitled 'We will clean up politics'. The document described what it saw as 'the debasing of democracy' during the Major years.

Party political funding was a source of ongoing angst, as it has been in one form or another ever since. New Labour made the specific pledge to the 'reform of party funding to end sleaze', with the commitment to legislate so that parties would be required to declare the source of all donations above a minimum figure, which Labour already did voluntarily in its own party reports. Blair won the election with a massive majority and was in a strong position to do virtually anything he wished. Foreign funding of parties was indeed soon banned by the Political Parties, Elections and Referendums Act 2000. This did not, however, prevent a series of scandals from tarnishing New Labour from virtually the start of its administration, and it was ironic that the first elephant trap into which the government stumbled related to the link between political funding and policy. The spark was the revelation that the chief executive of Formula One Motor Racing, Bernie Ecclestone, had given £1 million to the Labour Party, apparently in return for the promise of an exemption for his sport from the forthcoming ban on tobacco advertising. This special treatment would last until October 2006. To most people this did not pass the all-important 'smell test' – if it smelt like a scandal it probably was (an inexact approach we will encounter again).

The government originally denied that there was any form of *quid pro quo* for this legislative change. Sir Patrick Neill QC, then Chair of the CSPL (whose remit had been extended to political party funding), said, however, that the very appearance of taking Ecclestone's money raised questions of honesty and thus offended the rules. The donation was accordingly returned. Blair then found himself in the unaccustomed position of having to fight off the sort of sleaze allegations he had hurled so effectively at the Major government. He famously went on television saying that he was a 'pretty straight kind of guy' – a hipper version of claiming to be a member of the 'good chaps' tribe. He assured John Humphrys in the *On the Record* TV programme that he would never do 'anything improper. I never have.' [37]

This was not the only scandal to tarnish New Labour: there was the Coal Fund, which appeared to favour Labour seats (foreshadowing the allegations in respect of the Johnson government's Towns and Levelling Up

Funds),[38] the Union Modernisation Fund (UMF), which appeared to give trade unions money for supporting the government, and there were various 'Tony's cronies' rows about public appointments, including what the tabloids misogynistically dubbed the 'quango queens'. All of this knocked the sheen off the new administration.

The Blair government also saw the resignations of one of Blair's closest advisers, Peter Mandelson, while Secretary of State for Trade and Industry, and of Geoffrey Robinson, the Paymaster General, both over a loan from the latter to the former when one of Robinson's companies was being investigated by Mandelson's ministry. Ron Davies MP, the Secretary of State for Wales, resigned over what he called 'a moment of madness' on Clapham Common (a gay encounter) in 1998.[39] Tessa Jowell, the Culture Minister, failed to reveal a 'gift' of £350,000 to her husband from his client, the media magnate Silvio Berlusconi (later the Italian Prime Minister), which was used to pay off their joint mortgage.

During this period, the former Conservative MP and novelist Jeffrey Archer, who was competing to be the Conservative candidate for Mayor of London, was jailed for what the trial judge, Mr Justice Potts, said was 'as serious an offence of perjury as I have had experience of and I have been able to find in the books'. Archer had created a false alibi that helped him win £500,000 in a 1986 libel claim against a newspaper that asserted he had slept with a prostitute.

The most significant and long-lasting New Labour scandal by far was the cash-for-honours imbroglio in 2006 and 2007, concerning the apparent connection between loans to the party and the award of peerages (a recurrent theme throughout history). Loans were adopted as a means of exploiting an apparent loophole in the political funding system which New Labour had itself set up. To many, it looked to be straightforward corruption. Although anyone donating even small sums of money to a political party then had to declare this as a matter of public record, those *loaning* money at commercial rates of interest were not required to make any public declaration at all.

Blair's most serious travails began when Desmond Smith, a government education adviser, was arrested for an offence under the Honours (Prevention of Abuses) Act 1925. It was alleged that he had let it be known that those who funded school academies could expect knighthoods and peerages in return. In March 2006, several men nominated for life peerages by Tony Blair were rejected by the House of Lords Appointments Commission.[40] The one characteristic they shared was that they had loaned large amounts of money, totalling about £14 million, to the Labour Party, at the suggestion of Lord

Levy, chief fundraiser for the party and a close tennis-playing friend of Blair. It was alleged that the peerages were a *quid pro quo* for these loans, although Blair subsequently asserted that 'There were very good reasons for all of them being on the list',[41] without identifying those reasons.

The incident resulted in three complaints to the Metropolitan Police by political opponents of the Prime Minister for perverting the course of justice. There was a full-scale police investigation, during which senior members of the Labour Party (including Blair, his Chief of Staff, Jonathan Powell, and Ruth Turner, a political adviser) were questioned by the Metropolitan Police under the leadership of John Yates, the Deputy Assistant Commissioner. Powell and Turner were interviewed under caution and Blair was questioned, although not under caution, no less than three times, which was unprecedented for a Prime Minister (PM).

In July 2006, Lord Levy, who was not only Tony Blair's chief fundraiser but also became the PM's personal envoy to the Middle East, was enjoying a pleasant birthday lunch with his family when he was told by his solicitor that he had to report to Colindale Police Station, where he was to be arrested.[42] Levy was questioned under caution and later released on bail. A note from Turner to Powell came to light afterwards reporting Levy's request for her 'to lie for him' (which was denied by Levy).[43] Blair in his autobiography describes the period as 'Eighteen months of absolute hell for all concerned. It was a running sore of the most poisonous and debilitating kind.'[44] Many people would say there was justified concern.

In July 2007, the Crown Prosecution Service (then under Ken Macdonald as Director of Public Prosecutions) decided not to bring any charges against any of these individuals.[45] The Service's decision statement indicated that while peerages may have been given in exchange for loans, it could not find *direct* evidence that this *quid pro quo* had been agreed in advance, which would have been needed for successful prosecutions. The whole episode, however, sapped the morale and reputation of the Blair government. And there was more to come, although not involving the upper echelons.

While I was writing this book, records of the New Labour government were released by the National Archives. These showed that in 1998 Jonathan Powell had warned Blair that he needed to get to grips with a lack of discipline among ministers, especially because of potential issues of probity, and that the government should set up a 'commissioner for ministerial ethics'. Powell thought that Gordon Brown (then the Chancellor of the Exchequer) might be breaching rules on ministerial standards, especially by using official funds to pay for his newsletter to party members and for party fundraising receptions.

The expenses scandal: a plague on both parties' houses

Perhaps the most notorious of twenty-first-century sleaze stories – the MPs' expenses scandal – burst into public attention in the dying days of the Brown administration.[46] In this case, the stain spread equally across all parties. The affair started with a request in February 2008 under the Freedom of Information Act for the release of details of MPs' expenses claims. The House of Commons authorities announced that there would be publication of MPs' expenses, but with certain information that was deemed 'sensitive' removed, and that this would commence in July 2009. In the meantime, there was a massive leak of this information to the *Daily Telegraph*, based on a stolen computer disk the newspaper had bought.[47] In May 2009, the *Daily Telegraph* began publishing expenses claims made by all 650 MPs and members of the House of Lords over the past several years.

Some of the claims submitted were indeed astonishing. Those which made the most impact on the public included expenses claims for a duck house (Peter Viggers MP), 500 sacks of manure (David Heathcoat-Amory MP) and moat cleaning (Douglas Hogg MP).[48] A large number of resignations, sackings, de-selections and retirement announcements ensued, together with abject public apologies and the repayment of expenses by many.[49] Several members or former members of both the Commons and Lords were prosecuted and sentenced to terms of imprisonment.[50] Nothing else previously had generated such widespread anger against the political class as a whole.

Gerald Shamash is a solicitor who has been carrying out electoral legal work for the Labour Party since 1983. He told me, in a gap as we changed ends during a game of tennis, that 'The perception was that everyone was signed up to naughty stuff and they thought that they were not doing anything that was wrong; what is happening now in terms of declining standards shows that no one is learning from what happened then.'[51]

The expenses issue was apparently allowed to spiral partly because of a lax regime in the relevant Parliamentary Fees Office on the use of expenses as an informal supplement to the relatively low salary,[52] although this is clearly no excuse, and many committed brazen misconduct. The original idea of the expenses system was to provide the basic necessities to allow MPs to do their jobs. They could claim expenses, including the cost of accommodation, which were 'wholly, exclusively and necessarily incurred for the performance of a Member's parliamentary duties', according to the rules of the Fees Office, although the Office seems to have taken a somewhat liberal approach to this definition. MPs sought to justify it to themselves (and the public) on the grounds that their salaries had not risen greatly over the years and were well out of line with what they could earn in the private sector, a feeling which also permeates the attitude of some MPs to second jobs.[53]

The system was open to exploitation especially by the designation and redesignation of what was a first or second home, an egregious process known as 'flipping', which could net large sums of money for Parliamentarians. This involved them in ensuring their second home was the one that enabled them to claim the most in expenses. In at least one case, the nominated home was located neither in the constituency nor near Westminster.

The fraud was quite sophisticated, yet, as with most great crimes, it was also simple. Some MPs claimed for their 'second home' while they were, in fact, renting out other houses they owned. Others over-claimed for council tax on their second homes. Some 'second homes' were effectively businesses, since they were renovated on expenses and then rapidly sold. A panel was established to investigate all claims relating to the 'second homes' allowance between 2004 and 2008. The former Labour minister Tony McNulty admitted claiming expenses for a second home in Harrow, his constituency, just eight miles from his main home in Hammersmith. Under continuing pressure, he apologised to the House of Commons for this abuse. The then Conservative MP Eric Pickles (who is now the Chair of ACOBA) likewise was identified as claiming for a second home thirty-seven miles from his main home. The list of misdemeanours was seemingly endless and caused derision and contempt among the public.[54]

The penalty for some MPs was not just being put into the equivalent of the public stocks for humiliation but also subjection to criminal charges of false accounting, in the case of eight parliamentarians, all of whom were later jailed. Bad conduct may be contagious. Gerald Shamash told me:

> One of the lessons of the expenses scandal is that if the system is seen to be corrupt everyone gets down and dirty. There are others also who set bad examples of behaviour such as professional footballers.[55]

During a speech to the Royal College of Nursing conference, Gordon Brown, by now Prime Minister, apologised 'on behalf of all politicians' for the expenses claims that had been made.[56] Soon after, on 20 May 2009, Harriet Harman announced the creation of the Independent Parliamentary Standards Authority (IPSA), which was intended to manage Members' expenses at 'arm's length' from the House itself and has largely succeeded in cleaning up the stables.

This expenses scandal is both similar and different to the behaviour of the Johnson government, to which I turn in the next chapter – similar because it hit the same raw public nerve as partygate and Dominic Cummings' lockdown visit to Barnard Castle ('one law for them, a different one for the rest of us'), but different because it was Parliamentary rather than governmental.

The governments of David Cameron and Theresa May were generally scandal free,[57] with a few notable exceptions. They represented a relatively ethical period in British politics, at least at the level of political corruption. This would stand in stark contrast with what was to follow.

Corruption in the information age

As this brief survey shows, corruption or poor public standards have always been present in public life. But the rise of twenty-four-hour news and then social media (aided and abetted by a large number of freedom of information requests) means that we know much more than we used to about the activities of ministers, MPs and civil servants.[58] At the same time, it seems as though being 'economical with the truth' is increasingly common in public life.

To get a long view, I turned to Lord Patten of Barnes, who told me:

> Standards have declined over a period and this may be linked to the fact that we have a much more political class than when I started. Paradoxically, I suspect that as politics has been regarded as a career much like any others, the idea that it should be determined by a notion of professional standards has gone by the board.[59]

A pessimistic hypothesis holds that for several decades the UK body politic has been mired in sleaze, while at the same time we British have innocently told ourselves that we live in a country largely free of the taint of corruption. In other words, we may have been selling ourselves an entirely false prospectus about who we are and what we expect in our public officials. Our current knowledge depends on officials being more willing to leak and whistleblow, and in one sense it is a positive development that whistleblowing is better accepted.[60] I asked Lord (Robin) Butler about this, and he pointed to 'the greater pace of life, the celebrity culture'[61] and 'the desire to make quick money as well as the end of the age of deference as contributing to a decline in standards'.[62]

Sir Alistair Graham, a former Chair of the CSPL, put it this way: 'There has never been a golden age of standards, but we appear to be living through a particularly grim period'.[63]

But there is a counter-narrative, represented by David Howarth, a former Liberal Democrat MP for Cambridge and member of the Electoral Commission:

> We have much more transparency than in previous decades. Things were possibly even worse then but we knew less about it. There has never been complete propriety in our system, but it is of course difficult to measure this objectively.[64]

One cannot make politics available only as a profession for the saintly, as there are very few Mother Theresas in the world (and even fewer of them who want to go into politics). One of the big problems, however, is the lack of effective checks and balances in the British system. It is to the institutions designed to protect public standards to which we will turn after surveying the Johnson premiership.

Chapter 3

Boris Johnson and the downward spiral

He is late, rushed, chaotic, uncollegiate, unstrategic, sometimes inaccurate but he is also a bit of a genius.

Charles Moore, *Daily Telegraph*, 11 August 2018

He had long been a familiar English archetype, the gentleman amateur offering fluency, confidence and swagger in place of effort, experience and attention to detail…

Guardian, 8 July 2022

The philosopher Heraclitus some 2,500 years ago pronounced that 'character is destiny', and so it proved with the man universally known as Boris, a long-term classics scholar and a short-term Prime Minister. He tested almost to destruction the 'good chap' theory of government, which is a constant thread throughout this book. To assess his personality at a distance is difficult.[1] One minister likened him to 'a seafaring voyager from the ancient world – adventurous, reckless, dominant and storm tossed'.[2] As a boy his self-proclaimed ambition was to be 'world king'.[3]

Lying has been an enduring and encompassing theme of Johnson's career. There were the serious fictions peddled in the *Daily Telegraph* when he was a columnist in the 1990s, from the alleged EU attempt to straighten bananas to a suggestion that condoms would need to be a certain size to comply with EU law. These can be dismissed as semi-amusing riffs, but they may have had an effect in shaping the debate that led to the Brexit vote, which is less funny. He famously wrote one article for the *Daily Telegraph* damning the EU and another favouring it before deciding (momentously) that he was going to support Brexit in the 2016 referendum.[4] He was in 2023 sanctioned by the Commons Standards Committee for misleading the House of Commons on several occasions.

It is telling that the people who have worked most closely with Johnson often end up as his severest critics. This was taken furthest by Dominic Cummings, who was his Chief of Staff at the outset of his premiership and then turned on him with vengeance and vehemence. It began well; so keen was Johnson to have Cummings work for him that he cycled over to his Islington home to ask. Cummings was eventually forced out in a Number 10 power struggle in November 2020. He famously popularised the description of Johnson as veering all over the place like a shopping trolley from issue to issue.[5] He then said that removing Johnson from office was like 'fixing the drains … an unpleasant but necessary job',[6] and he seemingly dedicated his career after exiting Downing Street to doing just that, with quite vicious blogposts and leaks to the media.

Johnson's biographer, Sonia Purnell, who worked with Johnson at the *Daily Telegraph*, summed him up as 'the most ruthlessly ambitious person I have ever met'.[7] Max Hastings, his employer at that newspaper, described him as 'the hero of the Bullingdon Club, Houdini of the boudoir, most implausible prime minister in Britain's history' and a 'cavorting charlatan'.[8] The former MP Rory Stewart chose the term 'amoral figure',[9] while Camilla Cavendish, ennobled by David Cameron, described him as 'malevolent, cavalier'.[10]

As with most of us, Johnson's character may be traced back to his youth, upbringing and schooling. His housemaster at Eton recognised early that he did not think the rules applied to him. The family motto was said to be 'Nothing matters very much and most things don't matter at all'. This is a man never known for attention to detail. His influence was destructive: he found it much easier to knock people down than to build them up. As one minister was quoted as saying in the *Sunday Times* on 10 July 2022, 'Boris Johnson is the third prime minister to be brought down by Boris Johnson.'

But turning on its head the bitter barb directed by Ann Widdecombe against Michael Howard,[11] there has always been something of the glorious *day* about Johnson. He exudes positivity and optimism, and some clearly appreciate that. Many of the school friends with whom I grew up, in my hometown of Grimsby, were very supportive of him and Grimsby went Tory in 2019 as part of the 'red wall' of seats (constituencies which had been strongly Labour for decades). They saw in the person they all called 'Boris' someone who simplified things, was resolutely optimistic,[12] could speak easily to anyone and would be a good guy to spend the evening with in a local hostelry (perhaps only the latter was true). Somehow, they thought that he, unlike all the other politicians, was on their side and would not let them down. This cohort of my old friends, who generally have a low opinion of those in public life, thought that, if nothing else, he would at least inject fun into an otherwise miserable body politic. They would echo the sentiments expressed to Sebastian Payne, formerly the *Financial Times* politics correspondent, in his visit round the red wall seats, according to whom Johnson has 'the ability to connect, be human and self-deprecating while at the same time making people feel that it is within their gift and their opportunity to better themselves'.[13]

Johnson also has an anarchist tendency: he is a disruptor who is into breaking things, as can be seen most clearly over Brexit. There is indeed some irony in the fact that a government that was involved essentially in rule making was controlled for three years by an inveterate rule breaker, a man who could not stop himself even in the midst of the greatest public crisis since the Second World War, the COVID-19 pandemic. As just one small but perhaps telling example, as Prime Minister he failed to wear a mask in a hospital he visited when government advice was still to do so and everyone else in the room was masked and he revelled in telling everyone he had shaken hands with everyone he met.

It may be said that with him everything is a performance, and it is the performance art which sticks in the mind, such as when he got caught on a zipwire clutching two Union Jack flags during the London Olympics with a photographer on hand to record the event. He was probably the only politician who could turn this into a public relations triumph. He takes time, it is said, to make his hair messier than it really is. He is an insider/outsider and controlled chaos is part of his method of operation, indeed his shtick.

Johnson represented a new variant of populist politics with a strain of celebrity to it, and in this he resembled Donald Trump. As populists, both believed the will of the people gave them the legitimacy to take on elected chambers, the civil service, the so-called 'deep state' and politicians, and even, most worryingly, the rule of law. As with Trump, there was often a nastiness behind the showman's mask. The most notorious early exhibit here is a tape-recording from 1990 in which Johnson seemed to collude with Darius Guppy, a fellow old Etonian, in giving out the phone number of a journalist whom Guppy thought had crossed him so the journalist might be given a cracked rib and a couple of black eyes. That tape contains an unseemly discussion in which Johnson asks how serious the injury would be, which would inform his decision whether to provide the number.[14] In the end he did provide it, though fortunately for everyone involved the "beating" never took place.

The system meets a bad chap

A key question in this book is whether Boris Johnson was a one-off or whether changes need to be made in our political settlement in anticipation of another like him (or indeed his own Second Coming). One assumption behind the operation of the British constitutional system, built on conventions that everyone is expected to obey,[15] is that however many 'bad apples' there are in the ranks of the government, the Prime Minister will be someone of unimpeachable integrity and who can be trusted to orchestrate, together with a strong-minded Cabinet Secretary and independent Permanent Secretaries, the crucial ethical wiring of the government. That assumption is most clearly expressed in the Ministerial Code, for which the Prime Minister is responsible:[16] it states that ministers are expected 'to behave in a way that upholds the highest standards of propriety'. It was telling that in 2022, when Johnson was already under considerable pressure because of partygate, he removed any references at the start of the Ministerial Code to the traits of honesty, integrity, transparency and accountability which were formerly to the fore.[17]

Johnson's sporadic relationship with the truth was 'priced in' when he was selected as Conservative Party leader in 2019 and then elected by the people with an eighty-seat majority. No party in history had previously gained four successive general election majorities. Interestingly, that 'pricing in' was most eloquently expressed by a woman in West Bromwich when she said during the election to the BBC that 'I will definitely vote for Boris, liar, cheat and fool'.[18] Johnson's compulsive lying has been well documented.[19] He was sacked from his first journalism job at *The Times* for making up quotes, one purportedly by his godfather, the historian Colin Lucas, about (of all things) Edward II's catamite lover. Johnson does not care much about this and makes light of it. For example, when he admitted lying to Conrad Black, then owner of the *Telegraph* newspapers, he described how 'the blessed sponge of amnesia has wiped the chalkboard of history'.[20] In 2019 the Commons Committee on Standards said that he had demonstrated 'an over-casual attitude towards obeying the rules of the House' after failing to declare some of his property interests (see below).[21]

It could be said that Johnson's tenure as Prime Minister was chequered at best, going from embarrassment to shame. His own lack of the latter is demonstrated in the fact that he failed to attend a Commons debate on sleaze on 8 November 2021 that was considering his own conduct. Nor did it seem that his few apologies were laced with sincerity. Often he expected others to conduct the dirty work for him (e.g. to go out on the airwaves to defend his conduct) and this played a part in his downfall. There was a long decline in his credibility, support haemorrhaging as he obfuscated over what he knew about Chris Pincher, whom he had appointed as the Deputy Chief Whip despite knowing he faced allegations of sexual harassment (see below).

Ian Blackford in Parliament in late April 2021, while nodding to the restrictions on verbal abuse in the chamber of the House of Commons, said 'I can't possibly call the Prime Minister a liar in this House but … are you a liar, Prime Minister?' Bizarrely, there was an ominous, awkward silence from Johnson before he simply said 'No'.

This has proved a rich seam for journalists to mine. A video made by Peter Stefanovic about Johnson's lies went viral and clocked up some 13.5 million views. Peter Oborne, a fellow right-wing journalist, wrote an excellent book solely dedicated to the subject of Johnson's evasions. Summing up why they matter, he said: 'we can't let liars and cheats get away with it. This is because the liberal democracy we take for granted depends on a public domain with shared facts and assumptions upon which people of goodwill can agree.'[22]

Extraordinarily, Johnson started his premiership with a lie, saying outside Downing Street that he had a plan for social care when he manifestly did not. A particularly unfortunate example of the lie machine at work was when Johnson said that the government was building forty-nine new hospitals when in fact the most that it had actually built was six.[23] Johnson told the Commons in 2021 that crime had fallen by 14%, but this is so only if fraud and computer misuse were excluded, both of which were growing in importance, and there was no valid reason for excluding them (the only possible reason was to exaggerate the government's performance). In February 2022, he trumpeted the government's apparent success about the levels of employment, claiming that the number of unemployed people had fallen significantly since the pandemic,[24] but official statistics gathered by the Office for Statistics Regulation, the Institute for Employment Studies and Full Fact show it had in fact *risen*. He claimed for the fourth time that there were 420,000 more people in employment than before the pandemic, whereas, including the self-employed, there were 600,000 fewer.

Another example in this chamber of horrors (and we do not have space for many of them) was the denial that Johnson had any involvement in the decision to allow an airlift of animals from Kabul at the height of the fall of the Afghan government in August 2021. Johnson as Prime Minister said, specifically through Number 10 spokespersons, that he was *not* involved in the rescue of cats and dogs from a UK charity in Afghanistan run by Pen Farthing. Dismissing the claim as 'total rhubarb', he said he had 'absolutely not' intervened to save 170 dogs and cats. The claim was sensitive because many felt that people who were trying to escape the falling city in the chaos of the US withdrawal should have been given priority. Raphael Marsh, an official at the Foreign, Commonwealth and Development Office (FCDO), turned whistleblower however, released documents to a Parliamentary committee which showed that a Foreign Office official working in the office of Lord Zac Goldsmith, who was at the time a minister at both the FCDO and the Department for Environment, Food and Rural Affairs, had said in an email: 'PM has just authorised their staff and animals to be evacuated'. Perhaps he was mistaken. On 25 August 2021 a Foreign Office official said, 'In light of the PM's decision earlier today to evacuate the staff of the Nowzad animal charity…' – which suggests another animal charity was asking for something similar. Perhaps he was mistaken too. The emails also suggested that Trudy Harrison, Johnson's Parliamentary aide, helped secure a plane for the animals to fly out of Kabul. Jose Stewart, head of the FCDO's illicit finance team, also said that Johnson did have a role in the decision to evacuate the animals in her written evidence to the House of Commons Foreign Affairs Committee.

As *The Times* put it, 'No 10 has yet to explain how so many senior figures from across government could have become involved in the rescue of Pen Farthing's cats and dogs in the midst of the biggest airlift in decades believing themselves to be acting on the prime minister's authority when Boris Johnson himself is adamant he was not involved'.[25] Further clarification came there none.

There are two areas that show the extent to which Johnson disrespected standards in public life, the first of which registered with the public quite low on the Richter scale of scandals, but the second of which really burst through and nearly finished him off.

Flat refurbishment

First exhibit is the protracted saga of the flat refurbishment at Number 11 Downing Street,[26] otherwise known as 'Cash for curtains'. This allowed the Italians to mock that at least Silvio Berlusconi paid for his own wallpaper! It is still not clear that any agency has quite got to the bottom of what took place here, least of all Lord Geidt as the Independent Adviser on Ministers' Interests.[27]

The Prime Minister was allowed to spend up to £30,000 a year from public funds renovating the flat, which to most folks seems quite a large sum. Discussions about how the official and private areas of Downing Street might be re-presented, refurbished and funded started soon after Boris Johnson took office in summer 2019.[28] Johnson wanted an extravagant redesign, no doubt thinking that he and his wife were hunkering down for a long stay in Downing Street. He told Lord Brownlow of Shurlock Row, a businessman involved in recruitment and a major Tory donor (ennobled by Theresa May), that parts of the Number 11 flat were a 'tip' and needed to be redone.[29] They originally concocted a plan for this to be funded by a blind trust, but the government's legal advice indicated that this model was not viable. This cold water was poured in mid-June 2020, before Brownlow was (apparently) appointed as chair of the putative trust on 10 July 2020.[30]

Without the trust having been established, Brownlow very generously stepped into the breach and paid for the work himself.[31] He had just stood down as a Vice Chairman of the Conservative Party. And the problem was exacerbated because there was, as often happened during Johnson's premiership, only a drip feed of information from Number 10 until the truth finally emerged, which was in itself telling – this foreshadowed the approach taken in partygate. All that Downing Street would say initially was that Johnson himself had met the costs of the work. Further, he managed to condemn the allegations against him as a 'farrago of nonsense', a phrase reminiscent of his description of his alleged affair with Petronella Wyatt many years earlier (which also turned out to be true) as an 'inverted pyramid of piffle'.

The precise method of funding the refurb was later revealed, and it was as complicated as if it had been an overseas trust arrangement. Brownlow in March 2021 had refunded the Cabinet Office, which then refunded the Conservative Party for the society designer Lulu Lytle's charges,[32] with all of the final costs of wider refurbishment being met by the Prime Minister personally.[33] These details were, however, buried away on page 209 of the 282-page 2021 Cabinet Office *Annual Report and Accounts*, which is undoubtedly a good place to bury bad news, as most sensible people, if they read it at all, give up reading this exciting tome by page 10 or thereabouts!

It was envisaged that the Party would receive a refund from the proposed trust. Four months later, however, the trust could not be set up and the Party was short by £52,801. On 13 October 2021 Brownlow emailed the Party: 'Could you advise me of the total that the Conservative Party has lent the Downing Street Trust. I will then make a donation to The Party to clear the debt.' Johnson messaged Brownlow on WhatsApp two months after this, saying he wanted him to authorise further refurbishment work. Brownlow readily agreed and told a senior Party official that he would pay personally for it. The messages revealed an intimacy between Johnson and Brownlow, said Sir Alistair Graham, former Chair of the Committee on Standards in Public Life, that 'adds to the unsavoury nature of the whole exercise'.[34]

The only *quid pro quo* that Brownlow requested for this act of generosity was that his 'big idea' for a modern Great Exhibition should be seriously considered, as it apparently was by the then Culture Secretary (it was dismissed). This was a relatively modest ask, but someone else might have wanted more *quo* for this *quid*, and it is in this type of water that the bacilli of corruption thrive. The idea is that payment of such sums for private refurbishment can gain access, so that Brownlow's role does have a somewhat sinister tinge to it.

Dominic Cummings's blogpost in mid-April 2021 said that Johnson planned to 'have donors secretly pay' for the refurbishment. He went on to describe Johnson's actions as 'unethical, foolish, possibly illegal and [they] almost certainly broke the rules on proper disclosure of political donations if conducted in the way he intended'.[35] Money was being funnelled into the PM's private life without any proper paper trail.[36]

Several newspaper articles, notably in the *Sunday Times*, suggested that Johnson was finding it difficult to make ends meet as Prime Minister, stripped of his ability to make serious money by writing newspaper columns and on the after-dinner speaking circuit. The danger in a Prime Minister making clear to all and sundry that he needs funding hardly needs saying, because this is likely to attract those who will seek a tangible return for donating money, in terms of business arrangements or an honour.[37] It also appears that Johnson secured a credit facility of up to £800,000 to fund his life in Downing Street with the help of a distant Canadian cousin, Sam Blyth, an entrepreneur who acted as guarantor.[38] Richard Sharp was appointed as Chairman of the BBC after he had apparently introduced Blyth to the Cabinet Secretary, Simon Case. He did not reveal this involvement to the appointments panel and at length resigned in April 2023.[39]

Edwina Currie (the former MP) recalls that Margaret Thatcher was so fastidious that when ministers met in Number 10 to talk politics (as opposed to government business) she insisted they chip in a few pounds from their own pockets to pay for sandwiches. Today there is a different culture. Can one actually call this corruption? The journalist Michael Crick, an acute observer of the political scene over several decades, thinks not. He told me 'I do not think Johnson is himself corrupt' but he went on to say:

> He has lax standards of behaviour and a lax regard to the truth. He has an amoral way of working. His life is wholly chaotic. He needs strong people around him as he had when in charge of the Greater London Authority [as London Mayor] and the *Spectator*. He is in sharp contrast to Theresa May.[40]

Many of the abuses of public trust by Johnson would have probably brought down other figures earlier (and it was trust that eventually prised him from Downing Street). These include, as London Mayor, financially aiding his former lover from public funds. Jennifer Arcuri told the *Sunday Mirror* that she was having an affair with Johnson at the same time as he was including her on taxpayer-funded trade missions and giving grants to her technology company.[41] Arcuri received, all told, £126,000 of public money. An investigation by the Greater London Authority – which oversees the London Mayor's Office – was, however, inconclusive, which is in itself odd, given the admitted information that was available.

Despite the Labour Party exploiting them mercilessly, previous issues of sleaze like these gained very little traction with the public. Indeed, many probably thought that the state *should* pay for the refurbishment of the Number 11 flat and did not see what all the fuss was about.

Partygate

But the most monumental lack of judgement on display was over what became universally known as 'partygate'. This revealed a rich mixture of hypocrisy and mendacity and was fully appreciated as being serious well outside the Westminster and Whitehall villages. The public had a clear and simple idea that a lawmaker should not also be a lawbreaker.

There were three Ps in a subtle psychodrama that played out over months. The first was Owen Paterson, whose case is recounted in Chapter 12. Partygate followed afterwards, and this is in effect what brought Johnson to earth with a bang, although it needed the Pincher scandal to push him over the edge. Johnson's dishonesty over partygate was exposed by the Commons Committee on Standards, which recommended a ninety-day suspension from Parliament after interviewing Johnson. This would have triggered a byelection if there was a recall petition in the constituency. He resigned his seat in June 2023, before this could be implemented. Only seven MPs voted against the Committee's recommendation. Two of his long-standing supporters also resigned their seats. The Committee subsequently found several of his supporters to be guilty of contempt of the Committee.

Johnson over many months had insisted that the numerous parties held at Number 10 were not truly parties. It was a clear case of one rule for ministers and one for the public – and Teflon Boris finally lost his shine. This is a story of how birthday cakes, booze and Christmas quizzes became the backdrop to a grave constitutional issue.

To position the significance of this cake fest, we need to recall the dark days at the height of the COVID-19 pandemic. Think firstly of the evocative advertising campaign by the government itself over which Johnson presided, which was designed to persuade ordinary people to obey the strict rules against social contact. The campaign strapline was 'Look her in the eyes and tell her you never bend the rules'. The advert showed a woman being given oxygen and, importantly, also said that it required those in senior positions to set a good example.[42] The COVID regulations provided that indoor gatherings had to be 'reasonably necessary' for work purposes for them to be legal.[43] Enforcement was by fixed penalty notices issued by the police, although the degree of strictness of the enforcement of the rules by the police differed markedly between forces. Not only did the Prime Minister make the law itself (with minimal Parliamentary scrutiny), but he stressed nightly to the nation in broadcast press conferences the need to abide by it, under pain of criminal sanction. In these press conferences, flanked by the Chief Medical and Chief Scientific Officers, he looked gravely into the camera and brandished statistics about how serious the situation was.

Some of the parties took place at a time when schools were still shut, as were pubs and restaurants. One involved staff performing karaoke outside the Cabinet Secretary's office and was so raucous that it ended with one participant being sick and an altercation between two civil servants. The ball really began rolling for the public, however, when Allegra Stratton, the Communications Director at Number 10, was seen joking in a leaked video that she would have to portray for the public a party as a 'business meeting'. This was in a mock question-and-answer session with other Number 10 staffers. The footage showed Downing Street staff laughing uproariously in response to the line 'it wasn't a party … it was cheese and wine'.[44] There was a clear consciousness at the time that what they were doing was wrong. Some joked about the risk of being seen by drones while the partying was going on.[45]

Altogether, there were more than fifteen events in Number 10 and Whitehall between mid-May 2020 and April 2021. On 15 May 2020, Martin Reynolds, Johnson's Principal Private Secretary (who later paid for the party with his job), sent an email asking people to bring along their own booze so that they could 'make the most of the lovely weather'. Around the time of the parties Matt Hancock, the Secretary of State for Health and Social Care, when asked about Eid celebrations, replied: 'The clear answer for all faiths is people will have to adapt the celebrations around the current social distancing rules and everybody knows what those rules are and they remain the same for every community'.[46] The serious issue was not just the jollifications themselves but the significant steps that were taken to cover them up.

Over 100 staff members were invited to the May party, of whom forty joined what Johnson described as a 'work event', which suggests that some sixty had qualms about partying in these circumstances and decided not to stick around for it.[47] The Prime Minister attended at approximately 6 p.m. for around thirty minutes to thank staff before returning to his office. He was pictured in the capacious Number 10 garden eating cheese and drinking wine with senior members of staff, his partner (later wife), Carrie Symonds, and their baby. A suitcase was taken to the local supermarket to stock up with drink to add to the fizz the guests brought themselves. It was Dominic Cummings who revealed the existence of this party in his blog.[48]

The email traffic about this event was revealing in itself. A junior official wrote to Reynolds with sage advice: 'just to flag that the press conference will probably be finishing around that time, so helpful if people can be mindful … of not walking around waving bottles of wine etc.'[49] Reynolds replied 'will do my best!' (exclamation marks are often revealing). Lee Cain, the Number 10 communications chief, had his own qualms and said that 'a 200-odd person invitation for drinks in the garden is somewhat of a comms risk in the current environment', and how right he was. This was particularly so since in May 2020 the Metropolitan Police had warned people not to gather in groups to enjoy the hottest day of year.

One of Johnson's all-time favourite phrases was that he wanted to have his cake and eat it too (a philosophy known to his devoted followers as 'cakeism'), so it was richly ironic that his premiership was nearly brought down by a birthday cake. Carrie presented him with the said confection at a party attended also by Lulu Lytle, the interior designer, whom you will remember from the refurbishment imbroglio. There were some thirty people present in the Cabinet Room for this event. Food, alcohol and soft drinks were provided, and they had been organised in advance that morning. The event lasted only around twenty to thirty minutes. Simon Case, the Cabinet Secretary, attended for a short period. Johnson belittled the whole thing by saying that he was involved for only ten minutes and that it did not occur to him it was wrong.[50] Rishi Sunak, the Chancellor, received a fixed penalty notice too but he accepted what he did was wrong. However, it was the parties on the eve of the Duke of Edinburgh's funeral that resonated most powerfully with the public. They took place at Number 10 on 16 April 2021. One party was held for the departing Director of Communications, James Slack (who was leaving to join the *Sun*), and another for a Number 10 official. The last person to leave the party went home at 4:20 a.m. on the day of the funeral. This is not how good chaps were expected to behave.

There were some other events that never made it into the police inquiry.[51] Several sources claim that Carrie danced to the Abba hit 'The Winner Takes

It All' at a 'victory' party in the Number 10 flat when her nemesis, Cummings, resigned on the night of 13 November 2020. This gathering is not referenced in the Gray report, for reasons that are obscure.[52]

The Johnsonian failure to confess that these were parties at all did not land well. His denials drew incredulity and contempt. People had an intuition that if there was plenty of drink and food, and there were many people gathered after hours, it was likely to be a party. This demonstrated the worst sort of linguistic contortions adopted by politicians (and lawyers). Number 10 also tried to persuade the public that these were work events and that the garden was an extension of his home in Downing Street so did count as a work area (mixing was allowed at work events by this time). There was a lack of what President Obama once called 'a common baseline of facts'.[53]

The exact sequence of these evasions is worth noting in itself. The chain of distortion proceeded thus: Number 10 first said that there were no parties;[54] then that the Prime Minister was shocked to find that *his staff* were having them (always blame those below stairs); still later it appeared that he had actually *attended* some of them. Johnson also gravely told MPs that he had been assured that 'rules were followed at all times'. There was rising fury among Conservative Party supporters as well as others, although there was no consensus as to who would replace Johnson.[55]

The original investigation into the parties descended into farce when Simon Case had to recuse himself from investigating (as originally intended) because the Christmas quiz party had been held in his own office. He was replaced as the investigator by Sue Gray, whose appointment some initially doubted as she was an insider.[56]

Waiting for Gray's report[57] was like waiting for Godot, and some people's attention moved on to other things, but it was gone but not forgotten. The fact that the report was postponed made it easier for Johnson to ride out the storm. The term 'long delayed' became attached to the Gray report like superglue. In her first report, she could consider only four of the sixteen events, as twelve were being investigated by the police.[58]

This investigation led to calls for Johnson's resignation, but the necessary fifty-four Conservative MPs did not go so far as to deliver votes of no confidence to the Chair of the 1922 Committee. David Davis was, however, moved in the Commons to channel Cromwell and say 'In the name of God go', the very words that had been used by Leo Amery to Chamberlain after the Munich declaration, although Johnson, who was Churchill's biographer, affected not to understand the reference. Already the mood in the Conservative Party was described as 'funereal'.

Johnson's predecessor, Theresa May, then asked a devastating question in the Commons: 'Either [the PM] had not read the rules or did not understand what they meant … or they did not think the rules applied to No. 10. Which was it?', to which a convincing answer did not come.

An attenuated, first version of the Gray report was published on 31 January 2022, but it contained fewer than 500 words of findings.[59] Nevertheless, although neutered in several ways because of continuing police inquiries, Gray's initial report found serious failings of leadership at Number 10.[60] She concluded that 'At least some of the gatherings in question represent a serious failure to observe not just the high standards expected of those working at the heart of government but also of the standards expected of the entire British population at the time'. She went on, 'a number of these gatherings should not have been allowed to take place or to develop in the way that they did'.[61] She pointed generally to an unprofessional drinking culture in Downing Street.

The second Gray report surfaced after the police had completed their long investigations and had found 'multiple examples of a lack of respect for cleaning and security staff who tried to raise concerns'. As Gray wrote, 'even allowing for the extraordinary pressures officials and advisers were under, the factual findings of this report illustrate some attitudes and behaviours inconsistent with that guidance'.[62] Gray's third conclusion was damning: 'Many of these events should not have been allowed to happen. It is also the case that some of the more junior civil servants believed that their involvement in some of these events was permitted given the attendance of senior leaders'.

On 12 April 2022, the Prime Minister, Carrie (by now his wife) and Rishi Sunak received a fine for attending one party on 19 June 2020 in the Cabinet Room. There were nineteen other parties being considered by the police at that stage. Keir Starmer said that both Johnson and Sunak should resign for 'dishonouring their offices' by reason of their fines, but ironically he too became ensnared in controversy after a video emerged of him enjoying a beer in the Durham Miners' Hall during the lockdown period with his deputy leader and local party workers. The Durham police originally dismissed the idea of investigating this, but relented after a tabloid press campaign led by the *Daily Mail*. In mid-July 2022, however, they decided to take no action against the Labour leader and his deputy, who had (unlike Johnson) both said that they would resign if served with a notice. The Durham police did not however find liability in their cases.

The police in due course issued Number 10 staff with 126 fixed penalty notices. These went to no fewer than eighty-three individuals for parties held on eight separate dates, which made Number 10 the address with the most intense COVID law-breaking in the whole of the country. A then loyal minister, Brandon Lewis, said that such notices should be considered to be no more serious than a parking ticket (he later served briefly as Justice Minister). Lord Hennessy on Easter Sunday 2022 was more accurate when he observed on *The World This Weekend*, 'I think we are in the most severe constitutional crisis involving a PM that I can remember', because a Prime Minister (the guardian of constitutional proprieties) had been fined. In the same programme he also said for good measure that Johnson was 'a rogue Prime Minister unworthy of the Queen' and 'the great debaser in modern times of decency in public and political life and of our constitutional conventions – our very system of government'.[63] What can be safely said is that under no other PM (and probably no other Cabinet Secretary) would partygate have happened, although some of the Number 10 staff were the same people as in previous and subsequent premierships.

There are several striking things about the partygate scandal and its handling that are likely to have repercussions long after the (unfortunately literal) vomit was cleaned from the walls of Number 10. The first is the overall decline in public standards that it all graphically depicts. It was the biggest test for the 'good chaps' theory, and many proved not to be good chaps at all. The overall tone for the government seemed to be set by an amoral Prime Minister who had no respect for the pesky rules nor thought that they applied to him.

Sir John Major, in a well-timed address to the Institute for Government (IfG) in February 2022, warmed to this theme and said that Johnson had clearly broken lockdown laws and sent out ministers to 'defend the indefensible'. This made the government 'look distinctly shifty', with 'brazen excuses' being given. He was right to say that 'the lack of trust in the elected portion of our democracy cannot be brushed aside' and that 'deliberate lies to Parliament have been fatal to political careers and must always be so. If trust in the word of our leaders in Parliament is lost then trust in government will be lost too.' He concluded by saying 'outright lies breed contempt'.[64]

The second lesson was that the only real check on the Prime Minister appeared to be the electoral calculations of Tory backbenchers – there was also nothing informal done by the civil service, as would have probably happened in the past with a stronger Cabinet Secretary such as Lords Butler, Wilson or Heywood.[65] Simon Case was the youngest ever Cabinet Secretary and his authority was weak. This is probably precisely why he was chosen for the role. He was unlikely to speak truth to power.[66] Nor, save the Committee on Standards, was there anything that could provide a break to Johnson's career beyond political calculations.

Thirdly, the affair demonstrates the close relationship between press and politicians and the attempted manipulation of the media; indeed, one of the Number 10 parties was held for James Slack, who was leaving to join the *Sun*, a newspaper that conspicuously did not find much room for the parties in its pages. Probably as a 'dead cat' strategy,[67] to distract attention from the difficult news of the moment about parties, Johnson counter-attacked Sir Keir Starmer in the House of Commons over his record as Director of Public Prosecutions (DPP) decades before. Starmer was visibly furious as the Prime Minister pronounced on 30 January 2022 that 'when DPP, he spent most of his time prosecuting journalists and failing to prosecute Jimmy Savile'. This seemed to come straight from the Trump media playbook of distraction and deflection. The lawyer acting for some of Savile's victims said that the PM was 'weaponizing their suffering', and others said that the remark was 'Poundland Trumpism'.[68] The backlash against the coarsening of public discourse in the Savile attack was (surprisingly) led by Munira Mirza, who resigned as head of policy at Number 10, after working with Johnson since 2008, because, as she put it, 'there was no fair or reasonable basis for that assertion'. This was not the normal cut and thrust of politics and was exacerbated by Johnson's refusal to apologise. It was an inappropriate and partisan reference to a horrendous case of child sex abuse.[69]

Fourthly, this was a case where a full judicial inquiry would have been more appropriate, as a judge would not have been in the line of command below the Prime Minister, as was Sue Gray. I will return to this theme in the final chapter.

Sufficient signatures were sent in to the 1922 Committee of Conservative MPs for a vote of confidence in the Prime Minister in June 2022, but he won that vote handsomely by 211 to 148. However, this was not at all the end of the story, because of something that happened late one night in St James's.

Pincher by name…

Johnson's final demise – his 'Clownfall', as the *Economist* called it – came about in the strangest of circumstances. One could hardly make it up. On 29 June 2022 at the Carlton Club, a watering hole of the Right established by the Duke of Wellington, the Johnson ultra-loyalist and Deputy Chief Whip Chris Pincher got drunk and groped two men.[70] Johnson had recently brought Pincher back into government after a long period in the wilderness.[71] When questions were inevitably asked as to whether Johnson knew of previous such incidents, the Prime Minister said 'no'. But it soon emerged that there had been several allegations against Pincher of which he had indeed been made aware during his tenure as Foreign Secretary. This was confirmed in an unusual intervention on 5 July 2022, in a letter to *The Times* by Lord Simon McDonald. McDonald had been 'encouraged' to resign as Permanent Under-Secretary at the Foreign Office by Johnson. He said that Johnson was indeed told about the problems with Pincher when Pincher was appointed some years before as a minister in the Foreign Office when Johnson was Foreign Secretary. McDonald wrote to this effect to the Parliamentary Commissioner for Standards and spoke to the media about it. This opened the floodgate to criticism of Johnson from all wings of the Conservative Party. It was also rumoured, and not denied, that Johnson had made the comment 'Pincher by name, Pincher by nature' to colleagues. The incident opened Johnson to the charge that he did not take sexual harassment seriously.

Some fifty ministers and trade envoys resigned over a few days in July 2022 because they and colleagues were asked to defend the indefensible. At least twenty-seven MPs in government or in senior Conservative Party roles cited in their resignation letters concerns over conduct, standards or integrity.[72] There were, it appeared, not enough MPs left who were prepared to fill the ministerial positions thus vacated. Bizarrely, Michelle Donelan had come and gone as Education Secretary inside thirty-six hours. When Rishi Sunak and Sajid Javid[73] resigned as Chancellor and Health Secretary respectively within minutes of each other, it was the last straw for Johnson. Sunak said in his letter 'I believe standards are worth fighting for'. The government appeared to dissolve before our very eyes.

After two days of indecision, Johnson announced he would be leaving office. In a graceless resignation speech on 7 July 2022, he said 'them's the breaks', blamed 'the herd' (i.e. Conservative MPs) for turning against him and complained of the goalposts having been moved mid-game.[74] He positively signalled a comeback in the sign-off to his final Prime Minister's Questions (after which he gained a standing ovation from nearly all Tories, notably ex-cluding Theresa May) when he said 'Hasta la vista baby'.[75] He later described his ousting as 'the biggest stitch-up since the Bayeux [tapestry]'.[76] Sunak was punished by Conservative Party members for what many saw as his treachery in the subsequent leadership election, which he lost to Liz Truss, who was loyal to Johnson until the end. Sunak, however, was to have the last laugh, following Truss's rapid demise, although his subsequent victory was in a leadership contest limited to MPs.

Johnson resigned as an MP on 9 June 2023, after the Commons Privileges Committee found that he was guilty of misleading Parliament over partygate. For example, he lied 'when he said that guidance was followed completely in No. 10, that the rules and guidance were followed at all times, that events in No. 10 were within the rules and guidance, and that the rules and guidance had been followed at all times when he was present at gatherings'.

Other misdemeanours

The above is not the full list of Prime Ministerial indiscretions and failures to meet standards in the burgeoning charge sheet against Johnson. There was also the use of a taxpayer-funded plane for a visit to Hartlepool during a byelection campaign.[77] There was the series of text messages between Johnson and Sir James Dyson in which Johnson said that he would 'fix it' so that Dyson's staff would not have to pay extra tax while building ventilators in the UK during the pandemic. The exchanges took place in March 2020, at the start of the lockdown, when the government was appealing to firms to supply ventilators amid fears the NHS could run out. The government had to admit that none of Johnson's messages from his mobile phone prior to April 2021 were available.[78]

It is alleged that Johnson also tried to secure a job for Carrie Symonds at the Foreign Office as Chief of Staff when she was already his girlfriend;[79] Dominic Cummings made the further accusation that he had tried to secure a government job for her when he was the PM. Curiously, this story was withdrawn from *The Times* after the first edition appeared, at the request of Number 10. Downing Street described it as a 'grubby, discredited story'. The allegation regarding Carrie had originally appeared some years before in a book by Lord Ashcroft about David Cameron.[80]

How do you solve a problem like Johnson?

Under Johnson, political deceit became not just commonplace but almost, it seemed, an automatic reaction. Lord Patten of Barnes told me:

> The idea that you need to be told by an ethics adviser that it is a good idea that you don't have your flat refurbished by a Conservative Party donor is preposterous. It is astonishing you need to be told that.[81]

Lord Hennessy described the Johnson government as 'a bonfire of the decencies'.[82] Using a different metaphor, it can be said that he drained what was left from the public reservoir of trust. Sir Chris Bryant, Chair of the Commons Committee on Standards, said, 'if you break the rules, just rewrite the rule book is the motto of this despicable government'.[83]

There was a major contrast between Johnson and the person who sat across from him each week at Prime Minister's Questions, Sir Keir Starmer. Some saw the difference as being that Johnson was a great campaigner but poor at government, while Starmer would have governed well if elected but was poor at dealing with ordinary people. At the Bar, Starmer was known by some as an advocate for the judge, not the jury.

Johnson was probably a one-off, and eventually the system of conventions reasserted itself and he was removed, but we need to ask what lessons we should learn for the ethical ecosystem. An obvious point is that the Prime Minister should not be involved in any way in overseeing any investigation into himself; where the PM is involved, any investigation should be led by a judge (and not by a civil servant, who is inevitably down the chain of command from the Prime Minister). The system is reliant on people treating it as though it were the rules of cricket. Boris Johnson did not do so. The system needed robust regulators. We now turn to consider the regulators, to see what the system is and whether it is fit for purpose.

Part II

The ethical regulators

Chapter 4

The Independent Adviser on Ministers' Interests: bullying, wallpaper, parties

From the perspective of the average member of the public, who must look upon the arrangements from the outside and may see a system which relies too much on self-regulation, I can understand some of that scepticism.

Para. 62 of Lord Geidt's *Annual Report* of the Independent Adviser on Ministers' Interests, published in May 2022

The mysterious case of the Home Secretary

The case of Priti Patel and the Independent Adviser, which played out in 2019, was unusual and set many precedents.[1] It raises in particular the seventh Nolan Principle, which requires office holders to treat others with respect and to challenge poor behaviour. It was the first time a Permanent Secretary sued the government for bullying after he resigned. It was also the first occasion the Prime Minister refused to accept the views of the Independent Adviser on Ministers' Interests, otherwise known as his 'ethics adviser', then Sir Alex Allan.[2] Allan was the first (though he was not to be the last) such Adviser to resign in protest about his report being ignored by the Prime Minister, to whom he reported. In the aftermath, and this too had never happened before, the First Division Association (the mandarins' trade union) sued the government. The case brought to the fore the notion of 'unintentional bullying'. Allan adopted it in his report. It is not normally possible in law to rebut an allegation of bullying by saying 'I did not intend to harass or bully'. In December 2020 I wrote to *The Times* to make this point and the letter went viral.

Patel (then Home Secretary) is by any standards an unusual if not unique politician, in that she is extremely right-wing (she started her career as a communications officer in the pro-Brexit Referendum Party) and against many forms of migration, despite being a second-generation migrant of Asian heritage.[3] Her parents came to the UK when Idi Amin expelled the Asians from Uganda in 1972, and she might have been expected to have a soft spot for refugees, but this is so far from being the case that she introduced a vastly expensive policy to send refugees to Rwanda (a policy subsequently found to be unlawful by the Supreme Court). She has a fiery personality and always secured a long ovation from the Tory faithful at the Conservative Party conference. For these reasons at least, the Johnson team in Number 10 were desperate to retain her in her important office of state.[4]

The PM (like Houston) had a problem, however, because she was allegedly a serial bully of Whitehall civil servants. Her permanent secretary at the Home Office, Sir Philip Rutnam, claimed that she subjected him to a 'vicious and orchestrated campaign' after he had raised concerns about the treatment of civil servants working under him. This sustained campaign was, he said, conducted through several press briefings directed against him over a two-week period, and this became too much for Rutnam, a career-long civil servant, to bear. There is, of course, a fine line between bullying and robust management of officials who are thought to be lazy or incompetent.[5] This issue would have played out at an explosive employment tribunal, because Rutnam claimed constructive dismissal, but the case at length was settled.[6] I asked Sir Philip why he resigned and he answered:

> Because I wasn't willing to be involved in covering up unacceptable behaviour. And that behaviour included both the bullying of staff and the vicious media campaign that followed my attempts to challenge this. I saw that campaign as clearly aimed at intimidating me, and indeed other senior officials who might dare to challenge ministers in future.[7]

Sir Alex Allan, as Independent Adviser, was asked by Boris Johnson to report on the Home Secretary's conduct. He found the allegations against her to be proved in the two government departments where she served. Patel claimed in her defence that she had found civil servants at both to be so impossible to deal with that she had to tell them they were useless in *very* direct terms, which they did not like. The civil servants responded that this was not behaviour with which they should have had to put up; rather, it was, they felt, bullying and harassing. Some in her private office had asked to be moved. Lady Bracknell's comments come to mind: to lose one civil servant may be regarded as a misfortune; to lose both looks like carelessness.

One might have thought that this set of conclusions by Sir Alex was so important that it was in the interest of the public to know of them in detail and in short order after they were reached. The 'report' by Sir Alex was, however, slipped out by Downing Street only some six months after the matter was referred to him. That was on 20 November 2020, ironically just after the end of anti-bullying week.

No part of this process could be described as remotely transparent. On the contrary, it was messy and opaque. The 'judgement' of Sir Alex that saw the light of day is just one and a quarter pages long, has no proper heading, is unsigned and refers to 'the facts established by the Cabinet Office', which have still not been published. It is in fact a précis of the advice that was given by Allan to the Prime Minister. If transparency is a disinfectant, this case remains to this day very murky.

Allan's report included reference to Patel's 'forceful expression' (presumably a euphemism) and 'some occasions of shouting and swearing'. The conclusions were not, however, wholly one-sided. He raised concerns that Patel was not always supported by her department and implied that senior officials (unnamed) were also responsible to some extent for the poor relationship between civil service and minister. He said that 'The Home Office was not as flexible as it could have been in responding to the Home Secretary's requests and direction. She has – legitimately – not always felt supported by the department.' This is presumably mandarin-speak for 'there was some fault on both sides'.

One wonders how the facts could be 'found' at all without any full investigatory or hearing process.[8] The other important knight in this story, the aforementioned Sir Philip Rutnam, was not asked for his comments (although this was anyway problematic because he brought proceedings).[9] The two knights (Allan and Rutnam) did not get to joust with each other.

The ultimate decision on Patel's fate was to be taken by a Prime Minister who had not only made up his mind that he was not going to sack Patel but had even pre-announced it; this is what you call 'going through the motions', or not even bothering to do that. Michael Gove, the Chancellor of the Duchy of Lancaster (and responsible for the Cabinet Office), had actually said that he supported the Home Secretary when he had first announced that the inquiry was going to happen; this was, one might say, a reverse kangaroo court.

On the day the report was released, Johnson told Conservative MPs on a WhatsApp group to 'form a square around the Prittster' (a military term for a defensive manoeuvre). He also denounced the bullying allegations as 'mere trivia' when this was raised at Prime Minister's Questions. Given all this, it is not surprising that Allan (a retired senior civil servant) resigned. But it was shocking that the post was then left vacant for nine months. His successor, when one was finally appointed, was also to resign.

The Ministerial Code

What is the Ministerial Code on which Allan was advising, and is it fit for purpose? It is the wide-ranging and unwieldy bible for the conduct of ministers. There are some parts of the Code, for example on leaking to newspapers,[10] which are inherently political, while others are about the fundamental principles of holding public office (going beyond ministers). These must be subject to proper scrutiny and an inquiry process that is protected from politicisation and fair to those whose conduct is being criticised. The CSPL itself concluded that 'This combination of procedure and propriety confuses more than it enlightens',[11] and Rishi Sunak as Prime Minister did not take the opportunity to make real changes when he introduced limited reforms in December 2022. The Code encompasses such matters as collective Cabinet responsibility, the accountability of ministers to Parliament, the relationship between ministers and officials, and the avoidance of conflicts of interest and the general maintenance of personal probity.

The Code was first made public in 1992 as *Questions of Procedure for Ministers* by the then Prime Minister John Major. It became known as the Ministerial Code under Tony Blair in 1997, and it has been regularly updated, including under Prime Ministers Theresa May and Boris Johnson.[12] Johnson introduced stronger rules on harassment and bullying in 2022.[13]

The work naturally errs on the side of caution where the bullying of employees is concerned, and adopts a wide definition. It calls for positive conduct and says that 'Ministers should be professional in their working relationships with the Civil Service and treat all those with whom they come into contact with consideration and respect'.[14] The Code includes an 'overarching duty' to comply with the law, which became a sensitive issue when the Prime Minister received fixed penalty notices over partygate. Ministers must also abide by Nolan's Seven Principles of Public Life.[15]

The May 2022 edition of the Ministerial Code proved controversial because of what it lacked: the important phrase that ministers must 'uphold the very highest standards of propriety' was removed, presumably because the Prime Minister could not utter them with a straight face; it was amended to say that the Code should 'guide ministers on how they should act and arrange their affairs'. This points to the importance of not retaining the PM as legislator, initiator and judge in these cases.

An established breach of the Code will normally lead to the resignation of the minister, but the lack of due process can produce unjustified departures as well as undeserved exonerations. Peter Mandelson's second resignation as a minister (over the Hinduja brothers case) and Damian Green's removal are possible examples of the former.[16]

Back to the Patel case and Raab

The First Division Association (FDA) brought Priti Patel before court, but the result of the action was somewhat equivocal.[17] This was the first time a breach of the Ministerial Code had been the subject of legal action.[18] In any other area of engagement Patel would have been dismissed or have received a final written warning (even given the 'mitigation' found). The actual rules for ministers are clear. It is the adjudication and enforcement processes that are problematic. Several features are difficult about the affair (the first three of which are commonly found in such cases):

- the fact that the Prime Minister was in effect marking his own homework;
- the failure to publish the full report or even a précis of the facts (accepting that complainants should remain anonymous) or even to make the report available to the court;
- the long delays before the result was announced;
- the Prime Minister and his colleagues pre-announcing the result;
- Patel's failure to issue a proper apology.

A better approach was taken in the case of Dominic Raab, against whom a series of allegations of bullying were made in two different ministries. Fact-finding was delegated to Adam Tolley KC, an employment law barrister, who produced a meticulous forty-eight-page report.[19] He found that Raab had engaged in 'abuse or misuse of power' and was 'intimidating and insulting' in meetings at the Ministry of Justice.[20] Notwithstanding that senior officials had warned him about his behaviour, Raab's ungracious resignation statement took aim at 'snowflake' civil servants. He said he stepped down only because he had pledged to do so if criticised, which he was, but only over two of the several cases against him.[21]

What an unusual role!

We now need to look in more detail at the role filled by Sir Alex Allan, then for months by no one and then by Lord Geidt,[22] then by no one again for a long time and now by Sir Laurie Magnus (3rd Baronet of Tangley Hill), a former banker and the Chair of Historic England.[23] The role was introduced after the CSPL's sixth report in 2003 endorsed Peter Riddell's original proposal for an ethics commissioner. Riddell envisaged a Crown servant, appointed by the monarch. When the role was actually introduced, three years later, it was designed to remove the weight of dealing with ministers' behaviour from the shoulders of Permanent Secretaries, who naturally did not relish such a burden,[24] since they were effectively delivering judgement on their bosses.

Not all cases that might fall within the Adviser's remit are referred to him or her.[25] This is still a decision for the Prime Minister, which makes it doubly difficult when the concerns relate to the conduct of … the Prime Minister. When the role was introduced, it was a case of the Prime Minister proposing, disposing and adjudicating, an unholy and uncomfortable trinity. Jill Rutter, a former civil servant and now a senior fellow at the Institute for Government, rightly criticised the status quo in this way:

> The PM sets the rules. The PM chooses the person to advise on the rules. The PM decides whether to ask that person to investigate a breach and whether to publish the independent adviser's report. He then decides if any consequences should follow.[26]

This is inimical to the rule of law, which requires independence of operation.[27] As Professor Jim Gallagher, who used to head the Scottish justice system, told me, 'The Independent Adviser starts from the position the king can do no wrong'.[28]

In respect of the Adviser, the problems did not start with Johnson. The Adviser's jurisdiction should take in all alleged misconduct by ministers, but the Adviser was not asked by David Cameron to consider the difficult cases of Liam Fox and Jeremy Hunt (in relation to his role in the BSkyB TV channel takeover). Cameron chose instead to have confidential inquiries conducted by the relevant Permanent Secretaries.

After a hiatus of nine months following Sir Alex's resignation, Lord Geidt was appointed to fill his shoes. Geidt had served the Royal Family for many years (he finished up as Private Secretary to the Queen) and was Chair of Governors of King's College London, with a paid post at the defence company BAE Systems Ltd. He had a background in the military and diplomatic worlds. For a Palace courtier, the virtues most required and prized are discretion, loyalty and secrecy first, and probably not rocking the boat as a close second. The latter is not necessarily the qualification most obviously needed for the role of *Independent* Adviser on Ministers' Interests. Yet Lord Geidt came out on top in whatever process was run for this important post. And whether there even was a process is itself obscure, because a freedom of information request elicited the extraordinary reply from the Cabinet Office that even though the 'process' of appointment in this instance ran all the way from November 2020 to April 2021 there was not a single document generated in the Cabinet Office. There was not even an explanation for why no notes were kept. This was not a good look for someone tasked with increasing public confidence in standards. And it was not a first: Sir Alex Allan told a CSPL online evidence session in March 2021: 'I wasn't aware of any particular process when I was appointed, I was simply asked, would I be interested in taking on the role.'

At the pre-appointment scrutiny evidence to the Public Administration and Constitutional Affairs Committee (PACAC), Geidt put it rather laconically, saying that Johnson 'had alighted on my name as being a suitable candidate to fill the role. I was asked to give thought to whether I would be willing to accept appointment if offered.' He declared, 'I'm not here to tell Government what to do'. He also stated, 'Like my predecessor Sir Alex Allan, I believe that I may be capable of engaging plausibly with the Prime Minister, building trust', because 'much will depend on the extent to which a relationship of trust can be built with the office of Prime Minister'.[29] We will soon see how well that turned out. Geidt was probably in a strong position to influence the way in which his role was to evolve only *before* he entered upon it. Yet the single amendment to the rickety scheme that he secured was that the Independent Adviser gained explicit authority to *advise on* the initiation of investigations of alleged breaches of the Ministerial Code,[30] which is not much of a step forward, you might think.

Number 10 refurbishment

Lord Geidt's first challenge was a particularly hot potato and it came just as he took on the portfolio: to consider the refurbishment of Number 10 and the fund raising for it by the person whom he was advising (Prime Minister Johnson) and thus to advise him on his *own* misdeeds. This is (like Greensill[31]) a case of overlapping jurisdictions, since the Electoral Commission also held an investigation. It also raises questions about whether the Adviser has the means properly to delve into such a matter, especially with an uncooperative minister (or in this case Prime Minister).

The facts of the refurbishment case have been covered in the previous chapter. Here I touch on the way the Independent Adviser chose to deal with it. At paragraph 25 of his first *Annual Report*, published in May 2021, Geidt declares that his fellow peer Lord Brownlow had (according to 'the record') 'pursued this task [of assisting with the refurbishment] with energy and due regard for propriety throughout'. No light is let in on what 'the record' is, nor do we know whether Geidt pressed his fellow peer on whether, as a business person, the latter might expect even tiny favours in return, so that there might have been a hint of a potential conflict of interest.

But wait: according to Geidt, the real villains in this piece were civil servants, in particular those Cabinet Office officials who apparently did not advise the Prime Minister that if he were accepting large sums of money from private donors this might lead to perceptions of a conflict of interest. This question of advice assumes of course that an experienced politician (some thirty years in the business) would actually require it.

Apparently he did, because paragraph 28 of the Independent Adviser's *Annual Report* says 'the Prime Minister ... confirms that he knew nothing about such payments until immediately prior to media reports in February 2021'. The word 'confirms' is interesting, because it appears that Geidt just took Johnson's word at face value. One would have thought that with Johnson's form, Geidt would have carefully tested every assertion he made during the investigation.

Geidt decided that the refurbishment 'was not subjected to a scheme of rigorous project management by officials', which amounted to a 'significant failing'. This was, of course, no more than a slap on the wrist (and a metaphorical one at that), and Geidt chose to make no comment at all on the Prime Minister's integrity, even though this had to be the subject of two decisions by Geidt because of a failure by Johnson to disclose an important email trail for the first of these. Geidt says only that Johnson was 'unwise' and that 'a Prime Minister might reasonably be expected to be curious about the arrangements', but he still concludes that Johnson was 'ill served' by his officials.[32]

Following this investigation, the baton was taken up by the Electoral Commission.[33] It could go further than Geidt because of its statutory powers to call for documents and the team of investigators at its disposal. The range of parallel investigations also shows the need for some streamlining of the inquiry process.[34] It is instructive to compare the effectiveness of the Electoral Commission with its statutory powers with the feather duster of the Independent Adviser. In its *Report of Investigation into the Conservative and Unionist Party – Recording and Reporting of Payments*,[35] it concluded that there were 'reasonable grounds to suspect that an offence or offences may have occurred' under the Political Parties, Elections and Referendums Act 2000 (PPERA), because of the failure to disclose this gift for refurbishment.[36]

The Commission found that the Prime Minister had sent a WhatsApp message to Lord Brownlow asking him to make further payments towards the flat at a time when Johnson had said he knew absolutely nothing about requests for money or where the cash was coming from. The Commission accordingly fined the Conservative Party (not Johnson personally) £16,250 for the offence of failing accurately to report the full value of the donation from Huntswood Associates and £1,550 for contravening the requirement to keep proper accounting records.

As often when cornered, Johnson gave a 'humble and sincere apology' for not recalling those text messages when he first briefed Geidt. One might have thought, given this, that the investigation would be reopened in the light of the important new evidence found by the Commission, but he did not do so. He just offered mild criticism of the Prime Minister for not disclosing all of his messages about the renovation of the flat. Geidt then looked weak because *he* did not resign. His concern that he was not being provided with all the relevant information prompted the Prime Minister to promise 'access to all information you consider necessary and prompt' and 'full answers' in future investigations, perhaps to be underpinned by a 'legal instrument'. It did not take long to see whether this would happen; it did not.

Bizarrely, the blog *Popbitch* proved to be a key player in the issue, because Johnson said he changed his mobile phone when the blog published his number and that was the reason he did not disclose the documents, which were on the old phone. This is along the lines of the hoary old excuse 'the dog ate my homework'.[37]

And then along came partygate

The sorry saga of partygate again showed the fundamental weakness of the Independent Adviser position. To PACAC, Geidt said that it was 'reasonable to suggest that the PM being fined constituted a breach of Ministerial Code', but that he did not have any role in investigating this. This was because he had not been asked to do so by … the PM. This may be correct in law, but is surely worthy of a Gilbert and Sullivan opera plot. Strangely again, he refused to answer the question of how much interaction he had had with the Prime Minister while carrying out his job. But he revealed that he came close to leaving the position several times, before saying that there were 'legitimate' questions that could be asked about whether Johnson breached the Code over Number 10 parties. An MP accused him of acting like 'a tin of whitewash'.[38]

Geidt looked increasingly uncomfortable in the role as time went on. The only tool at his disposal to enforce his will against Johnson was indeed the threat of resignation. The leaving letter finally came following an appearance before PACAC on 14 June 2022, which John Crace described in the *Guardian* as 'a masterpiece of nihilism. The last word in futility. Existential despair reconfigured as rapture.'[39] He resigned the next day over 'Decisions related to the Trades Remedies Authority', on which he had been asked to advise. It was an issue about the rule of law.[40] In his plaintive resignation letter, he wrote that 'the idea that a Prime Minister might to any degree be in the business of deliberately breaching his own Code is an affront'.

It is not much of a job if the only way to get noticed is to resign. Geidt told PACAC that 'resignation is one of the rather blunt, but few, tools available to an independent adviser'. He said he had been put in an 'impossible and odious position' over the Trade Remedies Authority issue. Johnson responded that this seemed a curious basis on which to resign, given that he was being asked only to express a view on a hypothetical circumstance.

Given the history of the job and the moral character of Johnson himself, it seemed the PM would be faced with not having another Adviser any time soon. The farrago over Geidt's resignation led Johnson to consider abolishing the job or to replace one Adviser with three. Liz Truss, when standing to be party leader, said she would not appoint an Independent Adviser, as she knew the difference between right and wrong, which is also extraordinary. Sunak did not change the terms of reference for his new Adviser, Sir Laurie Magnus (appointed many months later), one jot. Magnus's first intervention, however, shows some hope that the position can be more useful with a different PM. On taking office, Sunak appointed Nadhim Zahawi to be Chair of the Conservative Party, notwithstanding that he had made a settlement of £5 million for unpaid taxes to HMRC (although Sunak said that he had not known at the time about penalties being exacted). A week before Zahawi was removed on 29 January 2023, Sunak announced that Zahawi had 'addressed this matter in full'. This had added piquancy, because the negotiation with HMRC took place during Zahawi's short tenure as Chancellor in July 2022, when he was responsible for that body. Zahawi's misconduct was exacerbated because he described the allegations as 'media smears' and hired lawyers to silence the whistleblower against him, a tax solicitor called Dan Neidle.

The system worked in this instance because Magnus reported swiftly and decisively against Zahawi, saying that he had misled Sunak and breached the Ministerial Code on no fewer than seven occasions, including making untrue public statements and repeatedly failing to act with openness and honesty.

Reform

It is necessary to unpack certain features relevant to potential reform. Firstly, ministers of the Crown are appointed by the monarch on the advice of the Prime Minister, which is always followed. The Prime Minister must retain the effective power to appoint, or at least most of it.

Secondly, there is a particular problem when it is the Prime Minister's own conduct that is under scrutiny by his own 'Independent' Adviser; in the case of partygate, one had the absurd position that Sue Gray could recommend Johnson be investigated under the Ministerial Code, but it would be he who would have to sanction the inquiry.

Thirdly, this position can be unfavourably contrasted with its equivalents in the other nations of the UK. In Scotland, an independent panel has existed since 2008 to investigate breaches of their code of conduct. This had a particular impact in the bitter dispute between Nicola Sturgeon and Alex Salmond over the handling of sexual harassment allegations against Salmond. The First Minister first referred herself to an independent investigation on whether she broke the Ministerial Code during the Scottish government's investigation of accusations of harassment against her predecessor. In January 2021, this was widened to investigate accusations she had misled the Scottish Parliament. A Northern Irish QC conducted the investigation and concluded that Sturgeon had not broken the Code.

Under the Northern Ireland Ministerial Code,[41] all complaints about alleged breaches are investigated by the Panel for Ministerial Standards. The Panel, however, does not possess powers to reprimand or sanction ministers. The Welsh Code provides that the First Minister can refer alleged breaches to an Independent Adviser for investigation, 'unless he is satisfied that the complaints can be responded to more immediately or routinely'.

In the Canadian system, the Ethics Counsellor administers the Conflict of Interest and Post-Employment Code for Public Office Holders. This independent commissioner can investigate potential conflicts of interest. He or she may act because something has been highlighted by media reports, by the opposition or by another group, or because of information the Ethics Counsellor has acquired – as the Parliamentary Commissioner for Standards may in the UK.

There is also a case for ministers to gain a right of appeal from these inquiries. There should not be just one judge, given the wisdom of the phrase *Juge unique, juge inique*, to which Professor Sir Vernon Bogdanor drew my attention.

The basic case for reform was put to me by Lord Wood of Anfield, who had served as an adviser to Ed Miliband:

> It is important that the Independent Adviser has the full range of ability to investigate across the whole ministerial slate including the Prime Minister. The best method of achieving accountability is by publicity. The Independent Adviser should be able to order publication of the full report. There should be consistency of approach. I find it curious that Lord Geidt was apparently asked about steel tariffs but not breaches of the Northern Ireland Protocol since breach of the law is a breach of the Ministerial Code. The Independent Adviser should have clear terms of reference and in a way this is more important than making it a statutory office.[42]

The Adviser should truly be *independent*. No one should mark their own homework, and it needs someone independent to investigate erring ministers and to check any acute conflicts of interest. This lack lags well behind similar arrangements for MPs, peers and civil servants.[43] The Ministerial Code at present makes the Prime Minister the prosecutor, judge and jury in cases of ministerial impropriety, which cannot be right.

Is the Adviser position necessary at all? Lord Evans of Weardale, the former Chair of the CSPL, thinks so. He told me that 'It is a useful mechanism for the PM to have an independent adviser as an "off ramp" to properly consider standards issues'.[44] The CSPL recommended that the rules regarding the conduct of ministers needed strengthening; they were 'below the bar' for effective standards regulation.

The centrality of the function means that the appointment of the Independent Adviser should be made not by Prime Ministerial fiat, but with the consent of opposition party leaders and by a panel made up predominantly of members independent of the government. There should be a further safeguard, as the CSPL has suggested: 'The Independent Adviser should be appointed through an enhanced version of the current process for significant public appointments' by Parliamentary scrutiny.[45]

The Adviser should have the express authority to determine breaches of the Ministerial Code. The office (independent also from the civil service) should also ensure that reports are published within eight weeks of their submission to the Prime Minister. Lord Evans, in a letter sent to the Prime Minister on 20 April 2021, said that the Independent Adviser should 'be given authority to initiate investigations where in their judgement that is necessary'. The Adviser should also be able to initiate changes to the Code.

As the CSPL has stated, 'Significant advances in independence in standards regulation in Parliament have highlighted the Independent Adviser's comparative lack of independence'.[46] Sir Alex Allan told me that he 'had sufficient resources to carry out my role', but surely an independent investigative function is necessary, whereas at present it is dependent on civil servants. The post does not have its own secretariat but instead relies on the Propriety and Ethics Unit in the Cabinet Office to provide support. The Independent Adviser's function should be statutory and operate more like the Parliamentary Commissioner for Standards, who possesses an independent power to investigate. The whole process should be placed under the general superintendence of a revamped Committee on Standards in Public Life.[47] The need is for a more streamlined method of adjudication on these matters, with rights to legal representation before a panel of retired High Court judges.

At present I would give this system 2 out of 10 on my admittedly subjective scorecard of the regulators.

There is a wider issue of reform of the mish-mash that the Ministerial Code now is. Firstly, the Code's provisions on ethics and standards should be separated from those describing the very processes of Cabinet governance. It should serve as a clear code of conduct of ethical standards for ministers, akin to MPs' and peers' codes of conduct, and based on the Seven Principles of Public Life.[48]

Secondly, although the Code must be owned and issued by the Prime Minister, rather than by Parliament, an obligation in primary legislation for the Prime Minister to publish the Ministerial Code would grant the Code a more appropriate constitutional status. The Independent Adviser should be consulted in any process of revising and reissuing the Code, as has sometimes occurred in the past. Options for greater oversight include that the Code must be laid before the House of Commons or that PACAC be consulted on the drafting of the Code.

One of the main problems with the Ministerial Code as it stood until May 2022 was that the menu of sanctions it provided was an all-or-nothing list, in effect resign or nothing. Sir Alex Allan told me:

> It is not every breach of the Ministerial Code which should lead a minister to resign. Formulating sanctions can be difficult however. For example, temporary suspension of a junior minister may be possible, but suspension of a Secretary of State would be more problematic.[49]

As from 2022, para 1.7 of the Code added that range of sanctions, so that those available 'include requiring some form of public apology, remedial action, or removal of ministerial salary for a period'. I would go further: there should be further sanctions on the specified menu, including:

- a ban on being reappointed as a minister;
- an informal then formal warning;
- loss of pensions.

There should be a time limit for complaints, say three months from the contravention.

The last word goes to the comedian Gráinne Maguire, who said that 'Boris Johnson Ethics Adviser sounds like something you'd have printed on a t-shirt for a stag-do'.

Chapter 5

The public appointments system and the Commissioner for Public Appointments: unmerited jobs and cultural cleansing?

The government seem hell-bent on only appointing people from a very small pool of like-minded individuals. The only criteria for appointment seem to be support for the PM and an opposition to the 'woke' agenda. Some say it was the same under Blair – but at least New Labour was a very wide tent.

Sir Chris Bryant, Chair of the Commons Committee on Standards[1]

There is a gradual chipping away at the independence of public appointments. The cumulative effect is a very uncomfortable position.

Nick Hardwick, former Chief Inspector of Prisons and Chair of the Parole Board[2]

Recent years have witnessed rampant corruption of the public appointments system.[3] A modern, fair and transparent system requires that those who have come through the proper independent appointment processes are not turned down purely on grounds of their political beliefs. But Jonathan Michie OBE,[4] President of Kellogg College, Oxford, was. A distinguished economist, he was approved by an independent panel as the new Executive Chair of the Economic and Social Sciences Research Council (ESSRC),[5] only to be rejected without interview by the then Secretary of State for Business, Energy and Industrial Strategy (BEIS), Kwasi Kwarteng, presumably because of his perceived left-wing politics.[6] It is true that he had, decades earlier, written a book with Seumas Milne, who later became Jeremy Corbyn's Chief of Strategy. However, Michie had not publicly voiced any political views for decades, although his sister was a prominent member of SAGE (the Scientific Advisory Group for Emergencies) during the COVID-19 pandemic who did not slavishly follow the government line and his former brother-in-law was a senior adviser to Corbyn.

The press release from the Department for Business, Energy and Industrial Strategy after this rejection simply said that no 'suitable' candidate had been found, and the search would be resumed to establish 'a wider range of candidates'. There was no basis for a finding of unsuitability about Michie other than his perceived politics.[7]

Kwarteng's negative views were not shared by the independent appointment panel, which was made up of some weighty public servants: Sir John Kingman, founding Chair of UK Research and Innovation (UKRI) and now chair of Legal and General, Dame Ottoline Leyser, UKRI's Chief Executive, and the economist and Brexit campaigner Gerard Lyons, with Mike Keoghan, a senior official in the Business Department as the secretary. The whole point of the independent appointment panel is to assess merit, and this panel could hardly be accused of covert left-wing sympathies.[8] It had told Michie during the interview that he had an impressive CV and a good background, and then subsequently in a letter that he had 'impressed' the panel. He asked for feedback from Kwarteng after the rejection, but feedback came there none.

This post is particularly sensitive because the government and the wider public depend on impartial social science research and research-based solutions to national problems. The Executive Chair of the ESSRC must be committed to that rigour. Setting detailed limits for what any governing party considers legitimate research is inappropriate and a slippery slope. Will Hutton, writing as President of the Academy of Social Sciences, commented:

> Undermining this principle has crossed an important line. It risks turning the post of ESSRC executive chair into a poisoned chalice—diminishing not only the institution and social science but the government's reputation for funding impartial research through arms-length bodies... it [is] all the more important that ministers exercise their prerogative sparingly and judiciously, otherwise these powers become progressively delegitimised.[9]

Kwarteng's approach was probably unlawful as well as unwise, in that it apparently constituted discrimination on the grounds of political belief, although Michie did not stoop to suing.

This is just one of many recent abuses that illustrate why the present system of public appointments is not fit. There have been problems in the past, but Boris Johnson's determination to remove possible dissenters (and people who criticised him personally, especially over his COVID policy) from public appointments was unprecedented. This led towards the hegemony of a narrow clique of Brexit supporters in such appointments. Many people now refuse to serve as independent members of appointment panels on the basis that they have no discernible impact on the outcome. Appointment has become rather like some aspects of the honours system, a bauble for supporting the party. Sir

Ian Kennedy, who was chair of the Independent Parliamentary Standards Authority and of many important public inquiries, told me that many such bodies lived in a 'grey world of legitimacy, accountability, authenticity and control'. They only had 'apparent independence'.[10]

One candidate of my acquaintance told me that she was not called back to sit as a member of an independent scrutiny board because she used to write for the *Guardian* and that in itself was anathema to ministers. The civil servants told her they wanted her back, but they were overruled. Another apolitical acquaintance was a member of a body in the labour arena and was not reappointed, for reasons that are entirely obscure. An ex-Labour minister and long-standing MP who lost her seat applied for twenty public roles but was shortlisted for only one (and not appointed). She would have been an excellent choice and had relevant experience. A Blair Cabinet appointee failed to reach the shortlist for the directorship for the British Council. This is a form of blacklisting, and over time strong candidates are not likely to apply for these posts.

Recent examples cannot be squared with the Code for Public Appointments, which stresses ministerial responsibility, selflessness, integrity, merit, openness, diversity, assurance and fairness. This area of public appointments engages most directly Principle 3 of the Nolan Principles, which says that 'Holders of public office must act and take decisions impartially, fairly and on merit, using the best evidence and without discrimination or bias'.

Lord Gus O'Donnell, the former Cabinet Secretary, told me:

> Many people will not go through with the big public appointments because they don't feel their interest will be kept confidential. There is also much greater politicisation of arts and culture. The risk is that we finish up with the old tap on the shoulder but this time coordinated by Number 10. Over the years, both parties have been partisan in their appointments and the merit principle has been lost sight of.[11]

Culture wars

Under Boris Johnson, many appointments were viewed through the prism of the culture wars waged from Downing Street. There was a particularly aggressive approach to board appointments at museums and other cultural institutions so that only those from a clique considered to be close in thinking to the government on issues such as the removal from public places of statues of now controversial historical figures would be considered for appointment.[12] Those who gained posts needed to commit to the government policy of retaining statues and to explain the context in which the statues were erected. This policy of course interferes with their autonomy. In an egregious example, the government opposed the nomination of the distinguished classicist Mary Beard as a trustee of British Museum apparently because of her pro-EU views.[13] In the end the Museum board discovered it had the power to make a few appointments of its own and chose … Mary Beard.

Checks and balances have gradually been weakened, in some cases to be replaced by cheques. Some of these cases have been high profile, while most were well below the surface. I have found it hard to prise stories out of people, who were naturally reluctant to talk (especially on the record) in case further applications they might make are stymied. I suspect I have uncovered only the tip of the iceberg in the list in the accounts below and in the Appendix.

Excellent people have just given up on the system, as they have found their applications have been a waste of time. There is a whiff of the pedigree chumocracy about all this: it represents a turning back of the clock.[14] People are being appointed who do not obviously have expertise or relevant experience in the particular area to which they are appointed.

Sir Alistair Graham, former Chair of the CSPL,[15] told me that 'All serious appointments are going through Downing Street, who look at the Twitter (now X) feeds for signs of disobedience to the line'. Social media have given special advisers in particular a welter of evidence for second-guessing appointments.[16] Professor Matthew Flinders of the University of Sheffield spoke to me of 'an insatiable desire at the start of government to put your own people in to give an architecture of change'.[17] This affects the recruitment companies. A well-placed source told me:

> I speak to many search firms on a regular basis. Some are quite glad to be used less at the moment as it's both embarrassing and professionally very difficult to be seeking people to apply when they know they would not gain the role.[18]

Two different processes are operating (both of which are also present in the US, and perhaps also in the case of appointments to the House of Lords). First, there is patronage: certain positions are being used as rewards for government supporters in general or donors to the Conservative Party in particular.[19] The rules need to be tightened to prevent jobs for mates or political supporters. Sir Peter Riddell, a former Commissioner for Public Appointments, said in one of his reports 'some at the centre of government want not only to have the final say but to tilt the competition system in their favour to appoint their allies…. I have on a number of occasions had to resist … attempts by ministers to appoint people with clear party affiliations.'[20]

Second, there is the ideological aspect (which has always been present), that the government is trying to implement a political project and is applying political tests for candidates. Government ministers want more like-minded people around them, more believers in them and their project. The argument proceeds that if the political agenda for which I have been elected is reducing poverty, I would want to ensure that the Chair of any body tasked with reducing poverty has the commitment and view of the world that I believe is needed to achieve this reduction (as well as the skills to drive it through). After all, in most organisations, being seen to support the values for which they stand is a key positive *sine qua non* in the recruitment process and goes towards merit. Professor Jim Gallagher, formerly head of the Scottish justice department and twice a member of the Number 10 Policy Unit in London told me that 'Merit is a slippery concept; it incorporates the notion that the appointee needs to be comfortable in the task they are being asked to pursue'.[21]

A distinct area of concern is the unregulated zone of tsars and non-executive directors.

There is also no real pressure on the government to obey the CPA's Governance Code for Public Appointments beyond the court of public opinion, and mostly such appointments do not arouse much public interest. This no doubt lies behind Riddell's comment that 'Ministers are in a strong, even dominant, position in public appointments but some are now seeking to tilt the process even further to their advantage'.[22] He was referring to in particular the pre-briefing and the use of packed selection panels.

The Public Administration Select Committee (PASC, as PACAC was previously named) concluded in 2015 that 'public appointments are not sufficiently transparent, representative, or accountable'.[23] Yet the Grimstone Report, commissioned by the Cameron government, ostensibly to review the system and render it less bureaucratic, concluded that the methods had been a 'major success'. Although doffing the cap to Nolan's sagacity, Grimstone represented a major stepping back from the principles derived from Nolan.[24]

What are public appointments?

The contours of public appointments covered by the CPA are not clearly drawn and are regularly changing as the shape of the state morphs and expands. Hundreds of public bodies play some part in the processes of national government, but are neither government departments nor part of them. They operate to a greater or lesser extent at arm's length from ministers.[25] Non-departmental public bodies (NDPBs) are of varying size and scope and include bodies like art galleries, museums, inspectorates, regulators, NHS boards and advisory committees. In 2020–2021 in the UK, 4,739 public appointments and 1,439 regulated appointments were made. The public bodies within the scope of the CPA are listed in an Order in Council (a form of statute),[26] and this can be easily amended.

Since the mid-1990s it has been Lord Nolan whose legacy has run in this arena to keep the necessary guard on the guards.[27] His Committee here stressed 'Integrity, Openness and Honesty' and bequeathed an independent system for public appointments supervised to some degree by the CPA, an office held by Sir William Shawcross since 2022. The pre-Nolan system was anything but formal; rather, there was the tap on the shoulder, sometimes occurring in the gentlemen's clubs around Pall Mall in London. The temptation was to appoint 'people like us' or chums (a caste formerly known as 'the great and the good').[28] The 'us' were generally white and middle class. A senior politician, however, told me of concern about civil servants' role in appointments, saying they have not done a job like this before, meaning you end up with a quangocracy, a self-licking lollipop, and it 'finishes up with the same people being appointed'. He said that Number 10 should 'spend more time looking for people'.

Although merit and patronage do not mate well, the Nolan Report said that 'ultimate responsibility for appointments should remain with Ministers' but that this process should be 'open', with fully documented and reviewable reasons for appointments.[29] All must now be advertised on the public appointments website, with a job description.

The fundamental question is, what system is most in keeping with a democratic mandate? But there are lots of subsidiaries: What does 'merit' mean? Is it most beneficial for ministers to mould public appointees to their political viewpoint, which, after all, represents what people voted for, or for there to be a wholly independent system that could resemble the Judicial Appointments Commission that limits ministerial involvement?

The argument is that, given that accountability to Parliament is through ministers, ministers should be centrally involved in selection and that the public appointments process for roles in quangos is inherently political. Lord Wasserman, who was for twenty-seven years a civil servant in the Home Office dealing with policing matters and is now a Conservative peer, offered this balanced assessment:

> The governing party should look for supporters who are keen to see the government succeed and are prepared to do what they can to make this happen. But,

of course, they must be competent and the ministers must appoint the best person for the job. It's in no one's interest to appoint incompetents to key jobs in the public sector.[30]

The view of MP Mark Harper is surely realistic and accurate:

Public appointments have always been political. People look back with rose-tinted glasses if they think otherwise. It is reasonable to appoint people who share the political approach of the government and it is ministers who are ultimately accountable. It is important, however, that appointees have a certain level of competence.[31]

The Governance Code for Public Appointments sets out the normal system. Pre-Grimstone, the interview panel for most appointments was chaired by a senior civil servant or the Chair of the relevant public body and included an independent member. For very senior appointments, the chair of the panel was a Public Appointments Assessor appointed by, and reporting to, the Commissioner. Following Grimstone, the process has been devolved to the sponsoring government department, which establishes an advisory assessment panel for each appointment. And each department takes a somewhat different approach to the task.

It is accepted as good practice to seek the minister's views about the quality of the field at the beginning of the process on the role, description, person specification and publicity options for the vacant post, as well as inviting the minister to put forward the names of potential candidates. At the start of the process is where ministers have the maximum chance to mould the pack of candidates in their own image. Chums can be inserted into the mix here, but the apparent (and sometimes more apparent than real[32]) safety valve of the system is that they have to go through the scrutiny of an independent panel, which often does not come out with the answer the minister wants, as happened in the case of Paul Dacre, considered below. Ministers are expected to leave this part of the process alone.

A shortlist is selected for interview by the panel, which is usually chaired by a senior official. The minister then chooses from the list of names submitted by the appointment panel at the end of the process as being appointable.[33] I have, however, heard many worrying tales of interference throughout the processes and of practices that would not pass muster in an employment tribunal if it happened in a normal employment context. The civil service sometimes takes the path of least resistance in giving ministers what they want, even if it is in breach of the spirit of the Code. As one person who operated the system told me, 'for Permanent Secretaries it was an issue constantly of which battles to choose to fight' over public appointments.

Back to the process: having conducted the interview(s), which may be a dry and formal occasion, given the perceived need to ask each candidate the same set of questions,[34] the panel then provides ministers with a list of perceived appointable candidates. Under the original Nolan plan, a panel only puts people 'above the line' or not, and the minister makes the final choice. The Code says they are not to be ranked in order by the panel unless the minister asks for this. Sir Peter Riddell observed:

> For a strictly limited number of regulatory appointments, there is a case for both strengthening the independent element on the advisory interview panel and limiting the number of candidates put forward. This would not be ranking candidates in order of preference but could be like the procedures adopted by the Judicial Appointments Commission where a single candidate is suggested by the interview panel and ministers have a right of veto. So, final ministerial choice would be preserved.[35]

I reluctantly disagree with Sir Peter and think ranking candidates in order of preference in all cases is the better solution. The overriding problem at present is, however, the opaqueness of the whole process. All discussions with ministers at the shortlisting stage should be properly recorded, as would be the case in any proper HR process.

The independent panels are powerless save as gatekeepers of who is above the line and is considered to be appropriate for appointment. Even if there is a candidate who is clearly miles better than the favoured candidate in a panel's view, it does not matter so long as he or she is above the line. Then it is for ministers to decide.[36]

Also, more rigour is needed in the carrying out of due diligence on candidates. Those considering the appointment to the board of the Office for Students of the journalist Toby Young in December 2017 had not checked publicly available tweets posted by him which many found offensive.[37] He resigned before taking up the position.

Under a 2016 amendment to the Governance Code for Public Appointments, a minister may even appoint someone who is deemed unappointable by a panel, but 'must consult the Commissioner for Public Appointments in good time before a public announcement and will be required to justify their decision publicly'.[38] Ministers can also reject the whole candidate list and ask for a competition to be rerun.[39] There are, as for most things in this space, however, no sanctions if this consultation is not carried out. There were no such incidents on Riddell's watch, he told me.[40]

The Commissioner for Public Appointments (CPA)

The post of Commissioner for Public Appointments (CPA) (and the associated Office of the CPA, OCPA) was introduced in 1995 and was designed to invest more confidence. Nolan intended that the CPA would 'regulate, monitor and report on public appointments'.[41] The Commissioner has a very large numbers of appointments to consider. In 2020/2021, there were 693 such positions within the remit. Of these, sixty-seven proceeded without competition.[42]

Broadly speaking, the CPA regulates non-executive part-time jobs in non-departmental public bodies.[43] The CPA is 'to oversee that system and to provide public assurance that these principles [on open public appointments] are observed'.[44] So, with such a challenging brief, and a bulging in-tray, you would expect the CPA to be well resourced. You would be wrong. The Office of the CPA has only three members of staff – including the part-time Commissioner – and is based within the Civil Service Commission Secretariat.

The Grimstone Review generally limited the power of the Commissioner to auditing departments' choices against the Governance Code, although he or she could be more active through informal and formal inquiries and by a wholly new process of audit (carried out by the Office, not by outsiders). Grimstone is a former civil servant, then Chairman of Barclays p.l.c., and was in 2020 created a Conservative peer.

The primary responsibility for ensuring that ministers behaved was put onto Permanent Secretaries and thus taken away from the Commissioner, who now has a more passive, reactive role. An informed insider told me that a determined team of a Secretary of State and their special advisers who want to push through a political appointment will simply not worry about the busy Permanent Secretary policing this to the same degree as would an external regulator operating in the public eye.[45]

The CPA has no enforcement power but can merely draw attention to abuses of the system that would normally remain behind the veil of official secrecy. There may, in particular, be a serious embarrassment factor for ministers and civil servants when the CPA puts a matter into the public arena. Riddell, a former journalist, was more willing to be in that public square than his predecessors and his successor. What is clear is that the CPA's responsibility is, overall, a duty of process, not of outcome. As Claire Perry

O'Neill (a former minister) told me, 'I have always followed the rules. But I don't think there is any penalty for failing to do so, and if you have brass neck enough to ignore the odd *Daily Mail* story it seems to me that it's a pretty lame standards regime.'[46]

It remains to be seen whether the cross-party goodwill that Riddell enjoyed will be transferred to the present incumbent, given the increased prominence of the issue and its particular divisiveness under the Johnson government. His close connections with that administration caused some controversy for William Shawcross on his appointment as Commissioner in 2021. He is a veteran, award-winning journalist. He came to this role from Chairmanship of the Charity Commission for England and Wales from 2012 to 2018. He attracted controversy as the independent reviewer of the counter-terrorism programme Prevent. He is also a former director of the Henry Jackson Society, a conservative think tank.[47] Having been appointed, he stood down from his first major investigation of the complaints made against the appointment of Richard Sharp as Chair of the BBC because he knew Sharp, although it apparently took him seven days before he 'realised' that he did.

Various abuses, then, need to be cleaned up in public appointments.

Leaking

Briefing the media in relation to forthcoming appointments before the process has had a chance to provide candidates makes a mockery of that process. It can make it appear to those outside the gilded circle of pre-preferred candidates that the result of a competition is a foregone conclusion (and thus put off other candidates from applying). This technique has gained greater traction recently, and has received the critical attention of the CPA.[48]

This happened most blatantly in two appointments made to important media bodies by the Johnson government. As just mentioned, Richard Sharp, a former Goldman Sachs investment banker who over many years has donated more than £400,000 to the Conservative Party, graced the board of the Centre for Policy Studies, a right-wing think tank, and used to manage Rishi Sunak at Goldman Sachs, was widely touted in the media in 2019 as likely to be the next Chair of the BBC, well before his actual appointment.[49] Only a few other serious candidates bothered to put their heads above the parapet. Indeed, only ten applied for the BBC Chair on that occasion, because of the widespread trailing of Sharp as the man anointed to assume the job.[50] This figure was fewer than would normally be expected to apply. What was not known to the appointments panel was that Sharp had introduced Johnson's cousin

Sam Blyth to Simon Case, the Cabinet Secretary, with a view to discussing Blyth guaranteeing the making of a loan (it is still not known by whom) in the sum of £800,000 to the Prime Minister.[51] Sharp discussed his becoming Chair with Johnson before applying for the job, even though, as PM Johnson would have to approve the appointment. Sharp, however, assured the Commons Culture, Media and Sport Select Committee several times, 'I believe I was appointed on merit'. The Committee decided that he had undermined trust in the BBC and that this was a significant error of judgement. It said that the omissions 'constitute a breach of the standards expected of individuals' applying for public appointments. The Scottish National Party MP John Nicolson described this as 'pals appointing pals donating money to pals'.

Sharp insisted on continuing as BBC Chair even though he had not complied with the BBC application form, which states that you must disclose any conflict of interest. Blyth appears to be a distant cousin of Johnson and it remains unclear why Sharp needed to be involved at all. What was also troubling was that Blyth was being considered for the post of Chief Executive of the British Council at the same time as this was in train, in particular in November and December 2020. After a report by Adam Heppinstall KC and months of poor morale for the BBC, Sharp resigned in April 2023. The KC decided that Sharp had created a potential perceived conflict of interest by failing to tell the interview panel he had discussed the job with Johnson. At the time, Johnson was struggling with his finances, not least because of the cost of his divorce from Marina Wheeler.

The BBC role has an intriguing history. Some decades ago, in less partisan days, Harold Wilson appointed Lord Hill to the same post, which was seen as hostile by the BBC (Hill had been a Conservative Postmaster-General). Tony Blair reappointed to it a known Tory, Sir Christopher Bland. In a cognate cross-party appointment, William Whitelaw under Thatcher welcomed the Labour peer Lord Thomson to the Independent Broadcasting Authority.

The second media furore concerned the controversial on–off process for Paul Dacre, who in 2020 was frequently trailed in Number 10 briefings as the soon-to-be-appointed Chair of Ofcom. Dacre edited the *Daily Mail* for twenty-eight years, and was the combative chief spokesman for many years of the Tory Right. Ofcom has an especially pivotal role because it regulates media companies, including the BBC, of which the Conservative government and Dacre were at times very critical. Indeed, for years his newspaper has been enemy number one of the BBC. This constant briefing again predictably had a chilling effect on other applicants coming forward. Oliver Dowden, the Secretary of State for Culture, Media and Sport, somewhat disingenuously said on the *Today* programme that the reason Dacre was not appointed and the process had to be rerun was that there were so few applicants.[52] In fact, the government, by its incessant leaking that he was the preferred applicant, discouraged others.[53]

Changing sponsors

Usually it is clear which government department will take responsibility for a particular appointment, but some jobs have vague lines of responsibility into a particular department, so that the sponsor department may be changed. This appears to be what happened in Dacre's case, as he was initially turned down as an appointable candidate for the role of Chair of Ofcom when the panel was, as it should have been most naturally, under the tutelage of the Department for Digital, Culture, Media and Sport.[54] A second panel, which would have been controlled by Number 10, was, however, announced before Dacre eventually withdrew.[55]

Subtle changing of the job requirements in the second round for the Ofcom post also shows how the department can mould the job to the person, which is the opposite of how things should be done in employment terms. These amendments were clearly designed to favour Dacre. The successful candidate originally had to demonstrate that she or he could work 'collegiately' with other board members and have a 'positive relationship' with the Ofcom chief executive. These were probably not seen as virtues obviously to be found in the former *Daily Mail* editor. The terms were, however, watered down the second time round so as to require only working 'effectively' with board members and creating a 'productive relationship' with the chief executive. There were also subtle features of the constitution of the second board for the selection which should be noticed for connoisseurs of the ancient HR science (or dark art) of 'advanced jiggery pokery'!

Then, in December 2021, there was an unexpected turn of events that rendered the second panel moot. Dacre was appointed to be editor in chief of DMG Media, the holding company for the *Daily Mail* and others, and withdrew from the Ofcom process. But, characteristically, he did not depart the field quietly. He described his own trauma in a letter to *The Times* that is a good example of the Tory critique of public appointments. He said that his experience of 'an infelicitous dalliance with the Blob'[56] had not been positive, and he went much further and claimed that senior Whitehall figures were determined to exclude from public appointments anyone who had right-of-centre convictions.

Ultimately, a media industry veteran, Lord Grade, was appointed as Chair of Ofcom; he had been Chair of the BBC between 2004 and 2006 and held a similar position at ITV as Executive Chair. The natural thing for previous heads of Ofcom was to have brandished their independence,[57] yet, significantly, Lord Grade appeared to do precisely the opposite when he said a few months before his appointment that just one more lapse in the BBC's journalism would 'bring the house down'.[58]

Panel packing

The appointment of the new Chair of the Office for Students in 2020 of Lord Wharton (who was a Stockton MP between 2010 to 2017 and helped run Johnson's 2019 leadership campaign) appears to involve the dark art of panel packing; a Conservative-dominated panel appointed a former Conservative MP without any obvious experience in the education sphere to this sensitive (and well remunerated) role. I have been told that Wharton performed very well at interview. He was seen as someone who would stand up for freedom of speech. The Office for Students was especially sensitive because it was at the heart of the 'culture wars' being waged by the Johnson Downing Street machine.

At the time, the CPA raised concerns about a packed selection panel for this role, but to no avail; this shows the limited power of the Commissioner. The interview team consisted of Baroness Wyld, a former Tory councillor, Patricia Hodgson, a former Tory candidate, Nick Timothy, the former chief of staff to Theresa May, Eric Ollerenshaw, a Tory MP from 2010 to 2015, and Susan Acland-Hood, the Permanent Secretary at the Department for Education.[59] Riddell was rightly strident in his public remonstrations about this particular process (although he only had jurisdiction over the senior independent panel member and she operated independently) and wrote to the House of Commons Education Select Committee with his concerns. He could huff and puff as much as he liked; he had no power to restrain the appointment going ahead with such a panel (although his public remarks led to greater caution in later panel appointments).

Appointments without competition

The Grimstone report noted that there will be 'exceptional occasions when ministers may decide that a full appointments process is not appropriate or necessary'. In those instances Grimstone recommended that 'there should always be an independent scrutiny before the appointment is announced'.[60] The OCPA's *Annual Report* for 2020/2021 states 'the Commissioner was notified or consulted seventy-nine times on either making appointments without holding a recruitment competition, or extending appointees beyond the two terms or ten years of service'.[61] Ministers and officials often leave decisions too late, and if the process is delayed interim appointments have to be made.

Appointing donors

Party donors should not have any special purchase on appointments, but in fact they do and increasingly so.[62] A *Sunday Times* investigation in February 2022 found that six Tory donors had been appointed to highly prized roles to run cultural bodies, among them the National Gallery, the National Portrait Gallery and the Tate Museum.[63] These appointments may indeed be of excellent candidates, but the look is wrong and the smell test is engaged. Between them the six had given £3 million to the Conservative Party.

Donors had access to a biweekly list of appointments from Number 10, although it is believed that this also goes out somewhat more widely. The Conservative Party also provides help to donors to apply for public appointments via the PM's appointments unit. The *Sunday Times* disclosed an email from Party headquarters that said: 'We thought you may be interested in the latest public appointments. It is important Conservatives rebalance the representation at the head of these important public bodies.'[64]

The businessmen donors

Mohamed Amersi illustrates the methodology. In December 2020 the staff of Ben Elliot[65] (co-Chair of the Conservative Party) lobbied for Amersi to be considered for the Chair of the National Lottery Community Fund. A Party employee wrote an internal email to someone in Number 10 saying 'Amersi is very interested in the chairmanship and certainly has the skills for it (I know the Fund). I have spoken to [another official] but know you work with the public appointments team. Can we see that he is at least considered for the role.' This cannot have held his application back (although it did not propel it forward much either). His interest was discussed with Amanda Milling MP, then the Party's co-chair. This was at a time when the Party was keen to keep Amersi in the Leaders' Group. Those in this donors' circle gained extra access to ministers on the basis of a minimum contribution to the Party of £50,000.

It seems to have accorded 'access all areas' tickets for those who contributed. In fact, Amersi did not gain the job, so that you could say that the system reasserted itself, although this was because the prize went to Blondel Cluff, a solicitor, academic, charity trustee and diplomat who was the wife of Algy Cluff, who used to own the *Spectator* when Johnson was the editor.

David Ross was appointed the Chair of the National Portrait Gallery. As well as being a major Tory donor he had (it was alleged) the extra advantage for Number 10 that he had arranged a holiday in Mustique for Boris Johnson at the end of 2020. He was due to receive a peerage in the Johnson resignation honours list but his name was taken off for reasons which remain obscure.

Dido Harding and Kate Bingham: appointments without competition

The appointments without competition of Dido Harding, former chief executive officer of Talk Talk,[66] and the venture capitalist Kate Bingham to important NHS bodies during the COVID-19 pandemic (Head of NHS Test and Trace[67] and Head of the Vaccine Taskforce respectively) merit separate consideration, not least because one of the cases (unusually) ended up before the courts. Bingham was spectacularly successful in her role with the vaccine rollout programme, Dido Harding much less so. Both of them happen to be the wives of Tory MPs – the former the spouse of John Penrose, who ironic- ally enough was then also the Anti-Corruption Tsar. Bingham, however, had lots of relevant experience for her role from years spent in biotech venture capital.[68]

These were not regular quango appointments: several people were brought into the heart of the executive branch, bypassing the civil service and its normal procedures for appointment. Bingham and Harding directed a massive amount of civil service effort for months, which is extraordinary in itself. A source within government tells me that when (s)he raised questions internally there was a general understanding that the appointments were 'irregular but temporary'.[69]

The Harding appointment, to run COVID Test and Trace, a vastly ex- pensive project, even bypassed the rules set by the Northcote–Trevelyan civil service reforms dating from 1854 and the public accountability principles put into force by the first Gladstone administration. In the book *Spiked*, Jeremy Farrar and Anjana Ahuja wrote that it was a grave error to appoint Harding.[70] Although Matt Hancock as Secretary of State for Health had praised Harding's 'significant experience in healthcare and fantastic leadership', Farrar, the then

Chief Executive of the Wellcome Trust, from close quarters could not see what skills she brought to the role.

Lack of due diligence

The appointment process for the Chair of the Charity Commission in 2021 was a major fiasco, illustrating several separate abuses. The body performs a sensitive role in keeping the voluntary sector within the law, supervising the extraordinary number of some 169,000 charities in England and Wales, and could be used as a key part of the culture wars agenda. A friend of Johnson was appointed, but he resigned before formally even taking up the role.

There was here a pre-emptive strike by a minister that effectively put up a notice that 'others need not apply'.[71] In advance of the competition starting, Oliver Dowden said that the new Chair of the Charity Commission would 'reset the balance' after he claimed that some charities had been 'hijacked by a vocal minority seeking to burnish their woke credentials'.[72] After a long drawn-out appointment process (about nine months), Martin Thomas was appointed Chair.[73] As a positive he seemed to have had some relevant experience, with a background in the charity sector and as the Chair of two charities. Before that, he was the Chair at Women for Women International UK.

He will, however, be remembered (unfairly for him) as the man who had been caught sending a photo of himself at a Victoria's Secret store to an employee of the latter charity.[74] He said that the chain of lingerie shops was thinking of putting money into that charity. This misconduct allegation had in fact been dismissed by the charity but it was too 'good' a story for the tabloid press to ignore (or check). His resignation before he took up the post was instead triggered by the fact that two other allegations had been upheld in relation to his conduct at other charities (and one of them had filed a serious incident report with the Charity Commission itself[75]). Bizarrely, this was not picked up in the due diligence process conducted by the civil service; it seems obvious that if a person is to become Chair of the Charity Commission his or her record of conduct at charities should be reviewed, and this information should not have been at all difficult to locate. The civil servants involved, however, admitted that they had neither taken up references for Thomas nor checked his track record in those charities. Sarah Healey, the Permanent Secretary at the Department for Digital, Culture, Media and Sport, defended this on the basis that each department had its own policy on whether to take up references and theirs was against taking them up, because it could be 'time consuming' and did not add much value, which seems somewhat odd.[76]

On 11 January 2022, the House of Commons Digital, Culture, Media and Sport Select Committee, after a full review, delivered a damning verdict on this appointment process, rightly deeming it to be 'shambolic'. Julian Knight, the Conservative Chair of the Committee, memorably said that this process showed the modern civil service as 'now more a Reliant Robin than a Rolls-Royce'. He also criticised the Department for carrying out fewer checks for a post overseeing a £70 billion sector 'than you would if you were employing someone to do a paper round'.[77]

Eventually, Orlando Fraser KC, a friend of then Prime Minister Johnson, was appointed in March 2022. He is the son of the author Lady Antonia Fraser.[78] It was also revealed by the *Sunday Times* that his wife's family was close to the Royal Family,[79] which is problematic given that several complaints to the Charity Commission involved charities linked to them.[80] He was apparently instructed by Johnson to leave the independent schools alone.

Delays

The length of time taken for appointments is also a major problem. A source told me that 'Chairs of public bodies are tearing their hair out about getting people appointed to their boards and in particular how long it takes to do so'. Sir John Kingman, former head of UK Research and Innovation and a former Treasury civil servant explained:

> There has been a step change in the politicisation, and even what some might call corruption, of public appointments. It is true that this was not unheard of in the past, but the scale and reach of it is now of a completely different order. Obviously, there is a perfectly arguable democratic case for elected ministers being free to appoint whoever they want to run public bodies. But there is an inescapable cost in quality, once a narrow political acceptability test is applied both to candidate pools and to appointment panels, and of course good people will be much less willing to chair public bodies where they now know they will have very little voice in board and CEO appointments which are made on political acceptability, not on merit. Political vetting at every stage, as well as a seemingly very limited pool of politically acceptable candidates, have also hopelessly gummed appointments processes up, resulting in crazy delays and leaving too many critically important roles vacant for very long periods, even years, such as the Chair roles at Ofcom and the CMA.[81]

Kingman also condemned ingrained habits in departments of treating time 'as a free good' without a clear enough focus on outcomes. He gave as an example the appointment of the head of Innovate UK with a budget of over £1 billion a year. Until the appointment of Indro Mukerjee, the post had been left vacant for more than three years, and Sir John says that 'the government process took us round and round in circles. It is just not sensible that an organisation of Innovate's importance can be left without a permanent head for three years.' He criticised the fact that there is 'the deployment of many political advisers around government, all of whose views are thought to be needed before every stage of every process for every minor appointment can proceed. There are a lot of appointments, and special advisers are very busy. As a result, they tend to do their collective political policing job extremely slowly.'

There was also a lengthy gap at the Competition and Markets Authority after Andrew Tyrie resigned as Chair. I have been told of many relatively minor appointments that have taken a year to be approved by Downing Street.

Birds of a rare plumage

Two significant areas escape the jurisdiction of the CPA.

1. Tsars

Rather vague tsar positions proliferated under the Johnson (and immediately previous) governments, becoming an important part of the 'patronage state' or chumocracy. They are not subject to any regulation at all. Some are unpaid and others are rather well remunerated. If you can set up a new body or tsardom and appoint whomever you like to the position, you can effectively bypass other institutions and the 'inconvenience' of the public appointments criteria altogether. These are often given out as rewards to buy political loyalty. There are no rules, procedures or codes to govern their appointment, role or indeed payment.

Four hundred such figures have been appointed since 1997.[82] Many of the roles fizzle away after a little while, such as the Shale (Fracking) Tsar, but some have real influence and staying power, such as the Tsar for Troubled Families. Tsars are mainly important in bringing matters to public attention. They did, however, lead core parts of the pandemic response, including vaccines, test and trace, personal protective equipment (Lord Deighton) and education catch-up. Successive Prime Ministers have relied on an informal approach of appointing them. It is all rather *ad hoc*.

They can be called on to appear before select committees, but are not bound to face other Parliamentary and even media questioning, notwithstanding the influence some may wield. I believe that they should fall within the scope of the CPA unless they are certainly going to be transient, say less than six months.

2. Non-executive directors

Unelected bodies have expanded rapidly, with little formal constitutional recognition.[83] There are decision takers who stand outside the normal domain of politics or the market, and they include non-executive directors (NEDs) of government departments, whose roles also do not fit within the public appointments paradigm or the regulated regime.[84] They were first introduced as a class in the early 1990s.[85] In 2005 the first Corporate Governance Code recommended that each Whitehall department should have at least two NEDs, to sit on the management board chaired by the Permanent Secretary. The 2010 Ministerial Code emphasised that NEDs should largely be drawn from the 'commercial private sector'.[86]

In 2011 the Code was significantly revised. Boards would be chaired by the Secretary of State, with at least four NEDs on them to advise on performance, delivery and strategic leadership. The influence of the NED depends very much on the minister and the Permanent Secretary in the department. Sometimes their roles are sinecures but NEDs are often asked to carry out informal reviews, help with personnel issues or conduct 'deep dives' into specific areas of a department's work. The 2020 Declaration on Government Reform gives a bigger role for NEDs, in assessing the performance of Permanent Secretaries. Lord Butler told me, however, 'I am very sceptical of the role of non-executive directors; they have a business background, which needs different skills'.[87]

Tom Brake of Unlock Democracy, a former MP, goes further: 'There is now strong evidence that cronyism runs as deeply in NED appointments as it does in PPE contracts'.[88] The Constitution Unit, however, offers a different view:

> non-executives have definitely proved their worth: they are high calibre people, who have shown real commitment, contributing a lot more time than they signed up for. Civil servants greatly value their input and expertise; but many NEDs find the role frustrating, and feel they could be more effective if the system only allowed it.[89]

Michael Gove was eclectic in his appointments of NEDs:

> I sought to give non-executive directors a more active role. They had been traditionally seen as an additional source of wisdom, another weight in the scale to

deal with the impetuosity of ministers. I wanted to bring them closer to having an executive role. I encouraged them to be tough on me and on other ministers, to hold our feet to the fire. There is no value in just having chums. I appointed excellent people who did not necessarily agree with me politically, for example Michael Barber, who had served the Labour government, Martin Narey, who was not politically aligned with me; I appointed a Lib Dem and at DEFRA a Labour supporter.[90]

These appointments should be as transparent as the rest of public appointments and should be within the ambit of the OCPA. The CSPL was categoric to this effect.[91] Lord Falconer told me: 'They should be used to bring in outside talent and not another group of donors and insiders'.[92]

Sir Peter Riddell, however, is not keen on NEDs being regulated:

> Regulation of public appointments only works if ministers and departments accept the principles of fair and open competition under the government's own Governance Code – with only rare exceptions. The problem with including non-executive appointments to departmental boards within the remit of the Commissioner's regulation is that some ministers have treated NEDs as personal appointments and there has been an increasing use of direct, largely political, appointments without any form of competition. You cannot operate a regulatory system where such direct appointments are regular rather than the exception.[93]

Many Tory MPs have been appointed as unpaid trade envoys and other such jobs, so that the 'payroll' vote of those signed up to support the government no-matter-what gets bigger, even though they are not paid. I catalogue various other abuses in the Appendix.

The long view

We need to revert to the key question of politicisation. Riddell as CPA complained of repeated 'attempts by ministers to appoint people with clear party affiliations', which he tried to rebuff.[94] This is similar to what happens in the USA for senior governmental appointments, but without the independent institutional check of Senate confirmation for important roles. Nick Timothy, joint Downing Street Chief of Staff to Theresa May until his resignation in the wake of the 2017 general election, gave me some insight into the mentality: 'Ministers are inclined to circumvent or game the system on public appointments because it is rigid and dominated by the civil service'.[95]

Dame Sara Thornton offered an interesting practical contrast between politicians and public appointees as she saw it:

If you are a politician, you know that your position is precarious and you may lose office at any time. Taking a public appointment is quite different. I fear that good people are being put off applying for such posts because they are becoming so political; and there is less certainty about reappointment.[96]

My informants inside Number 10 claim that this appointing of chums is by no means a new phenomenon and David Prout, a former civil servant, told me that 'ministers have over a long period sought to appoint people in their own image'. Here we need a little history. One of the most notorious examples of nepotism was under Labour, when Peter Jay was appointed by his father-in-law Jim Callaghan as ambassador to Washington in 1977 at the age of forty, notwithstanding that he had zero diplomatic experience. In the 1980s virtually all public appointments were blatantly and unashamedly political. Margaret Thatcher famously often asked the question 'Is he one of us?' before an appointment was made (it was rarely a 'she'). Even for minor appointments to local consumer councils, ministers' private offices were told to check with the relevant local Conservative Association to see whether those put forward were of the right persuasion.

In the 1990s, this started to change, particularly after the Nolan Report, and by the end of the decade most public appointment procedures were much more objective and independent. In the 2000s the Nolan Principles were largely adhered to. But as it became more transparent, it also was clear that the final stage of some appointment processes was being interfered with by ministers and Number 10. In one case, a household name for a culture job was found to have 'liked' a tweet about a race riot in the USA in the 1950s and a red mark was put against her. She did not gain that job.

As to when this politicisation really got going, many point the finger at the practice of picking political allies adopted by New Labour.[97] The Blair and Brown governments, it is said, ensured that the Chairs of most NHS trusts were Labour-leaning. There was also the phenomenon of the 'quango queens' (as the tabloid media dubbed them), who were close to the government and who acquired a clutch of appointments.[98] Gordon Brown, however, answered my written questions by saying:

I appointed people that would be said to be more of a right wing persuasion to Governor of the Bank of England on two occasions and the same was true of the important Monetary Policy Committee. These were probably the most important appointments a government made and they were made without regard to political bias.[99]

Brown's appointment of Gavyn Davies to the Chairmanship of the BBC, however, raised eyebrows, as he was the husband of Sue Nye, Brown's Director of Government Relations and former diary secretary.

In the 2010s, interference became more obvious and more widespread. Under the coalition government there was a deep frustration that public appointments were perceived to be still dominated by what government ministers saw as the soft left and a New Labour legacy. The Right argue that Britain is still, so many years after his retirement as Prime Minister, run essentially by a Blairite elite of 'liberal metropolitans'. The Conservative Home website has a regular feature entitled 'Calling Conservatives: New Public Appointments announced' that encourages its readers to apply for vacant posts. The Taxpayers' Alliance reported in 2018–2019 that of 1,844 appointments where the political allegiance was declared (and this is a small percentage, below 10% and falling), 47.4% were Labour-supporting, while 31.6% supported the Tories.[100] This is, however, a contested area, given that the 2019/2020 CPA *Annual Report* cites the figures of 38.3% and 36.8% respectively.

Bipartisanship can, however, be seen, for example in two big appointments made by the coalition government: Alan Milburn, a former Labour Health Secretary, to the sensitive Chair of the Social Mobility Commission and Andrew Adonis, a Labour peer, to the National Infrastructure Board.

Political interference became more centralised in the 2020s, to such an extent that the Nolan Principles were no longer recognisably in operation. Laura Wyld was put in charge of public appointments at Number 10 and most key appointments went through her. Theresa May as PM redressed the balance a bit. For example, she asked Matthew Taylor, who had worked for Tony Blair, to report on the gig economy, and another Blair adviser, Simon Stevens, ran the NHS under successively May and Johnson. Things, however, got much more political under Johnson.

It is difficult to assess whether New Labour were as bad as Johnson. I asked Ed Richards, a member of the Number 10 Policy Unit under Tony Blair, who denied that there were overly political appointments in that period and gave a reason:

> Tony Blair said in keeping with his overall stance as far as I witnessed it that always 'we want the best person for the job'. He was meritocratic about these matters, but it was more than that; the New Labour project was designed to be capable of absorbing ideas and capability from a broad group, so there would always be room for people who were not Labour to gain public appointments.

This seemed to me to be part of wanting to make Labour a more natural party of government.[101]

Tony Blair himself told me:

> Appointments were always based, fundamentally, on ability and suitability for the role. It's important to note that after long periods of Opposition – and we were out of power for eighteen years – the culture and values within public life mirror the government that defines it. We were elected on a bold manifesto with a landslide majority but with many institutions geared instinctively against our proposals. We were never party political in that regard, but there were institutions where an overwhelming party political bias necessitated an extensive rebalance which viewed out of context could appear excessive.[102]

All my research suggests that politicisation was taken to new lengths by the Johnson government, with much greater centralisation of the process in Number 10. SpAds became more involved.[103] There were weekly public appointments meetings. The 'cultural cleansing' of those who disagreed politically with them was spearheaded by Dougie Smith, often described as the most important person in the UK of whom you have probably never heard. Sheridan Westlake, a senior Number 10 adviser who unusually survived from Cameron to Sunak, was also a central player. As one anonymous source expressed it to me, the rules had not changed but the way in which they were being interpreted and administered had. I was told by another source that the only way to circumvent Westlake was to appeal to the Prime Minister himself.

The former civil servant Jill Rutter made a more fundamental point to me, contrasting the political parties:

> Many Conservatives think their supporters have not in the past had a track record of securing important public appointments. This may be because fewer of them were interested. So recent governments – Cameron, May and Johnson – have all thought they needed to put extra effort into getting their people into such posts, and Number 10 has become much more actively involved in appointments which previously would have been rubber stamped by the PM.[104]

The journalist Michael Crick detects a difference between the supporters of the two parties which accounts for some of this:

> Public appointments are more likely to appeal to Labour supporters because they are less likely to gain high-paid business appointments. Each government appoints its own and then the next feels they need to roll the clock back again. So, a more extreme approach is taken.[105]

Parliament's role

Some think that the answer to this covert politicisation is actually open discussion in Parliament, although this would risk a different sort of politicisation *between* parties and would be time-consuming.[106] It would, however, render it a more transparent process.[107] The current role of Parliament in public appointments is, surprisingly, somewhat vague, confined to pre-appointment hearings for preferred candidates to chair more than fifty public bodies as set out in a Cabinet Office list, which serves as guidance. There are anomalies, so that five Chief Inspectors are on the list, yet the Independent Chief Inspector of Borders and Immigration, Insolvency Service, National Infrastructure Commission and Medicines and Healthcare Products Regulatory Agency are outside. To these positions might usefully be added: Chairs of the House of Lords Appointments Commission and the Legal Services Board; the Chairs of Ofsted and Ofqual (in addition to the Chief Inspectors, already included), and the National Schools Commissioner; and the Chairs of NHS Improvement and of Health Watch.[108]

Some of the cases considered by Parliament are prescribed in legislation, such as the appointment of the Comptroller and Auditor General, while others are treated as such by convention, like the Parliamentary and Health Service Ombudsman, and others by agreement between the minister and the relevant committee.[109] The Parliamentary Commissioner for Administration is a Crown appointment. Since 2011 the Parliamentary and Health Service Ombudsman has been appointed following a process led by the House of Commons Service, involving both a Permanent Secretary and the Chair of PACAC as members of the selection panel.

Parliament cannot veto these appointments; it can merely give an advisory opinion. In several cases, a candidate has withdrawn when it has become clear that a select committee would recommend against their appointment – but in others, ministers have proceeded to appoint notwithstanding an adverse view from the relevant select committee. On only six occasions did this result in the relevant committee recommending that the preferred candidate should not be appointed. Ministers, however, rejected this recommendation in four of those six cases. Examples include the appointment of Amanda Spielman to head Ofsted and that of Baroness Stowell (a Conservative peer) to chair the Charity Commission, although Stowell served only one term. In another case, commitments given during a hearing led to a later resignation.[110]

The list of the posts subject to Parliamentary scrutiny has not been updated since 2013,[111] and, as Riddell says, there is 'no obvious logic' as to what positions are covered in this net. He has rightly proposed that for pre-appointment hearings select committees should have the right to summon the relevant Secretary of State.

The Public Administration and Constitutional Affairs Committee was scathing:

> The Government has appeared to approach the pre-appointments process as a tick box exercise rather than an important component in the public appointments process. The Committee's patience in this respect is not limitless. We are aware that this frustration is shared by other Select Committees. When making appointments that require a pre-appointment hearing, sufficient time must be allowed for this stage to be completed.[112]

Conclusion

Most public appointments are non-political and non-contentious – the practical issues on an everyday level are delay, low or no pay, and lack of social and geographic diversity in recruitment. Shawcross has already emphasised that he is seeking candidates for appointment from the north of England. It is helpful that an apprenticeship scheme for appointments has been established. The record on gender and ethnic diversity is now in fact far better than in the rest of the public sector, the private and voluntary sectors and universities.

On my informal impressionistic system of classification, I give the public appointments system just 4 out of 10. We will consider reform in the final chapter, and you should look at the list of abuses in the Appendix. Prepare to be shocked!

Chapter 6

The Advisory Committee on Business Appointments: revolving doors and dogs with rubber teeth

I think it is desirable and beneficial to the country that men of considerable experience should be available, when they leave government to the service of industry and commerce.

Harold Macmillan[1]

Civil servants go into industry or finance. Now it is almost the exception not to. It is not so much specific corruption as atmospheric pollution.

A Labour minister[2]

Introduction: the conundrum

The doors revolve ever faster. But as they revolve, the glass in the doors becomes more opaque. A 1909 cartoon in the *Evening Standard* summed up the issue brilliantly when it showed a board of directors waiting to start a meeting. The caption had one of directors saying 'I am very sorry. We have just received a telephone message from the chairman. He has not yet quite resigned from the Government.'

In 1968, Conservative MP Anthony Courtney openly explained that 'Election to the House of Commons not only consolidated but also improved my business affairs. I had acquired for the benefit of the firms with which I was connected improved personal contact with the Board of Trade and other ministers.'[3] When one Cabinet minister left the government in 1990, a fellow Tory MP referred to his resignation letter as akin to a 'Situations Wanted' advert.[4] This interacts most directly with the Nolan Principle of Integrity.[5] There is of course nothing wrong in going from one job to another, building up skills in one place and using those skills elsewhere. There are many examples of this being beneficial to policy making. It can drive innovation and enable the sharing of best practice and expertise, as well as providing an opportunity for individuals to develop their careers. This may benefit the consumer and taxpayers.[6] Interchange between the private and public realms is an overall positive, as Macmillan's quote above attests. There is, however, a sense that public roles are a stepping stone on the way to private riches. The main problem is risk management, including harm from people who accidentally let slip something confidential from their old job when they move to a new one. Proper regulation of the afterlife of civil servants and ministers is necessary for transparency and accountability, and ultimately for the good of democracy. It is partly what Nolanism was trying to control.[7] The task – in the words of Cabinet Secretary Simon Case, is 'to stop people making direct personal financial gain from the privileged information that they have gained in government'.[8]

The other danger is that a hidden 'cohort system' operates in which the present set of officials are lenient to those moving on in the hope they too will be permitted to take lucrative jobs when they depart from public service. Worse still, there may be questions about whether decisions made in government are influenced by the possibility of jobs to be taken afterwards, so that the interests of the private sector are disproportionately taken into account in quite subtle ways. This may even be a corrupting influence.

Often expensive consultants are hired from the private sector. Lord Wasserman, who was for seven years a civil servant in the Home Office dealing with policing matters and is now a peer, told me:

> There is a natural tendency in civil servants who work alongside successful consultants for any length of time to see themselves in those positions, either on retirement or even earlier. As there is no longer a mandatory retirement age, civil servants naturally begin thinking of other career opportunities at an earlier stage than we did.

The dangers in this area were clearly illustrated in the Greensill Capital scandal.[9]

A particular danger is that a minister or civil servant may give improper advantage to companies, groups or think tanks because he or she intends to seek a berth there at a later date. A vast number of civil servants are involved in regulating businesses, and these businesses may employ them after they leave public service in the hope that they can open doors for them in the public sector. The extensive regulation of the culture sectors makes these areas sensitive too. And many companies are more interested in the connections made by the ex-public servant than by any actual expertise they may bring. Occasionally, there have been issues of abuse of official secrecy too.

As the government put it in evidence to the Committee on Standards in Public Life, there is 'moral and reputational pressure on people leaving public office'.[10] Jill Rutter, formerly a senior Treasury civil servant, says:

> There is nothing wrong – and indeed potentially a lot of benefit – in bringing people from the outside into the civil service, but you do need to iron out areas of potential conflict of interest. In the case of tax, for example, HMRC lose staff regularly into the big accountancy practices, and the government can gain expertise by allowing people from those practices into government on secondment. But, as with all interchange, those need to be managed properly to ensure they do not gain an unfair advantage from misuse of inside knowledge.[11]

A little history

There is now increased porosity in the boundary between the state and business, although some movement between private and public sector is by no means new. This used to be primarily at senior levels: for example, Edward Heath as Prime Minister brought in Derek Rayner from Marks and Spencer to advise on efficiency in the public sector.[12] Under New Labour, there was a renewed attempt to open up the senior ranks of the civil service to people with skills from outside. The Blair government put delivery units in the Cabinet Office and the Treasury that were led by outsiders such as Michael Barber.[13] Gordon Brown made ten appointments of ministers from the outside to his 'Government of All Talents' (and they inevitably became known as GOATS[14]).

Francis Maude as Cabinet Office minister under the Conservative-led coalition of David Cameron gave this further momentum. The issue has become increasingly difficult because ministers and civil servants are leaving the public sector for private jobs at a much younger age. This applies to Prime Ministers too. Between 1900 and Thatcher in 1979 the average age coming into office was sixty; from Major onwards it has been forty-eight. Being in government can greatly enhance the earning potential of politicians too.[15]

The Advisory Committee

At the moment, there is an abundance of rules on the employment of those leaving public office, although only for ministers and those in the upper echelons of the civil service, and the rules are not necessarily meaningfully enforced. The system is presided over by the Advisory Committee on Business Appointments (ACOBA), which can only advise and offers little by way of strategy. People are still expected in this area, as in others in the ethical sphere, to be 'good chaps', but they do not necessarily behave as such. Some conveniently 'forget' that there is such a system in place when they leave office, while others merely evade something they find inconvenient. The main problem is people honestly forgetting, or not knowing, what they should or should not be passing on from one employer to another.

One can detect that something is wrong when, unusually, the Committee's own Secretariat stated, in response to a Freedom of Information request in 2018, that 'ACOBA has no enforcement power and therefore depends upon voluntary cooperation from applicants'.[16] The Committee's Chair wrote on 9 October 2022 that 'the system is advisory and widely criticised as toothless. We agree.'[17] He cranked it up further in an article in the *Daily Telegraph* in December 2022, where he called for repayment of salary by those proven to be in breach.

The different stages of public and private career

Of course, it is the appearance of conflict rather than actual impropriety that lies at the heart of this issue. So how are we to achieve this balance without encouraging concern about conflicts of interest and, even worse, corruption? The process for application for clearance by ACOBA is different for civil servants and ministers, and the rules differ also between job offers which come during the public employment or engagement and afterwards.[18] During employment, the Civil Service Management Code says 'Departments and agencies must require staff to seek permission before accepting any outside employment which might affect their work either directly or indirectly'. Under the Business Appointment Rules (BARs), former senior officials, in-cluding SpAds, and ministers are expected to make an application to seek advice from ACOBA before accepting new posts within two years of leaving public service.[19]

Once a minister has left office, he or she is no longer bound by the rules on disclosure of financial interests that govern MPs, or by the Ministerial Code, which precludes ministers from conflicts of interest between their official position and their personal financial interests.[20] There are various possible abuses.[21] Who should be the guards of the process and what sanctions should those guards possess? Each case is different, as indeed is the context, and restrictions and sanctions must be proportionate in each case.

The Ministry of Defence (MOD) is a particular arena of concern because of the constant 'traffic' between it and the private sector, the very large sums spent on procurement and concern that what someone wants to do afterwards may influence their decision making while in government.[22] For many years ACOBA *Annual Reports* have shown that the highest proportion of applications have come from this Department and the Cabinet Office.[23] One of my interviewees (who wished to remain nameless) expressed disgust at the way senior military figures assumed that they would 'glide effortlessly' into private sector jobs with companies from which they had procured equipment often running into billions of pounds. The most insidious and complex issue is how (if at all) it is possible retrospectively to judge whether favouritism has been given to a company, PR firm or think tank in the expectation (merited or otherwise) that it will smooth the way to such a berth.

The rules are designed to avoid:

- any suspicion that an appointment might be a reward for past favours;
- an employer gaining an improper advantage by appointing a former official who holds information about its competitors, or about impending government policy;
- a former official or minister improperly exploiting privileged access to former contacts in government.[24]

Most OECD countries have implemented basic post-employment standards to avoid such conflicts.[25]

The area requires sensitive drawing of boundaries. It is indeed a bit of a blancmange. Civil servants should not be wrongly restricted in their activities after leaving service. To do so would render it harder to attract them to public service at all. Restrictions should be no greater than those that are reasonable in all the circumstances and are legally necessary. This is called the 'restraint of trade' doctrine and such clauses in the private sector are strictly construed with the aim of placing as few restrictions as possible on the freedom of employees to earn. This concept is set out well in the Civil Service Code:

> When making a decision, the Committee [ACOBA] must strike a balance between any justified public concern about the circumstances of an outside appointment as set out in the Government's Rules; and the right of individuals to earn a living after leaving the Government, reflecting the law against the restraint of trade.[26]

The issue has in fact been kicked around for many decades. In 1936 the Royal Commission on the Private Manufacturing of and Trading in Arms criticised the movement of civil servants and members of armed forces to weapons manufacturers. The Business Appointment Rules have been in place since 1975 for senior civil servants and senior members of the armed forces, introduced under the second premiership of Harold Wilson. The supervisory body was then called the Advisory Committee on Civil Service Appointments. The name was changed to the present moniker in 1995. The situation it is meant to cover has shifted because of retirements at a younger age; the rickety institution set up to deal with it has not.

In that same year, 1995, Lord Nolan heard substantial evidence on the point, but it was based on the proposition that 'in most cases, senior civil servants will leave public service at a retirement age which is known in advance, and that on departure most will receive a full pension'.[27] This is not so now. There may now be several interchanges between the public and private sectors in an official's career. There were no doors marked clearly 'in' and 'out' in Nolan times: once in, it was normally a one-way ticket.

The Nolan Committee concluded that the system for civil servants after they left public service was tested and could be easily adopted for ministers.[28] There is, however, a marked diffidence about the Committee's conclusion on whether the system should be statutory or advisory, which is another theme which has run and run. The Committee thought advisory was sufficient, no doubt influenced by the fact that there were two then-members of ACOBA serving on the Nolan Committee. They called for it to be wholly transparent, since 'the threat of hostile public reaction and media comment would be a powerful disincentive'. The Nolan Committee also said 'In reality ... the publication of the committee's advice, and the subsequent public scrutiny would stop an unwise application [for permission for a minister to take up another role] in its tracks'.[29] The disincentive has now run out, and yet the subsequent plea by the CSPL (and now by ACOBA itself) for tighter regulation has fallen on deaf ears. For ministers departing office, Nolan recommended that there should be an automatic period of three months as a general waiting time before taking up any other employment, a suggestion that has not been implemented but should be.

A critical critique

The body governing this area of leaflet quasi-law is a curious, flimsy structure, and it considers only top-end roles. It is the *Advisory* Committee on Business Appointments. ACOBA counts as an NDPB and is sponsored by the Cabinet Office, with its members appointed by the Prime Minister. The central characteristic is the adjective 'Advisory': ACOBA is often ignored or bypassed.

As Sir David Normington told me 'ACOBA advises the government – it has no powers to enforce its advice. So, it is not really a regulator at all, as many, including PACAC, have pointed out.'[30] Sometimes ACOBA is a mouse that roars, but more often it is just a mouse. It issues detailed letters that can be laid to one side and it operates only in the two years after the minister or civil servant has left their public position (a loophole that was exploited by David Cameron in joining Greensill Capital[31]). It may only apply delays, conditions and restrictions to an applicant, and it cannot decide, enforce or regulate. Still less does it administer any sanction beyond publicity for default, and clearly some politicians could not care less. ACOBA does not even 'own' the Business Appointment Rules: it is the government that is responsible for them.

Lord Pickles, the present Chair of ACOBA, recognised that 'there are no sanctions' for breaches of the Business Appointment Rules. It is for this reason that 'ACOBA is not a regulator nor a watchdog'.[32] The political scientists David Hine and Gillian Peele conclude:

> It is too small for the range of tasks it confronts and its own members resemble too closely, in social extraction, career experience, and in the way they have themselves benefited from combining public sector and private sector careers those whose motives and sincerity they are asked to judge.[33]

Sir Bernard Jenkin, then Chair of PACAC, said in a 2013 letter to *Civil Service World*[34] that it 'represents a failure of governance in public life – it inspires no public confidence, nor does it protect the reputations of those it is intended to protect'.[35] *Private Eye*, which regularly reports on the revolving door (often scurrilously), is more effective in tracking post-ministerial appointments than ACOBA itself.

The machinery is neither well set-up nor well oiled nor properly resourced. It operates with only four staff. It relies on folks playing the game by the rules. It is a Heath Robinson-type jalopy contraption in a motorway age. The Committee considered a total of 142 and 204 cases in 2018–2019 and 2019–2020, respectively. The limitation on its range can be gauged from the overall statistics for 2020–2021: 34,000 people had left the civil service in the previous year and the Committee addressed only 108.[36]

One obvious point can, however, be made in its defence: ACOBA's impact on inappropriate business appointments *not* being taken up is less visible. There is an asymmetric flow of information since information is not given out about the employment that it states cannot be taken up (for reasons of confidentiality) if the minister or civil servant abides by its advice.

The Committee aims to provide its advice within fifteen working days from receipt of the required information, recognising that complex applications will take longer, but many people to whom I spoke were disappointed at how long the process took when they applied to the Committee for advice, although it does seem to have speeded up.

ACOBA membership

Members are appointed for a single non-renewable term of five years. Three are political appointees who are nominated by the three largest political parties. A further six are independents, determined following open competition (as was the appointment of Baroness Browning as a former Chair of the Committee, following her earlier political party nomination to the Committee). Membership needs to be reviewed, because of a lack of diversity in career experience and in the way members themselves have benefited from combining public sector and private sector careers.

On occasion, ACOBA is quite demanding. There was, for example, a detailed intervention in the case of Lieutenant General Tyrone Urch, former Commander, Home Command and Standing Joint Command in the UK. In July 2021 he proposed to set up a consultancy which he broadly defined as work 'aimed at Non-Executive advisory roles in non-defence sectors and comprise of leadership, team building, mentoring, project delivery, and construction programming advice'. The Committee recognised that it would not be improper for Urch to operate a consultancy that draws on the generic skills and experience he had gained from his time in the armed forces, but noted that there are risks. Given his sensitive role, ACOBA stated that 'he will have had sight of a wide range of information and policy that may provide an unfair advantage to organisations, especially those operating in the defence sector; further there are risks attached with his access to contacts within government'.[37] Urch was thus required to seek advice from the Committee for each commission he wished to accept. He was also advised not to become 'personally involved in lobbying the UK government, the MOD or any of its Arm's Length Bodies on behalf of those whom he advises under his independent consultancy' and from making 'use, directly or indirectly, of his contacts in the government and/or Crown service to influence policy, secure business/funding or otherwise unfairly advantage those he advises under his independent consultancy'.[38]

There are, however, numerous appointments that have been allowed recently that do raise eyebrows because of closeness with areas in which the public servant was engaged while in public service. The following is a partial list:

- Emma Barr was special adviser to the Transport Secretary until the end of September 2020, yet the following month she became associate director of lobbying firm Grayling, whose clients include Uber and First Group.
- Katharine Braddick, Head of Treasury's Financial Services Directorate, responsible for advising on policy on banks, gained a job at Barclays as Director of Public Policy.
- Farazana Dudhwala, who worked at the Office for Artificial Intelligence within the Department for Digital, Culture, Media and Sport and then at the Government Centre for Data Ethics and Innovation, joined Facebook in January 2022 to work on AI and governance.[39]
- Sir Philip Jones, First Sea Lord, became Senior Military Adviser to the MOD'S main supplier, BAE Systems, which gained 13% of the total spend of the MOD. ACOBA said there was 'a risk that BAES may look to gain insight from employing the former Chief of Naval Staff that it could not otherwise gain and which may provide commercial advantage', so that he had to agree not to share any privileged information. The MOD said his job would have 'benefits for the UK's prosperity and security, involving as it does the export of UK manufactured capability to trusted overseas partners', which is a good example of the cohort principle mentioned already.
- Major General Colin McClean, who was MOD Land Equipment Director and Head of Vehicle Support, became Tactical Vehicles chief executive officer of the Rheinmetall defence firm in August 2020, months after he left the MOD. This was one of the consortium of companies building 500 new Boxer infantry vehicles for the British army. This was just below the ACOBA threshold rank for consideration, but the MOD said that for twelve months he should not work on Boxer supply.
- Nick McPherson, the former Permanent Secretary at the Treasury, is now a bank director.
- Sir Kevin Tebbit joined Finmeccanica, a defence contractor, after many years at the MOD, where he finished as Permanent Secretary.[40]
- Mark Sedwill, the most senior government official as Cabinet Secretary, joined BAeS in November 2022 as a non-executive director. This was just outside the two-year period, but he had been allowed to work for Westbury Partners to offer 'strategic advisory services' and insights 'into the global political economic and business environment' during the period.

- Lord Undy Lister, who was Chief of Staff to Boris Johnson as Prime Minister, discussed becoming adviser for Finsbury Glover Herring, a PR firm, while serving as a trade enjoy to the Gulf.[41]
- Sue Gray, who carried out the partygate investigation into the Johnson Downing Street, was allowed to move to being Chief of Staff to Sir Keir Starmer in June 2023.

There are also some ministers, including Secretaries of State, whose subsequent roles may occasion surprise (some were taken outside the time limit for ACOBA to be involved):

- Chris Huhne, the Energy Secretary in the 2010 coalition, became Europe Chair for Zilkha Biomass Energy.
- Sir Michael Fallon, a former Defence Secretary, was allowed by ACOBA to work for Wilton Engineering Services, despite meeting the leadership of the company when he was Energy Minister and awarding a contract for an offshore wind farm to that company.
- The former Energy Minister John Hayes accepted a role at an energy company soon after leaving office.
- Chris Grayling earnt £100,000 as a strategic adviser to Hutchinson Ports after having been a failure as Transport Minister (and in several other portfolios).[42]
- Julian Smith was allowed to lobby in areas for which he had had responsibility as Secretary of State for Northern Ireland. He was paid £3,000 per hour as an 'external adviser' on 'business development' to a hydrogen company owned by a Conservative donor who runs a Northern Irish bus factory and cruise ship refurbisher based in Newry, as well as the UK subsidiary of an Irish offshore wind company exploring expansion into Northern Ireland.
- Charles Hendry, a former Energy Minister, became Chair of Forewind Ltd, a group of four companies in the energy sector.
- Savid Javid took a £150,000 second job (in addition to his role as MP) at JP Morgan and said confidently 'it's good to have experience that is not all about politics'.
- Steve Brine, MP for Winchester and Parliamentary Under-Secretary for Public Health and Primary Care at the Department of Health from June 2017 to March 2019,[43] works for a healthcare company which gained COVID contracts.

The list could go on for pages. In fact, half of the ministers who had left the May or Johnson governments by November 2021 took up jobs related to their former posts.

MPs are not required to seek the advice of ACOBA when they take up outside roles, and face no comparable scrutiny of or restrictions on their post-Parliamentary employment. One former Permanent Secretary told me that the Permanent Secretaries get the worst hit (because they are in the ACOBA net), whereas it is those in the second or third tiers down where the procurement decisions are actually made; those officials escape the scrutiny of ACOBA as they are the substructure in the undergrowth. These decisions as to what can and cannot be done afterwards are taken within departments by the Permanent Secretary.[44]

Lord Pickles is concerned about this feature of the system. He told me: 'I regret that we deal with only the higher echelons of the civil service. The rules on the rest are administered by departments, which vary greatly in their dealing with the issue.'[45] In his evidence to the CSPL, he 'characterised the approach of some departments in this area as "slapdash" and "verging on negligent", while praising the approach of others',[46] although he did not say which departments deserved these negative adjectives.

SpAds are included in the regulatory regime but not the now-vast array of informal appointments, from trade envoys to Crown representatives or tsars of one sort or another.[47] As Pickles told PACAC, 'Contractors, consultants and people who arrive and offer assistance – maybe during the pandemic, or maybe as Mr Greensill did – are not covered at all'. Crown representatives (such as Greensill was at one time) are a curious and little-known category, appointed 'to help the government act as a single customer' because of their understanding of the private sector and procurement.[48]

Several 'big beast' ministers have escaped the ACOBA net altogether by not mentioning their new jobs to it. George Osborne, the Chancellor of the Exchequer under Cameron, did not even tell the Committee about one of the several big jobs he took soon after leaving office.[49] Johnson told ACOBA only half an hour before his *Daily Mail* job was made public. David Cameron avoided scrutiny of his Greensill Capital appointment by delaying taking it up for two years after he left office. Philip Hammond, another former Chancellor, did not acquaint the Committee with his appointment to OakNorth until he had taken it up.[50] No action could be taken against Hammond by ACOBA, despite a finding that his actions had not been 'in keeping with the letter or the spirit' of the rules.[51] I don't suppose he lost much sleep over that slap on the wrist.

Dame Priti Patel, when on the backbenches, took a consultancy job with a company called Viasat and, despite becoming a minister again, failed to consult ACOBA until a month *after* she started in the role. By the time she received the body's guidance, she had already earned £10,000 (for ten hours' work). Viasat was planning to bid for a large government contract.

Carwyn Jones, the previous Labour First Minister of Wales, ignored the clear advice of ACOBA and accepted the board role it advised him against taking. It is also not surprising that the rule breaker in chief, Boris Johnson, in July 2018, within a week of resigning as Foreign Secretary, signed a contract with the *Daily Telegraph* to write a weekly column, and did not tell ACOBA.

Pickles' evidence to the Greensill Enquiry included his statement: 'Whilst there are some examples of non-compliance, these remain a tiny percentage of the casework and applications that ACOBA considers'.

All lawyers will tell you that a rule without a remedy for its breach is not much of a rule. Many folks will not pay ACOBA much attention when there are large salaries or fees at stake. ACOBA does not have any power to 'veto' an appointment, however unsuitable it may appear to it. The strongest sanction it possesses is to *recommend* a delay in an appointment being taken up, with the maximum delay being two years from the last day in service, and even then it cannot enforce this against the recalcitrant. The strongest whip it has to crack is publicity.

In the private sector, if an employee does not abide by a restrictive covenant or confidential information clause, the employer will go to court to enforce the restraint. This is a ban on those who are leaving abusing confidential information collected during their employment. This should be clearly set out in the contract of employment, breach of which can be difficult to identify so that there is a ban on entering a particular narrowly defined area of business (often by reference to a geographical area near where the individual formerly worked, although this is less common now). These can be struck down by the courts if they are unreasonable in scope, given the commercial interests to be protected.[52] If a person disobeys, all the sanctions for contempt of court are available, including imprisonment and fines. ACOBA needs a power to seek a court injunction to prevent a minister or civil servant acting in breach of its edicts for it to have credibility.

Greensill and reform

There have been reviews galore of this system. A committee under the chairmanship of Austin Mitchell (MP for Great Grimsby) in 1984 wanted the maximum period of delay ACOBA could enforce to be raised from two to five years, the withdrawal of pension as a sanction if rules were broken and a ban on officials discussing jobs with employers in the last twelve months of service. Then along came Sir Patrick Brown, a former civil servant who reported in 2005 and called for a single standard sanction in case of perceived conflict of interest between the last civil service role and new private sector. He said that ACOBA should be wound up.[53] Next up was the Public Administration Select Committee in 2012 agreeing to its proposed abolition.[54] David Cameron as PM told the Treasury Select Committee, however, that ACOBA's examination of appointments should be mandatory and comprehensive, and its decisions should be enforceable.[55] The CSPL diverged from this consensus in its sixth report, saying that 'The system appears to be working well at present',[56] before adding that former ministers should have a right of appeal to the Prime Minister of the day.[57]

The Greensill scandal led to a review by Nigel Boardman (of the firm of solicitors Slaughter and May), which, among other things, looked at post-ministerial jobs.[58] An eyebrow-raising – or perhaps that should be jaw-dropping – part of the Greensill tale was the revelation that in 2015 Bill Crothers, the government's Head of Procurement, was expressly given permission to keep that important job alongside becoming an adviser to Greensill, which might of course be a beneficiary of government procurement. Crothers double-jobbed in this way for two months in what became known amusingly as 'Twohatsgate'. This was, he said, a means by which he could continue to contribute to developing the Civil Service's commercial capability while transitioning back to the private sector. He argued that he had been entirely transparent about his actions and intentions and had sought advice from his Permanent Secretary, Sir John Manzoni, and the Head of the Propriety and Ethics Team in the Cabinet Office, Sue Gray, who herself had to seek permission from ACOBA in March 2023.[59]

In his evidence to PACAC, Lord Pickles said of Crothers in a classic understatement: 'It is fair to say, to misquote P. G. Wodehouse, that my eyebrows did raise a full quarter inch when I heard about this.' This revelation indeed aroused puzzlement across the board.[60]

The proposals made by Nigel Boardman in his review of Greensill included that ACOBA should cease to be purely 'Advisory' and should gain the power to enforce its edicts by a legally effective 'deed of undertaking' for ministers, a new concept, and a more traditional restrictive covenant as part of the contract for civil servants. The difference is necessary because ministers do not have an enforceable legal contract.

Ministers should set an example and at least be bound by the same rules. The code of conduct for members of public bodies should be put on a statutory footing. It is, however, a major defect of Boardman's Greensill report that there are no recommendations that the Ministerial Code itself also be given statutory force.[61]

Boardman also recommended that anyone breaking the spirit or letter of their post-employment restrictions should be deemed ineligible for appointments to positions in public life. He rejected the suggestion made by Gordon Brown (among others) that, as a general restriction, ministers should not lobby government for five years after leaving office, and in doing so made the obvious point that any period of time would inevitably be arbitrary. He said that ACOBA should decide to impose longer periods in particular cases, but it is unlikely it will. It is of course a truism that any fixed period would be essentially arbitrary, but it would serve to put clear blue water between public service and private gain. This would increase public confidence in the system, which is sadly lacking at present.

Conclusions on reform

I would, overall, give this rickety system only 3 out of 10, if that. Daniel Greenberg, who was an experienced Parliamentary counsel and is now the Parliamentary Commissioner for Standards, described to me the dilemma thus:

> Ethical issues in public life are contextual. It is important to gain initial trust with those regulated. A dog with rubber teeth needs to bark selectively, because while it barks rarely people will take some notice and that gives it some deterrent power – if it barks regularly and apparently randomly people get used to its barking and ignore it. So selective barking requires publication of credible criteria against which the selection of when to bark is carried out. For example, ACOBA needs to publish a set of criteria to be satisfied for jobs in the private sector to be acceptable.[62]

There will inevitably be differences of view about what should be done, dependent on how individuals have been treated in the ACOBA process. Helen Goodman, the former Labour MP for Bishop Auckland, told me:

> ACOBA is weak; it advises and has no teeth. It also seems to be inconsistent. I was advised not to take up a role in a housing association because I had dealt with housing benefit when a minister at the DWP [Department for Work and Pensions], which seems wrong.

Sir Edward Troup, who worked both for a private sector accountancy firm and HMRC at different times in his long career, concurred, telling me:

> I found ACOBA difficult. There are anomalies: you can write articles for the *Financial Times* but if you want to do a little bit of consultancy there is this vast rigmarole.[63]

The CSPL's judgement is that ACOBA and government departments should be able to issue a lobbying ban of up to five years in cases where an official had a particularly senior role, or where contacts made or privileged information received will remain relevant after two years (the current maximum ban).

There could also be special rules about how those in government should engage with those who have recently left. Such principles would make it easier for those who wanted to say 'no' to inappropriate lobbying, such as conducted by David Cameron for Greensill.

The present system of naming and shaming is, however, clearly insufficient, and the Boardman recommendations do not go far enough. A rational, modern system to regulate this area would include:

- clear paragraphs in the statement of terms and conditions of civil servants saying precisely what they can and cannot do while they are in post and after they leave;
- an investigatory power to look into what the new private sector job is truly likely to involve;
- prompt, predictable and consistent advice on an informal basis to those who are seeking permission to move into the private sector;
- applications to be made before the minister or civil servant takes up the role and not permitted retrospectively;
- a system covering all senior civil servants, SpAds and tsars and any more exotic roles which have real influence;[64]
- a proper system for administrative enforcement, probably not with criminal sanctions but with a restraining order which could be enforced by the courts;
- ensuring that the system does not put burdens on the compliant while not affecting the non-compliant.

Most importantly, ACOBA should gain a significant investigation power. Non-compliance with the Rules should a former civil servant wish to return to the civil service should also be a consideration in deciding on the application and in the event that honours are being awarded.[65] Withdrawal of pensions would be too harsh a sanction and would be open to challenge in the courts.

The Code of Conduct for Members of Parliament should be revised to allow complaints to be made against an MP who is a former minister and who takes on outside paid employment but does not follow advice provided by a newly minted COBA.[66] ACOBA should also publish its assessment of overall compliance with the Rules by departments (and other bodies) in its *Annual Report,*[67] as this would permit transparency about which departments are failing.

ACOBA mark II

The institution itself needs wholescale reform. France relies heavily on hard law and sanctions contained in legislation to regulate its system. COBA should lose the A and be chaired by a retired High Court judge, preferably one with a background in employment law and judicial review. He or she would be used to conducting matters fairly and speedily, to set precedents and to use injunction-type powers. Given the greater powers, the new COBA needs to hold hearings at which ministers and civil servants can present their case for the appointment they seek and groups with a genuine interest should be able to present objections.

COBA should at least be put on a clear statutory basis. As PACAC concluded, 'Statutory status, even without enhanced powers, could bring significant gains in terms of status and visibility, perceptions of independence, and moral leadership'.[68] Lord Pickles, the Chair, disagrees. He told me:

> There should be consequences if a person breaks the ACOBA rules. We now write to the government pointing out breaches. After all, part of the civil servants' contracts are to abide by ACOBA. I do not, however, think that making the committee statutory is the right way to go, not least because it would mean all of our rulings would become subject to judicial review.[69]

There are, however, ways in which judicial review might be limited by good drafting. Lord Pickles has introduced some beneficial changes at ACOBA (including a consistency matrix for guiding decision making), and there is a danger in judges making rulings in this area (not least in injecting delays), but it does represent an adjudication on clashes of rights, which is the judges' normal area of operation.

Secondly, the Committee should report to PACAC so that the latter may provide full oversight of its remit. A beefed-up system should provide scope for appeal against a decision of a new COBA to either the Upper Tribunal (an existing legal body which hears administrative appeals) or the new Commission on Standards and Integrity.[70] No retrospective applications should be allowed.

Sanctions mark II

The employment contracts of senior civil servants should build in the public service equivalent of restrictive covenants, which are found in the private sector. It should be made clear that the relevant Permanent Secretary is accountable for all the management of these issues within the department.

Real sanctions are needed, as the CSPL spelt out:

> On the finding of a breach of the rules, ACOBA should submit a report to the Cabinet Office. It is necessary to go beyond the suggestions of the CSPL which were that as a breach of the rules would constitute the breaking of a contract with the government, the Cabinet Office should then decide on sanctions or remedial action, as well as any possible appeals process.[71]

There should be special rules on how those in government should engage with those who have recently left. They would make it easier for those who wanted to say no to inappropriate lobbying. As PACAC has recommended, 'The Government should … extend the scope of the Business Appointment Rules to prohibit employment in sectors where the applicant has had "significant and direct" responsibility for policy, regulation or the award of contracts rather than only with firms they have had a relationship with'.[72]

Latterly, a very frustrated Lord Pickles has gone on the offensive and called for his watchdog to be given the power to ensure that ex-ministers lose up to three months' salary for ignoring ACOBA's guidelines. In an article in the *Daily Telegraph* on 27 December 2022 he said that 'The rules have not kept pace with a world where … the average span of a ministerial career is two years'. So far, the government has turned a deaf ear.

In March 2023, Sue Gray, well known as the author of the damning report on partygate, announced that she would join the Labour Party as Chief of Staff of the leader's office. Many thought that this was a compromise of the civil service's reputation. She apparently thought she had been overlooked for promotion by Simon Case, the Cabinet Secretary. Johnson supporters subsequently questioned the impartiality of her report on partygate. There were also suggestions that Starmer had broken rules by wooing Gray while she was still a senior civil servant. There is civil service guidance on meeting opposition MPs and the allegation is that she broke that guidance, which says that contacts between civil servants and leading members of opposition parties should be cleared with ministers. The Cabinet Office inquiry decided that she had broken the Civil Service Code by holding undeclared talks with Starmer about joining his office while still a civil servant.[73] ACOBA did not, however, place any restrictions on her.

Chapter 7

Appointments to the House of Lords: ermined disgraces

I suppose that peerage cost the old devil the deuce of a sum. Even baronetcies have gone up frightfully nowadays, I'm told.

Bingo Little to Bertie Wooster in *The Inimitable Jeeves* (P. G. Wodehouse, 1923)

The Lord Lebedev of Hampton and Siberia

Consisting of an eclectic mix of nearly 800 Members as of July 2023,[1] the House of Lords is the second largest legislature in the world, after the National People's Congress of China. Membership bestows a legislative role for life and significant social status as well as a nice title, even into one's nineties. The point of being a Member of the House of Lords has moved essentially from being an honour to a job over the last fifteen years in particular. This needs proper gatekeepers.

To elevate persons of dubious merit reduces confidence in an institution whose legitimacy is anyway seriously under question.[2] We encountered a few historic scandals about such appointments in Chapter 2. Few thought they would come back like an ermined Groundhog Day, but they have in droves, and they demonstrate weak regulation. Several mates, cronies and culture warriors were dressed in ermine in the Lords by Boris Johnson in particular, and successive resignation honours lists have been a subject of ridicule. Even Liz Truss' short reign as Prime Minister led to a long honours list, including three new Lords.

The most egregious failure of due diligence in recent times occurred in the case of Lord Lebedev. What is unprecedented here is that Johnson pursued a nomination when the House of Lords Appointments Commission (HoLAC) said 'no no no', and the security services apparently had concerns too.[3] Lebedev was by no means an obvious candidate for elevation to the Lords, save if one wanted to demean the institution itself. Johnson once wrote that 'the putrefaction of the honours system is a suspected crime that is quintessentially British'.[4] Perhaps he saw himself as an active agent in achieving this.

The relationship between Johnson and Evgeny Lebedev is as hard to explain as it is clearly close and warm. So attached were they that on the night after the enormous victory of the Conservative Party in the 2019 general election, instead of the Johnsons going to the Party's office to thank party workers (or indeed to put a programme together for running the country), the couple found time to attend the lavish sixtieth birthday party of Evgeny's father, Alexander, a former KGB agent stationed in London. Part of Alexander's work for the KGB had been to read the UK newspapers on behalf of the Soviet Union, and, in a delicious irony, he finished up buying one of the most influential, the London *Evening Standard*. In 2009, he picked up 65% of the newspaper for a knock-down price of £1, later reducing that holding by selling part to Saudi Arabian investors. This organ was put at the disposal of Johnson as Mayor of London and was influential in shaping opinion, which contributed to a largely Labour city twice electing Johnson to the highest municipal office.

The attendance by Evgeny Lebedev at a dinner in February 2016 to discuss whether Johnson should back Brexit is also highly significant. Johnson's decision to do so had fateful consequences for the UK, which one might think were broadly helpful to long-term Russian interests. Johnson has also visited the Lebedev family-owned Terranova castle in Perugia at least six times. In 2016, when he was the Foreign Secretary, he went without his Metropolitan Police protection officers. In April 2018, he attended again after two Russian military assassins poisoned Sergei and Yulia Skripal in Salisbury,[5] which sent out a surprising signal of 'business as usual' to the Kremlin. He went there after attending the NATO foreign ministers' meeting in Brussels, which, among other things, discussed relations with Russia. And he had a 'personal' meeting with the Russian-born oligarch just days after asking the British public in March 2020 to avoid 'non-essential contact' with Russians.[6] This was shortly after Lebedev's initial rejection by HoLAC. Johnson said in a letter to Conservative MPs in July 2022 that 'as far as he can recall' no government business was discussed. Lebedev family parties at Terranova castle and elsewhere are apparently on the decadent side. An attendee described one such gathering as a 'vodka assault course'. David Cameron and Tony Blair are among other politicians who have paid court to Lebedev, both the father and the son, but none have done so as slavishly as Johnson.

The security services had concerns about Lebedev senior as far back as 2013. The then head of MI6, John Sawers, deemed him an unsuitable person to meet.[7] Johnson thus apparently ignored security concerns as well as the views of HoLAC to nominate Lebedev. The HoLAC vetting was conducted against a published set of criteria.[8] Nevertheless, in December 2020 Lebedev was sworn in with the grand title of Baron Lebedev, of Hampton, in the London Borough of Richmond upon Thames and of Siberia in the Russian Federation. The confection of the title in itself may be taken as putting two fingers up to the British establishment. Since then, as might have been expected, Lebedev has made virtually no contribution to the House of Lords beyond his maiden speech and one other. The title no doubt comes in useful for business, however.

When the story broke about the security services not being happy about Lebedev, Johnson doubled down. According to the *Sunday Times*, he responded to criticism by saying 'this is anti-Russianism'.[9] This mimicked Lebedev, who described it as 'farcical Russophobia'. Johnson added that 'It is very, very important that this should not turn into a general sense that we are against Russians'. Johnson also rejected the idea that he had overruled security concerns to push through Lebedev's nomination, calling it 'simply incorrect'. A government spokesperson said that 'All individuals nominated for a peerage are nominated in recognition of their contribution to society'.

The Parliamentary Intelligence and Security Committee in May 2022 announced that it was investigating the elevation. In response, Michael Ellis, Minister for the Cabinet Office, said that 'Lord Lebedev is a man of good standing. No complaint has been made about his personal conduct. He has been vocal in his criticism of the Putin regime.'[10] Lebedev did indeed condemn the invasion of Ukraine. This was a point emphasised in the government's response to the Humble Address on the issue, which in March 2022 directed ministers to release information about the elevation. The government, however, declined this, on the grounds that it would undermine the confidentiality of the process, which seems a less than compelling response.[11]

Dominic Cummings in one of his blog posts claimed that HoLAC was given 'a sanitised/edited/redacted version of security reports'. Sir Keir Starmer sought an inquiry into the peerage[12] and also wrote to the Committee to ask what advice it had provided when Johnson sought to nominate Lebedev, but this was not disclosed. Starmer said: 'I understand that the role of the Commission has never been to publicise the advice it provides on political nominees but reports of the political views, personal links, and financial interests of Lord Lebedev are deeply troubling.'[13]

Lord Bew, the Chair of HoLAC from 2018 until late 2023, gave guarded answers about Lebedev to PACAC in June 2022. This was a classic example of obfuscation, which served only to deepen the mystery around the appointment. He said:

Lord Lebedev is, among many things, a *rara avis*. I am not going to say to you that what happened in this case is exactly the same as what happened in numerous other cases. First of all, it would be an incredibly stupid thing if it had been. If you are asking me if it is the case that everybody is subject to a variety of checks, the answer is that, yes, everybody is subject to a variety of checks. No doubt, this is a unique case.[14]

This fiasco caused the Lords Speaker, Lord McFall, to call for tightening up of the processes.

Of course, the issues about preferment to the Lords did not start with the Johnson government. There was a major concern about the use of the honours list by Harold Wilson at the end of his term as Prime Minister. The recipients included Lord Kagan, who had been funding Wilson's leader's office and was later convicted of fraud, and Sir Eric Miller, who committed suicide in 1977 while under investigation for fraud.[15]

Jeffrey Archer was thrice turned down by HoLAC. In the end, John Major forced his appointment through, suggesting he would abolish the Commission in order to make it bow to his will. It is reported that Tony Blair had to withdraw five names from HoLAC. Of twelve people who gave loans to the Labour Party before the 2005 general election, seven were recommended for peerages. In February 2006, stockbroker Barry Townsley, who had donated £6,000 (and loaned £1 million on commercial terms) to the Party withdrew his acceptance of a peerage on the grounds of press intrusion into his private life.[16]

Blair in 1997 also used the possibility of a peerage to encourage MPs to announce their retirement from the Commons at the last possible moment. John Gilbert in Dudley in 1997 had already printed his election posters when he was enticed to stand down in favour of Ross Cranston, whom the Blairites wanted to install in that seat. It is understood that Cameron had to insist on two of his nominees over initial concern by HoLAC.[17]

There have been other recent incidents which throw doubt on the integrity of the process and the fitness for purpose of HoLAC. Lord Spencer of Alresford was granted a peerage in 2020, four years after being blocked by HoLAC, apparently because of concern about his company's involvement in the Libor interest rates scandal.

In December 2020, Peter Cruddas, a former Conservative Party Treasurer, was appointed as Lord Cruddas of Shoreditch no less, apparently over HoLAC's objections. He had been a prominent backer of the 'Vote Leave' campaign in the Brexit referendum. This was the first time the Committee has ever been known to have been expressly overruled, although it has from time to time rejected candidates. The reason on this occasion relates to the fact that Cruddas was caught by the *Sunday Times* on tape in 2012 promising 'access for cash' to potential donors to the Conservative Party. He lost a libel case against that newspaper over its article at the Court of Appeal,[18] but Johnson in the little that he has said on the matter indicated that it was okay for him to join the Upper House because he had been 'cleared' by an internal Conservative Party inquiry. This seems a little underwhelming as a reason. Cruddas has donated over £1,000,000 to the Tory Party,[19] including a cool figure of £500,000 just after becoming a lord. Lord Bew, the Chair of HoLAC, was reported to be 'incandescent' over the snub, as well he might be. Cruddas remains one of Johnson's firmest supporters.

What is HoLAC?

HoLAC is an independent, non-statutory, advisory, non-departmental public body with some independents and three members nominated by the Conservative, Labour and Liberal Democrat parties.[20] It was established in May 2000 as an interim measure,[21] pending Lords reform, which was envisaged by the then Prime Minister (Tony Blair). Since then it has dealt with several thousand cases, Lords reform having been derailed. The big problem as encapsulated by its Chair, Lord Bew, is simply that 'The Prime Minister, the elected leader of the country, has the ultimate responsibility for nominations for the House of Lords. We are an advisory body only.'[22] Lady Deech took over the chairmanship in November 2023.

Its primary role is to recommend at least two people a year for appointment as non-party-politicals, who sit on the cross-benches. It also vets (but only for propriety) most other nominations for membership of the Lords, including those nominated by the parties, those put forward by the Prime Minister for ministerial appointment and for public service, and nominations in the honours lists.

Propriety in this context is defined minimally, as follows:

- an individual should be in good standing in the community in general and with the public regulatory authorities in particular;
- the past conduct of the nominee would not reasonably be regarded as bringing the House of Lords into disrepute.

HoLAC thus does not look at the *suitability* of the person for such service but it does highlight issues of concern that might not in themselves prevent an appointment, but which it considers nonetheless to constitute relevant propriety or presentational considerations, were an appointment to be made.[23] Any suitability considerations are a matter only for the leader of the political party making a nomination or for the Prime Minister of the day,[24] who can override HoLAC.

If the recommendations of the Committee can be ignored on such flimsy grounds as was apparently the case for Lebedev, what is the point of HoLAC? Lord Bew, in his evidence before PACAC in 2022, accepted that 'HoLAC is teetering on the brink, to put it bluntly'. This question led to a House of Lords debate being held on putting the body on a statutory footing, and Lord Norton put forward a Bill to give it stronger powers. Lord Clark of Windermere, who sits on HoLAC, said: 'The committee takes every case seriously and investigates it as thoroughly as we can'. That is the rub of the issue of course because it is not clear what information is received and nothing goes into the public domain.

Party donations

Non-domiciled status for tax purposes disqualifies anyone from membership of the House of Lords,[25] but what if someone appears to have bought their peerage by party donations? The official line is that 'The making of a donation or loan to a political party cannot of itself be a reason for a peerage', but that, equally, 'nominees should not be prevented from receiving a peerage just because they have made donations or loans'.[26] The Commission's approach of assessing 'whether or not the individual could have been a credible nominee if he or she had made no financial contribution' is correct.[27] There were several important donors to the Conservative Party who were raised to the ermine by the Johnson government. For example, Matthew Offord, the founder chair of the Edinburgh-based boutique investment company Badenoch, who donated £150,000 to Conservatives, was created a life peer.

There is, indeed, an extraordinary correlation between gifts to the parties and access to the House of Lords, just as there is in respect of public appointments. Studies by Seth Thévoz and others at Open Democracy, with additional data analysis from Ben Parker of Brunel University, have found that the chance of so many significant Tory Party donors' ennoblements being unrelated to their donations is equivalent to entering the National Lottery twelve times in a row and winning the jackpot every time.[28] A discussion paper from the Department of Economics at the University of Oxford reported that one in nine peers were 'big donors' to political parties, and if retired politicians and those in occupations that inevitably resulted in a peerage were discounted, the ratio increased to one in three.[29]

The odds are even higher for Treasurer of the Conservative Party. This position offered better prospects of a peerage than having been a Cabinet minister.[30] The *HoLAC Guidance on Political Donations*, issued in December 2019, provided at paragraph 5 that 'What HoLAC must have in mind is the perception that peerages can be "bought" in this manner. The Commission should not support a candidate if it concludes that such a perception may be a reasonable assumption in the individual's case.' Further, by paragraph 6, 'The overarching consideration for Commission members should be whether the level of donation is matched by other work done for or on behalf of the party. In other words – would this be a credible nomination even if donations had not been made?'[31] You could conclude that HoLAC is not doing a great job on this aspect.

Buying loyalty

Johnson appointed ninety-two peers, and it is tempting to imagine that he wanted by his approach to undermine the institution itself. In an article for the *Guardian*,[32] Gordon Brown revealed an outrageous memo from the C|T Group (run by Lynton Crosby, the Conservatives' Antipodean elections guru) that contained a plan to appoint between thirty-nine and fifty new Conservative peers towards the end of Johnson's premiership. Each one was to be asked to agree to vote with the government as a condition of appointment. The document said that compliant Lords would be rewarded with special envoy positions and those who failed to attend would be 'named and shamed'. The C|T Group denied that this was a considered position; rather, it claimed that it was 'a working draft of a discussion paper'.

Johnson's resignation honours list in 2023 was controversial. One of the most notorious nominations was of the thirty-year-old Charlotte Owens, who had served as a political adviser to various MPs and for a short time at Number 10. People wondered what she had done to deserve a possible sixty-year spell in the Lords.

Conclusion

The Prime Minister decides how many peerages to recommend and the proportion between the parties. This should be regularised broadly to reflect the proportion that each party gained in the last general election. As Andrew

Rawnsley wrote in the *Observer* on 20 February 2022, 'The House of Lords is tainted every time the bloated ranks of unelected peers are further swollen by the introduction of more party donors and muckers of the Prime Minister, a sleazy game that did not start with Mr Johnson, but one that he has played with characteristic brazenness'.[33]

My scorecard gives only 3 out of 10 here to HoLAC.

The Committee on Standards in Public Life is spot on in believing that there should be a statutory HoLAC as part of a broader House of Lords reform agenda.[34] Parliament should pass Lord Norton's bill, introduced into the House of Lords as the House of Lords (Peerage Nominations) Bill, which provides that:

(1) Before recommending any person to the Crown for a peerage, the Prime Minister must refer the name of that person to the Commission

(2) The Prime Minister must not recommend a person to the Crown for a peerage until such time as the Commission has advised the Prime Minister as to whether the person meets the criteria for the conferment of a peerage specified in section 7.

The principles set out are that:

(a) not less than twenty per cent of the membership of the House of Lords shall consist of members who are independent of any registered political party

(b) no one party may have an absolute majority of members in the House of Lords

(c) the membership of the House of Lords must be no larger than that of the House of Commons.[35]

There should be strict criteria for the appointment of peers.

The more fundamental question is whether the entire existence of the House of Lords gives too much power of patronage to the Prime Minister – and a little to other party leaders – which inevitably seeds corruption. But that question is beyond this book.

Chapter 8

Party funding and the Electoral Commission: how to get the party started

Are we in a post Nolan age: Quite simply, the perception is taking root that too many in public life, including some in our political leadership, are choosing to disregard the norms of ethics and propriety that have explicitly governed public life for the last 25 years, and that, when contraventions of ethical standards occur, nothing happens.

Lord Evans of Weardale[1]

After the scandals of recent years people have lost faith in politics and politicians. It is our duty to restore their trust. It is not enough simply to make a difference. We must be different.

David Cameron[2]

Sir Ben Elliot, a nephew of Queen Camilla, is incredibly well connected and raised the prodigious sum of £37 million for the 2019 Conservative election campaign. He is the founder of a high-class concierge company called Quintessentially, which, among other services, provides peacocks for its wealthy clients, who double as donors.[3] Many of these clients constitute a new breed of tycoon funders who are not necessarily rooted in liberal democratic values. Some may simply want to exercise influence over Britain's politics. The issue overlaps with lobbying regulation, which we look at in the next chapter, and there is a geographical connection too. Many of the Tufton Street think tanks which were particularly influential during the short premiership of Liz Truss in 2022 take foreign money and do not publicise their source of funds.[4] This all needs some disinfectant.

Mohamed Amersi, who has contributed about £750,000 to the Conservative Party, describes the present process as 'access capitalism'.[5] According to the journalist Will Hutton, this 'is especially problematic in the UK because so much capitalism here is concerned with capturing and then holding a privileged market position'.[6] This desire for access is especially problematic at times of shortage, such as with personal protective equipment (PPE) during the height of the COVID pandemic.[7] Sir John Major told the IfG: 'The present system of funding of our democratic system leaves it prey to special interests. The Conservative Party is too dependent upon business and a small number of very wealthy donors.'[8]

Why *do* folks open their wallets so generously? An experienced donor told me that there were broadly three types of people who give money:

- Category 1 is the 'dumb money'. This is the donor who simply wants to be photographed with politicians and mix with the powerful.
- Category 2 is the 'transactional donor'. This kind of donor thinks: what is in it for me? He (and it usually is a man) may for example secure privileged access into the VIP lane for PPE and gain some lucrative government contracts.
- Category 3 is the donor who questions 'what can I do for you?' He craves access to public appointments and being around politicians and this provides a network for him.

Many give for the honours they imagine (or expect) it will bring them, a rational decision given the fate of some recent Conservative Party Treasurers already considered.[9] James Milne from Aberdeen was, according to *The Times*, quite 'taken aback' when he received his knighthood in 2022.[10] He should not have been so surprised, since his company, Balmoral Group, had contributed more than £240,000 to the Conservatives over ten years, and by the law of averages he might have expected some recognition. As is becoming increasingly common, he spread his favours to other parties, handing £75,000 to Labour and £45,000 to the Lib Dems.[11] Lubov Chernukhin paid a healthy £205,000 to play a few sets of tennis with Boris Johnson and has donated £1.7 million altogether to the Tories. Her husband was one of Putin's ministers.[12] Sometimes food is the key to the come-on. The apogee of gastronomic giving was probably the bidding for a three-course dinner at a Tory fund-raising event in June 2022 held at the Victoria and Albert Museum. This went for a princely £120,000, and again Chernukhin was one of the bidders. She had won the right to have dinner with Theresa May and six of her Cabinet ministers in 2019 for a cool £135,000.[13]

One disadvantage of meeting a minister in a formal setting is that there is almost always a civil servant present taking notes. The best way round this is to attend a political donors' dinner, as Richard Desmond did with Robert Jenrick, whom he found himself conveniently sitting next to at another big fundraising shindig. Jenrick then held the powerful post of Communities Secretary, and his empire took in planning decisions. Desmond found this a very useful *placement*, even without the food. The businessman subsequently avoided having to pay the Community Infrastructure Levy to the local council, Tower Hamlets, which would have cost his company £40 million, because he inveigled his neighbour at table into quickly approving his planning application.[14] Bizarrely, Nadhim Zahawi MP, then a senior Cabinet minister, explicitly said that anyone who wants access to a Tory politician can pay to go to a Tory fundraiser. He told the BBC: 'If people go to a fundraiser in their local area, for example in Doncaster for the Conservative Party, they'd be sitting next to MPs and other people in their local authority'.[15] Of course, not everyone has thousands of pounds to throw around nor necessarily wishes to go to a Tory dinner.

Questionable money: some exhibits

Foreign money tends to come within category 2 on the list above. The Parliamentary Intelligence and Security Committee found that Russian influence in the UK had become a new normal.[16] So it was no great surprise that the daughter of a banker with alleged connections to the Russian security services had contact with Savid Javid, Suella Braverman and Mark Spencer (all Tory ministers) through her carefully targeted donations.

In terms of influence, Exhibit 1 is Sir Ehud Sheleg, a Conservative Party Treasurer under Theresa May and Boris Johnson. Inquiries by the *Guardian* concluded that the money he contributed ultimately came from his father-in-law, Sergei Kopytov, who was, according to *The Times*, a close associate of Putin.[17] Some have suggested that the Party should return his donations.

Exhibit 2 is Alexander Temerko. The Conservative Party has been given £1.8 million by Temerko or companies linked to him. His company, Aquind, sought permission to build an energy cable worth £1.2 billion to connect the UK and French power grids.[18] He lobbied ministers, including Kwasi Kwarteng (then Secretary of State for Business), for support for this project. This cable was indeed given 'nationally significant infrastructure status' by the Department for Business, Energy and Industrial Strategy in 2018, which was, perhaps, unrelated to his political donations. Kwarteng, however, wrote to him: 'I will ensure that my officials continue to take suitable opportunities to communicate the benefits of the project in discussions with the French government'.[19] Eventually, the proposal was rejected in the planning process, which is probably another case of the proper value system eventually reasserting itself. The privileged access still grates.

It is not just the funding of parties that raises eyebrows: Liz Truss garnered £500,000 for her leadership campaign in 2022, around half of which came from donors linked to hedge funds, venture capitalists and other city financiers. Those contributing cannot have thought this to have been a good investment, as it turned out. She lasted no longer than the lettuce.

Influence is guaranteed through the Tory Party advisory board, which holds regular meetings with senior Cabinet members. It was not so subtly known as the 250 Club, as each person had to donate more than £250,000 to gain entry to it. This model was primarily developed by Sir Ben Elliot, as Party Co-Chair under Johnson, although it was foreshadowed in other guises. The Labour Party also runs a Chair's Circle, which guarantees access to the highest level of the Party purely for cash. And these groups can lobby, intimately. The Tory one, for example, pressed, *inter alia*, for an early relaxation of lockdown measures and for lower taxes on the wealthy, causes which were, no doubt, close to their collective hearts. The *Sunday Times* estimated in 2019 and 2020 that the fourteen members of that board together with their families had a combined wealth of at least £30 billion. It also alleged that the advisory board was given the phone numbers of ministers to facilitate contact.[20] Under Cameron and May the party published quarterly attendance lists, but this stopped under Johnson.

Nolan did not go far enough. People are clearly buying access and influence with their cash (or seeking to). Transparency should be the key in terms of both the ultimate source of all monies donated and what access they give rise to. There is a strange form of bipartisanship operating here against change. Nick Timothy, the former Joint Chief of Staff to Theresa May, told me:

> Some individuals in public life do behave inappropriately, some with an eye to financial gain in the future. The parties differ in terms of their weaknesses; the Tories are influenced by donors but not in a direct way. A donation may buy precious time with a minister who is normally surrounded by officials. This can influence greatly the environment in which you are operating.[21]

The Labour Party is over-reliant on funding by trade unions. An opposite (and not often heard) view was, however, voiced to me by Michael Foster, a successful businessman, who has given considerable sums to the Labour Party. He told me that 'there is a risk that if you donate to a political party you are seen as less than a decent human being, and your name gets splattered across the press and your motives are challenged. Long-term this could lead to fewer people donating.'[22] This is not healthy either.

The Electoral Commission

The institution that should hold the ring is the Electoral Commission, which was set up in 2000 by the Political Parties, Elections and Referendums Act (PPERA). Its role is to ensure integrity and transparency in the finance of elections. It is a good example of a statutory body that can bare its claws by investigations and enforcement. It supervises the conduct and financing of elections and referendums, UK political parties and their recordable donations. It regulates party and election finance – in particular, it may make regulations prescribing the form and content of political parties' annual accounts and returns of their campaign expenditure. PPERA enhanced its investigatory powers and gave it a wider jurisdiction to impose civil sanctions on political parties (and other regulated actors) to support its regulatory functions.

Tony Blair told me:

> The only reason that there is transparency around party political funding today is because of the legislation my government brought in with the Political Parties, Elections and Referendums Act 2000. I think we got the balance just about right, but there's always a risk of trial by media where there's seen to be alleged corruption. PPERA was a necessary step to restore trust in the government and honour New Labour's election pledge to tackle sleaze in politics. It was arguably the largest and most significant reform to public standards since the Corrupt and Illegal Practices (Prevention) Act of 1883.[23]

The CSPL's 1998 report, which was the genesis of the Electoral Commission, naturally emphasised the fundamental importance of independence for the proposed Commission, stating that 'in a democracy like ours [it] could not function properly, or indeed at all, unless it were scrupulously impartial and believed to be so by everyone seriously involved and by the public at large'.[24]

The Act creates a ringfence around the Commission's independence in its supervision by a committee chaired by the Speaker: this appoints its members and provides its funding. There are nine or ten Electoral Commissioners, each appointed by the Monarch on an Address from the House of Commons on the recommendation of the Speaker's Committee on the Electoral Commission (SCEC). Four Commissioners are nominated by party leaders, with three representing the three largest political parties and one for the smaller parties at Westminster. Commissioners may be appointed for a maximum term of ten years and may be reappointed if the Speaker's Committee so recommends. The party leaders need to consent to the appointment of Commissioners (including the Chair).[25]

The danger now is that the Commission's reputation for being 'scrupulously impartial' is slipping away. The Conservative administration of 2019 had the Commission firmly in its sights, probably because of its forceful investigation of the Vote Leave campaign (and this led to the non-reappointment of the Chair in 2021, Sir John Holmes, a career diplomat). Amanda Milling, the Chair of the Party, in September 2020 threatened ominously that the body should either become 'more targeted' or it should be abolished.[26]

Most tendentiously, the government inserted into the Elections Act 2022 a power for the government to issue to the Commission a 'Strategic Policy Statement', to which it 'must have regard'. This is designed to direct the Commission on how it should operate. This was introduced against the vociferous objections of all the other parties and of the House of Lords and many academics.[27] Any such Statement is subject to a consultation process and must be approved by Parliament (although this will cause little problem to a government with a large majority). The Commission's compliance with this Statement is to be assessed by the Speaker's Committee, whose remit is expanded under the Act. The politicians are put back in the saddle on what should be an independent process.

Under the chairmanship of Conservative MP William Wragg, PACAC thought that there should have been a broader review.[28] *Guardian* journalist Jonathan Freedland was clear:

> Reform of the Electoral Commission is placing a hand round the throat of democracy's referee. The aim is to corrode the checks and balances that make democracy function, to allow the government to do what it likes, for itself and its allies by ensuring those who might hold it to account – whether judges, press or protestors – are too weak to stop them. It ends in a government that is, in effect, beyond the law.[29]

Gerald Shamash, who has been carrying out electoral work for the Labour Party as a solicitor since 1983, agreed, telling me: 'The attack on the Electoral Commission is corrosive and comes from a Trumpian play book'.[30]

David Howarth, the former Lib Dem MP for Cambridge and a former Electoral Commissioner, commented:

> The central problem is that the Conservative government is trying to subject the Electoral Commission to political control just as it is seeking to take over other

supposedly independent regulators. The big question is what the Conservatives are going to do with that power in respect of the Electoral Commission. A particular danger is that they tell the Commission how to interpret legislation, although ultimately the courts could intervene.[31]

Another issue is the directing of the Commission's budget away from priorities that might be seen as contrary to the Conservatives' political interests, such as helping hard-to-reach people register to vote, which may be an even more serious danger.

The appointment of Stephen Gilbert as a Commissioner also raised eyebrows, not least among other members of the Commission, although it was a party and not a public appointment, so it was entirely a matter for the Conservative Party whom to nominate. He was no stranger to the Commission: he had been involved in election expense problems for the Conservative Party in several byelections. He had moved from serving as David Cameron's Political Secretary to Conservative Party Deputy Chairman early in 2015.

Events in the South Thanet constituency in 2015 resulted in criminal proceedings, following the Commission's finding that the Conservative Party had included within its return in relation to *national* expenditure, on which there is (curiously) no limit, expenses which the Commission considered should have been included in *local* expenditure, which is capped. This included the visit of a national 'battle bus' of Conservative Party activists to the constituency.[32] Evidence was given in the subsequent criminal trial by, among others, Mr Mabbutt, Ms Little (a Conservative central headquarters official) and Mrs Goff. In his remarks on 9 January 2015, sentencing Little to nine months' imprisonment, suspended for two years,[33] Mr Justice Edis pointedly said that 'Mr Mabbutt gave evidence [on candidate expenses] which was more careful and more accurate than that given by Victoria Goff and *Lord Gilbert*'.[34] Gilbert was one of Little's bosses. This is not an obviously positive 'reference' for someone subsequently to serve on the Commission itself, but points up the danger of the parties making appointments.

What should be done?

I met the Electoral Commission's impressive Chair, John Pullinger, who has a background in statistics and the House of Commons Library Service, in his functional office in Bunhill Row, London. He told me: 'We have to get ahead of the curve, checking out the risks and threats to the integrity of the electoral system'. This is a major job, not least because, as Pullinger put it: 'We live with antiquated electoral laws; for example the Ballot Act is 150 years old'.[35]

It is difficult to disagree with Nick Timothy, who told me:

> There should be a serious investigation of the taxpayer funding political parties as the way to break this cycle. Our political expenditure and campaigning rules date from before the internet.[36]

There should also be a 'fit and proper person' rule about donations, with adjudication on the test by retired High Court judges, who are independent and have experience of deciding such issues. This is required for a person seeking to serve as the owner of a football club and should also be a requirement for donors. Parties should also have to declare the name of the person who actually provides the money given, so that the person(s) truly behind them cannot remain anonymous, as they can now. No business, bank or financial institution should be able to donate to a political party.

An overall cap on donations is also needed. In Canada the maximum is set at C\$1,700 to party and constituency. In addition, no political party should be able to nominate a person for honours where that person has provided financial or other support of more than £100,000 in any one year to that party.

Further, as Pullinger told me, 'On company donations we should ensure that not only does a company have to be registered at Companies House but that it has enough money in the UK to fund the donation'.[37]

Generally, the Electoral Commission does a good job and uses its powers sensibly and forcefully, as seen in wallpapergate.[38] I would give it 7 out of 10. We now move on to the overarching body that from time to time has considered political funding as well as many other matters. Happily, this one is also a success story and I couple it with another success.

Chapter 9

The Committee on Standards in Public Life and National Audit Office: two success stories

It is necessary to take the politics out of ethics (but very difficult – and it will never be perfect!). The CSPL can be a thorn in the side of government but a somewhat odd thorn (not least by allowing it to distance itself from issues – as when Gordon Brown asked the Committee to look at MPs' expenses).

Mark Philp, Chair of the Research Advisory Board to the CSPL[1]

The CPSL is not a direct ethics regulator, still less an 'anti-corruption' agency. Its role is to recommend strategies to improve standards of ethics and propriety.[2]

David Hine and Gillian Peele, *The Regulation of Standards in British Public Life*[3]

The Committee on Standards in Public Life

There is a cluster of independent offices on the ground floor of 1 Horse Guards Road. The Committee on Standards in Public Life (CSPL) resides there, along with the Civil Service Commission, the Commissioner for Public Appointments and the Advisory Committee on Business Appointments. Not far away can be found the Honours Secretariat and House of Lords Appointments Commission. It could be called Nolan Avenue. Some, however, see it as forming a ghetto for bodies that the rest of Whitehall find inconvenient. A former civil servant informed me that he was told in no uncertain terms a decade or so ago that taking a job in 1 Horse Guards, as he wished to do, would not be career-enhancing for him, so he stayed away.

John Major in 1994 saw the CSPL as 'standing machinery to examine the conduct of public life and to make recommendations on how best to ensure that standards of propriety are upheld'.[4] Tony Blair extended its terms of reference in November 1997 'To review issues in relation to the funding of political parties'.[5]

The issues have moved on with time but in some ways they have stayed much the same. In the 1990s, the Committee aimed to create an integrity system whose values would act as a deterrent against impropriety, whereas in the 2000s attention turned to the efficiency and accountability of the new regulators it had established. Further, as the state itself has morphed and grown,[6] so the Committee has had to respond. Since 2013 it has encompassed all bodies with a responsibility for delivering public services, even if the bodies themselves are in the private sector.

The CSPL has survived more than one attempt to kill it. Some senior people under Tony Blair, in particular, saw no need for its continuation. Many informants indicated to me that Francis Maude as a minister under the 2010–2015 coalition government had felt the same way. Mark Philp told me that 'Several backbench Tory MPs were markedly hostile to the Committee in 2012–2013 largely because it was seen as stirring public discontent and as interfering with MPs' self-government in Westminster'.[7] 'Mothballing' was also considered, that is, reducing the CSPL to a 'care and maintenance' basis, to be activated by the Prime Minister only when necessary. Peter Riddell, then Director of the Institute for Government and later the Commissioner for Public Appointments,[8] carried out a seminal triennial review for the Cabinet Office in 2012 that essentially saved it as a permanent body, although there was a cut in its staff and their seniority.[9]

The Committee is designed to be above politics, and this means refraining from comment on cases of current political controversy, however central they are to public concern about ethics.[10] It proceeds by consensus and this broke down completely only when the thorny issue of the funding of political parties was put on its plate. The Conservatives would not accept a cap on donations; Margaret Beckett, the member of the committee nominated by Labour, dissented from the final report, which did not recommend this.

So, the Committee is the standing body that keeps the spirit of the Nolan Report alive. Technically, it is an independent, advisory, non-departmental public body that advises the Prime Minister on ethical standards across the whole of public life in the UK. It is 'not a regulator, but offers a perspective on the ethical landscape'.[11] Its secretariat and budget are provided by the Cabinet Office, so to that extent it is dependent on the goodwill of the government of the day. The Cabinet Office as sponsor has responsibility for exercising the powers of appointment, dismissal and funding. The Prime Minister is answerable to Parliament for its policies and performance, including the policy framework within which it operates.

Government often views it as an opposition. Lord Evans of Weardale,[12] its previous Chair and head of MI5 from 2007 to 2013 told me:

> We certainly do not want an antagonistic relationship with government and would like government to ask us to investigate particular matters. We want to help.

The Committee must consult with the government before commencing any inquiry, but ministers have no veto.[13] For example, the Blair administration did not initially want it to look at party election expenses. It was, however, because of funding cuts stopped from conducting its valuable survey on public trust, which provided a platform for review of how ethical standards are operating.

Notwithstanding the formal position, the pressure on the CSPL from government is, it seems, minimal. The Constitution Unit, an important think tank, after many interviews with interested parties for its report *Parliament's Watchdogs*, recorded that:

> Those chairing the CSPL said that they had come under little pressure, with one chair saying that he had no contact from the Prime Minister while in office, and another responding that any governmental queries were merely a 'healthy tension' and no threat to the Committee's independence.[14]

The Committee is also specifically responsible for:

- conducting broad inquiries into standards of conduct;
- making recommendations about changes in present arrangements;
- promoting the Seven Principles of Public Life.[15]

It has no formal powers to compel particular behaviour, but it has a convening power and most importantly a moral impact as it represents a continuing Ethics Incorporated.

Under Lord Evans it has been through a revival, and there are few recent standards issues of importance on which he has not opined and in an authoritative manner.[16] Lord Norton of Louth, a Conservative peer and constitutional expert, told me that Evans 'possesses gravitas and manifold connections and is doing an excellent job with the CSPL. He is listened to with respect across the spectrum of opinion.'[17]

Recent reports have spanned such knotty issues as public standards and artificial intelligence, intimidation of Parliamentary candidates, local government ethical standards, MPs' outside interests, a wider review of standards in public life, and the role of leadership in embedding those standards. A recent set of investigations, called *Standards Matter 2*, was more wide-ranging in scope, looking at the essential values underpinning the regulation of ethics.

The Committee seeks to maintain a sense of 'ethical buoyancy', which focuses on organisational culture. Lord Evans told me:[18]

> High standards require more than just rules; they need to be embedded in the organisational culture and part of the day job. To maintain 'ethical buoyancy' you need to build a culture where this is discussed and people feel able to speak up.

He described the CSPL as 'an ethical workshop for running repairs'.

The CSPL can claim several lasting achievements. For example, it recommended the creation of the Parliamentary Commissioner for Standards, which injected an independent element into a system whereby MPs adjudicated on other MPs, and the Independent Parliamentary Standards Authority governing House of Commons expenses is essentially its creation.

The Committee meets approximately ten times a year. Since 2017, its minutes have been published together with an annual report. It used to operate by hearing evidence in public from interested parties, on the model of a Parliamentary select committee, but this method has been phased out and its budget and secretariat were significantly cut in real terms after the Riddell review.[19] This method has been largely replaced by seminars, which have improved effectiveness through the ensuing discussion, as well as being cheaper.

The CSPL's board members and Chair are appointed for a single, non-renewable term. Three members are nominated by parties, one each by the Conservatives, Labour and the third largest party in Parliament, previously the Liberal Democrats but now the Scottish National Party. They sit alongside four independent members (although for a long time in recent years it was not up to full strength). Baroness Finn was appointed to it as the Conservative member at the caretaker end of Johnson's premiership.

Controversy attached to the appointment of Ewen Fergusson in 2021. He had been a solicitor partner in the Finance Department at Herbert Smith Freehills from 2000 to 2018 and ranked consistently as one of the City of London's leading individual lawyers in his sector in the main independent directories. He had, however, little if any background in standards in public life or public policy more generally but was a long-term friend of the then Prime Minister, Boris Johnson, and had also been a member of the Bullingdon Club. It looked like another case of the chumocracy at work,[20] even if in fact it was not.

The CSPL is generally a story of success, and it is enjoying a particularly strong period at present. Arguably the Committee's most valuable role in the last decade is that of a long-term public institutional memory for handling standards issues across all areas of public life. It also convenes an informal network of the chairs of ethics bodies, and this could be strengthened and formalised. The Committee could be better known. The Financial Conduct Authority, for example, probably has greater public recognition. Michael Crick concurs: 'The CSPL is effective because it can stand back and reflect on generic issues. It is good to separate this from the day to day.' As Mark Philp put it: 'We have got better at systematising the rules, although there is less consensus amongst the political elite.'[21]

The CSPL secretariat is small and relatively low in funds. Some of the Committee's reports were not even debated in Parliament. It should be mandatory that they are. Lord Evans expressed to me 'disappointment that the government failed to implement or respond positively to the electoral finance and local government reports'.[22]

In recent years government has often delayed its responses to CSPL reports for long periods, and then produced only a boilerplate brush-off or the long-grass response. It is, however, an indicator of decreasing government attention to the standards agenda, as is the habitual delay in making appointments to the Committee, which is not confined to the CSPL.

There have been several proposals for flexing the Committee's powers. The Public Administration Select Committee, for example, thought that it should acquire the status of a full regulator for post-employment rules for ministers and civil servants. We will return to this in the final chapter.

The CSPL is not underpinned by statute, and it could be abolished without any legislative scrutiny. It is thus presently more vulnerable than the Boundary Commission for England, the Electoral Commission and IPSA, which all have statutory protection of some sort. The CSPL should be enshrined in an Order in Council, as is the case for the Commissioner for Public Appointments.

The CSPL does a good job and perhaps deserves the status of a national treasure. It needs more funding, prestige and public understanding and probably fewer MPs serving on it.[23] I would give it 9 out of 10 on my score card. We now move seamlessly to another excellent body.

The National Audit Office

Boris Johnson believed in big infrastructure projects that would forever be associated with his name (possibly bearing it in big letters) and would provide a legacy, as often happened in the time of the Classics. One epic folly was the Garden Bridge Project, which he proposed when Mayor of London as a magnificent new pedestrian bridge spanning the River Thames in London (it was originally the idea of the actress Joanna Lumley). It would unite the top of Temple underground station with the South Bank of the Thames. It was, however, approved only on the basis that it would be privately funded to the tune of £125 million.[24] The Department for Transport and Transport for London each committed £30 million towards the scheme (the former being announced in the 2013 Autumn Statement).

It was never built and must count as one of the biggest wastes of taxpayers' money in recent years. Colossal sums were spent on design work and planning applications. It needed investigating. Step forward the National Audit Office (NAO), whose detailed report on the scandal is entitled *Investigation: The Department for Transport's Funding of the Garden Bridge*. Although blandly titled, it was completely damning of the vanity project.[25]

The NAO is an independent Parliamentary body that is responsible for auditing central government departments, government agencies and non-departmental public bodies.[26] Its writ extends to any of the bodies funded directly by Parliament. It is based in London and Newcastle upon Tyne and has a staff of about 900.[27] This one gets close to top marks on my scorecard, 8 out of 10, and might provide a template for others. It has a direct line in to the legislature. It works closely with the Public Accounts Committee (PAC; see below), which considers its reports.

Unusually, it reports directly to a special office holder, namely the Comptroller and Auditor General (C&AG), who is an officer of the House of Commons appointed by the monarch through an Address to the House of Commons. The Prime Minister, with the agreement of the Chair of the PAC, who by convention is a member of the Opposition, moves the motion for that Address. Crucially, the candidate must have cross-party approval to be selected. This gives the C&AG enormous freedom to carry out examinations into public expenditure.[28] By section 8 (1) of the National Audit Act 1983, the C&AG 'shall have a right of access at all reasonable times to all such documents as he may reasonably require for carrying out any examination'. This gives the C&AG the authority to receive all the information which is deemed necessary for a proper audit.

The inclusion of the Lords in the process further ensures greater in-dependence for the C&AG. This could provide the model for Chairs of all the key ethical regulators. The NAO in turn is subject to the PAC, a statutory body. It has a *post hoc* audit function and is, in the relevant obscure jargon, the Supreme Audit Institution for the UK. Besides reporting on the money, it is an important watchdog of governmental propriety more generally. In effect, it gives other actors (such as the media and Parliamentarians) the informa-tion necessary to scrutinise government spending. The general perception is that it works well, although there is a persistent criticism of the time taken to produce reports.

Gareth Davies, who was appointed as C&AG in 2019, has a long history of auditing. He spent twenty-five years at the Audit Commission, and seven subsequent years leading Mazars' UK audit services.

The introduction to the Garden Bridge report says: 'We conduct investiga-tions to establish the underlying facts in circumstances where concerns have been raised with us, or in response to intelligence that we have gathered through our wider work'. There are two main forms of audits carried out by the NAO: performance audits (also known as 'value for money' studies) and financial audits (which study the financial accounts to ensure everything is in order). The former focus on a specific area of government expenditure and seek to reach a judgement on whether there has been value for money. They are non-financial audits, and measure the effectiveness, economy and efficiency of government spending.

These are some recent examples of financial benefits deriving from NAO work:[29]

- savings arising from more cost-effective prescribing of drugs;
- reductions in government expenditure on consultants;
- improvements in departments' procurement capabilities;
- recovery of revenue by reducing the use of offshore accounts to evade tax;
- efficiency savings in local bus services;
- savings in custody costs through more effective use of electronic tagging;
- the rescue of British Energy;
- PPE contracts;[30]
- the Public Private Partnership to maintain the London Underground.

The NAO also produces Departmental Overviews, with a summary of how government departments have spent their money in the past year, their major areas of activity and performance, and the challenges they are likely to face in the coming year. They are based on insights from financial audit and the value-for-money work.

In 2020, the NAO's work led to a positive financial impact through reduced costs, improved service delivery or other benefits to citizens, to the tune of £926 million.[31] It does good work – not least recently on the procurement of PPE in the early phase of the COVID-19 pandemic[32] – but it works relatively slowly and some feel that it lacks teeth. One important question is whether the NAO should have power to direct sanctions itself or to do so only through the PAC.

Like many other public bodies, the NAO has seen a significant real-terms cut in its expenditure since 2010. Data collected from its annual reports shows an increase, from £94.6 million for 2009/2010 to £103.6 million for 2021/2022. This, however, corresponds to a 15% cut, based on the Bank of England's Inflation Calculator. If funding were tied to inflation, then the 2021/2022 financial year would have had an audit expenditure of roughly £122 million.[33]

The general criticisms of the NAO that I heard from my sources are that it:

- cannot effectively scrutinise the policy objectives of the government;
- is generally too conservative (small c) in its approach;
- has failed to lead to systematic change because of its relatively narrow focus.[34]

As to time, the NAO's figures show that from inception to publication, a value-for-money study will generally take between three and twelve months. It is difficult to keep ministers accountable for decisions over such a time-frame, especially when the turnover of ministers is so high (for instance, there have been twelve Housing Ministers in the last twelve years). It also makes it more difficult for Parliament and the media to carry out effective scrutiny; the political agenda will have changed considerably during that time.

The NAO cannot ensure impartiality and expert choices in its selection of targets.[35] Instead, it must use the targets and policy objectives that the government has itself set. For example, in a January 2023 report on sport and levels of physical activity, the targets against which the value for money of spending was measured were set in conjunction with the Department for Digital, Culture, Media and Sport itself.

Political arguments have also been made against the NAO from the right. During a speech at the Politeia think tank in October 2013, Michael Gove (then Education Secretary) contended that the NAO and the PAC are the 'fiercest forces of conservatism'. His argument was that these institutions unfairly criticise ineffective but innovative ideas:

> Time after time the NAO and PAC report in a way which treats any mistake in the implementation of any innovation as a scandalous waste of public money which prudent decision-making should have avoided. And yet at the same time it treats the faults of current provision as unalterable facts of nature.

Messrs Wiggan and Talbot, in their article 'The public value of the National Audit Office',[36] argue that the NAO has not in fact led to a systematic increase in value for money in UK spending. The authors contend that the fact the NAO saves between £8–11 a year for every £1 spent on it shows that government departments and public bodies are not becoming any better at spending money effectively, so that its dissuasive effect is actually limited.

The critique made by the Constitution Unit suggests that perhaps the NAO is *too* independent and that its work cannot be properly scrutinised by MPs. In practice, Parliamentarians do not have the time for the level of sustained scrutiny that is required for the oversight of such a body. Notwithstanding these criticisms, the NAO clearly carries out really important work and its independence is (unlike that of some other regulators) properly protected. I agree with the positive view given to me by Marcial Boo, based on his experience as a former Director of Strategy and Communications at the NAO:

> There is value in authoritative reports, even if they have taken time to produce, if they consider all of the evidence and will be treated with respect. As such, if the NAO think something is true, people will generally think that it is. This gives the NAO credibility and weight to what they say. But the need for authority sometimes means that punches have to be pulled and that reports may be published well after the fact. The NAO is strengthened by reporting to the PAC which is seen as the queen of select committees.[37]

This relationship between watchdog and select committee could be a model for other committees to have a specialist investigative function to enhance their work,[38] such as the Independent Adviser on Ministers' Interests. We consider later the PPE debacle, where the NAO burnished its credentials, but now we turn our attention to a billion-pound industry.

Chapter 10

The Registrar of Consultant Lobbyists and the vast lobbying industry

Lobbying is a serious hidden feature of British politics. Lobbying is best done when no one is watching.

Tamasin Cave and Andy Rowell[1]

This Committee has a long-standing interest in the implications of the cumulative effect of money, influence and power for standards in public life. Lobbying is one activity whereby those with vested interests seek to influence decision makers; it therefore raises issues of transparency, accountability and equality of access.

CSPL, *Strengthening Transparency Around Lobbying*, November 2013

Calling an Uber

Decades ago, Sir Winston Churchill described lobbyists as 'the touts of protected industries', while Tory Robert Adley MP referred to them as 'leeches'.[2] But they are indispensable to companies like Uber. Ubers are convenient, ubiquitous and usually cheaper than taxis. But not everyone likes them. Taxi drivers definitely do not appreciate the upstart tech company, and neither do many regulators. Trade unions despise Uber and took the company all the way to the Supreme Court to secure a change to their employment model, which many find toxic. To counteract these powerful forces, Uber feels it needs a direct line to legislators and civil servants, local and national; it needs to buy some friends and influence the right people. Uber is one of the biggest clients of lobbying firms. So big is its spend that it is difficult to know how far its reach actually extends.[3]

As Mayor of London, Boris Johnson planned to attack Uber's position with minicab reforms,[4] but these were watered down. People suspected a vast lobbying effort. Interestingly, when he was asked pointed questions in the Greater London Assembly about whether there had been 'enormous lobbying' by the company, Johnson responded 'I do not deny that'.

Ministers are, however, rather shy about revealing the extent of their contacts with this company as with many others. The *Guardian* disclosed that at least six ministers, including George Osborne, did not declare meetings they had held with Uber as part of the company's formidable lobbying efforts.[5] Interchanges between the company and the Conservative Party are legion. Rachel Whetstone, who worked for Michael Howard when he was Conservative leader, went on to be a senior manager there. She was also a friend of both Cameron and Osborne.[6] Lottie Dexter, an aide to Matt Hancock, later became Uber's PR chief. There are many more examples of the lobbying chumocracy.

The clients who spend most on lobbying are usually those involved in industries that are generally unpopular but depend on government for support and want to influence the regulation of their activities and to mould public opinion. This is traditionally so in the areas of defence, nuclear power, fossil fuels and pharmaceuticals,[7] but lobbyists are also active with companies that are trying to break into public provision, such as in the private healthcare and education sectors.[8] The gambling industry is another big spender on lobbying, flashing no less than £280,000 on MPs in the run-up to an overhaul of gambling laws.[9] The *Guardian* found that in that period thirty-eight MPs shared in this sum, earned for example as fees for speaking engagements, in supporting salaries for their advisers and in the form of hospitality.[10]

More recently, in a novel development, the lobbying firm Crowne Associates (described as a 'strategic advice agency'), whose clients include BP, provided 'administrative support' to a committee of Conservative MPs conducting an inquiry into the energy crisis.[11] It should not, then, come as any surprise that the 1922 Conservative backbench Committee on Business, Energy and Industrial Strategy recommended policies favourable to oil and gas. Crowne's links to BP appear nowhere in the report it produced. Dame Andrea Leadsom, the Chair of the Committee, assured everyone that Crowne had no influence over the conclusions of the Committee, but the process was far from transparent, and transparency is key to regulating lobbying.

Mark Fullbrook, Chief of Staff to the short-term Prime Minister Liz Truss, was found to have been lobbying on behalf of Fathi Bashagha, who led a failed military coup in Libya. The strongman's 'government' was not recognised by the UK government.[12]

Who is lobbying whom is surprisingly difficult to discern. Not enough is in the public wing-mirror. The consultant lobbying industry is far too well connected to politicians, and the schmoozing takes place behind an iron curtain, far away from public scrutiny. We need to ask: is the nexus between business and politics properly policed? Duncan Hames, a former MP and now Director of Policy with Transparency International UK, thinks not. He told the *Financial Times*: 'When you look at integrity in public life, there are a number of indicators around the relationship between money and politics-lobbying, the revolving door and political donations. Britain has problems in all three.'[13]

Lobbying works in quite insidious and hidden ways. This is usually an enemy of good standards. The present mini-watchdog, the Office of the Registrar of Consultant Lobbyists (ORCL), finds it difficult to keep up with their activities.

Who are the lobbyists? What do they do all day (and night)?

The word 'lobbying' dates back at least to the nineteenth century and derives from the gathering of MPs and peers in the hallways ('lobbies') of Parliament before and after Parliamentary debates, when members of the public could meet their representatives. The UK now plays host to the third biggest lobbying industry in the world, after Washington, DC, and Brussels, and it is a well-connected sector worth billions of pounds.[14] The Alliance for Lobbying Transparency estimates that about 4,000 people work in the industry.

Broadly speaking, lobbying is any action seeking to influence a legislator or civil servant on any issue. Often it is the special advisers (not the ministers) whom the lobbyists target, as they have the ear of ministers on matters of policy and are more accessible than the senior politicians whom they serve. Sometimes the politicians find it convenient to be lobbied. As President Franklin Roosevelt once reputedly said: 'You've convinced me. Now go out and put pressure on me.'[15]

It is not possible to tell how much time and money is devoted to influencing the political process and precisely what tactics are being used. Susan Hawley of Spotlight on Corruption summed it up: 'There is an appalling lack of transparency in lobbying with minimalist description of meetings and no centralised uniform system of compliance.'[16] When government gives special access to business interests, however, the public is effectively left outside that door.[17] The rich and powerful can afford sophisticated approaches and follow up, but the rest have to make do with doors only a little bit open, and not much greased, although the trade unions are among the most powerful lobbyists on behalf of ordinary working people. Too close links between policy making and pressure groups suggest that certain groups will receive unfair advantages. Public opinion polling shows the depth of public concern about this. In a 2019 survey, 63% of respondents thought that the British system of government is rigged to the advantage of the rich and powerful.[18] Linked with this, the IPPR think tank in a survey found that only 6% of voters think their views are the main influences behind government decisions. The survey also discovered that 25% believe major donors to parties have most influence over shaping policy.[19]

Lobbying is so pervasive in the corridors of power that Austin Mitchell, the late long-standing Labour MP for Great Grimsby, once said that 'our vaunted constitution is really a framework of lobbying'.[20] David Cameron, who worked in PR for Carlton TV before he entered Parliament, was correct when he warned, in a speech delivered soon after he became Conservative Party leader:

> I believe that secret corporate lobbying ... goes to the heart of why people are so fed up with politics. It arouses people's worst fears and suspicions about how our political system works, with money buying power, power fishing for money and a cosy club at the top making decisions in their own interest....[21]

Cameron also expressed in 2010 his view that lobbying was 'the next big scandal waiting to happen', but it is unlikely he envisaged that *he* would be in the centre of the storm, as he was in respect of the Greensill Capital scandal, covered in Chapter 14.

Lobbying is an important and legitimate aspect of public life in a liberal democracy.[22] Some would say that it actually enhances the democratic process because it enables a better-informed debate and ensures that expert information can be fed into the policy development process. Politicians and decisions makers cannot have specialist knowledge of all the areas on which they legislate, and lobbyists can give this essential insight. It is therefore said to be essential that those holding such expert knowledge should seek to educate, inform and advise decision makers.

This is true if all is open, but, as the CSPL said in a strongly worded statement, lobbying 'which is secret without good reason inhibits even-handedness, results in distorted evidence and arguments, fuels suspicions, facilitates excessive hospitality, corruption and other impropriety, hides or clouds accountability, undermines trust and confidence in political processes, and is inconsistent with modern democratic standards'.[23] Under such circumstances chumocracy thrives, leveraging and maximising contacts made while in government into serious earning potential afterwards. Key Cameron ministers such as William Hague and Francis Maude subsequently became lobbyists, as did Sir Craig Oliver, his head of communications, Kate Fall, Robbie Gibb and several others.[24] Lord Wood of Anfield, a Labour peer who was an adviser to Ed Miliband, told me: 'There is a close link between public affairs/lobbying organisations and appointments. So many of the Cameron political team went to work in public affairs and firms like Brunswick then recycled people back into government.'[25]

The Nolan Principle this area engages is the fifth, openness, which includes the requirement that 'Holders of public office should act and take decisions in an open and transparent manner'. It is difficult to draw a line between what is acceptable and what is not, but it is clear that the public should know who is pushing a particular line and who is behind a particular campaign. If a think tank is pontificating about climate change,[26] the public should understand whether its research is sponsored by a fossil fuel company operating behind the façade of a lobbying company. Only then can they judge the nature of the claims being made.

Calls for legislation to restrict lobbyists date back to 1969. In January 2009, the House of Commons Public Administration Select Committee published *Lobbying: Access and Influence in Whitehall*. In October of the same year, the government rejected a mandatory register of lobbying but instead decided that it would cover this from the other end of the telescope (but still inadequately), that is, by government transparency, so that:

- All departments would have to publish online quarterly reports detailing ministerial meetings with interest groups and hospitality received by ministers and their advisers and also details of meetings between officials and outside groups.
- The list of civil servants who have to publish details of hospitality and expenses would be extended.

There are also significant breaches of the rather minimal compulsion on government departments to declare. Transparency data is scattered, disparate and not easily cross-referenced, and information is often excluded from data releases completely.[27] Information is released well after the lobbying has taken place, and descriptions of the content of government meetings are ambiguous.

An IfG report launched in the wake of the Greensill affair,[28] which, among other things, featured key meetings between ministers and lobbyists that were not registered, recorded that:

- The Home Office published the required data on senior officials' meetings in just three of twenty-three quarters between the 2015 general election and March 2021.
- The FCDO, which was created by merger in September 2020, did not publish any information on meetings held by ministers or officials until September 2021.
- The Ministry of Justice often published data late and failed to publish any information on five occasions.

Transparency International UK cites twenty-six lobbying scandals since 2010 where 'critical information … was not captured either by the statutory lobbying register or departmental disclosures', and academic analysis has shown 'major discrepancies' between reported ministerial meetings and the Registrar of Consultant Lobbyists,[29] whose far too limited jurisdiction we will soon review. There are obvious gaps of coverage too. Communications with SpAds by lobbyists do not have to be revealed at all, and individual communications made on behalf of a client do not need to be listed. Another loophole is that ministers' meetings are sometimes referred to in these returns by generic phrases such as 'introductory meeting', 'general meeting' or 'not recorded by the department', which gives nothing away at all.

Iain Anderson, chief executive of the lobbying firm Cicero/AMO, told me:

> Lobbying has had a reputation of operating in the shadows, but it should not be so. Shine a light on it. I always underline the word 'public' in the public policy process as there needs to be transparency. Many more people now than in the 1990s understand that transparency is important for public policymakers and the ESG [environmental, social and governance] debate has helped.[30]

The minimalist Act

There should be further regulation of the industry beyond the Act currently on the statute book, which is a mouse, although it boasts a very long title: the Transparency of Lobbying, Non-party Campaigning and Trade Union Administration Act 2014. The government of David Cameron introduced it when the call for reform became more incessant (with his own speech being quite influential).[31] Defining lobbying, and distinguishing it from the simple provision of information, proved difficult, and the statute shows all the signs of a compromise between the two sides of the coalition government, which is what it was.

Section 1 requires registration by those 'carrying on the business of consultant lobbying'. The definition of such lobbying is restrictive because it only applies if

(a) in the course of a business and in return for payment, the person makes communications … on behalf of another person or persons,
(b) the person is registered [for VAT], and
(c) none of the exceptions in Part 1 of Schedule 1 applies.

A lobbyist so defined must give details every quarter of 'the name of the person or persons on whose behalf the lobbying was done'. Some MPs dubbed this the 1% lobbying bill, as that is about how much of the activity by lobbyists they said it would capture, although more accurate estimates range between 5% and 10%.[32] Either way, it is far too narrow and it is hard to think of any other regulation of an important profession that reaches so few practitioners. Helen Goodman, a former Labour MP and minister, told me that 'The definition of lobbying under the Act is too wide and catches too much in the net'.[33] By 'too much' she meant that it unnecessarily covered charities and trade unions.

The restriction to those lobbyists who are registered for VAT is hard to defend and excludes many one-man bands. The major get-out, however, is located in Schedule 1, which provides that a person does not qualify if he or she carries on a business that consists mainly of non-lobbying activities and the lobbying is incidental to the carrying on of those activities. This exempts most law, accountancy and management consultancy firms, even though they may be involved in extensive lobbying activities, but certainly that would not be the majority of their work. This is in fact a major sector of present-day lobbying activity, but it was less so when the statute was passed. This area has been somewhat encouraged by the wording of the law. The statute also does not catch the lobbying of MPs or local councillors, nor the staff of regulatory bodies or the private companies that provide public services. All of them may be the object of major lobbying operations.

The definition of lobbyist also excludes those who are *employed* by companies, charities and other bodies, both 'in house' and on a fee basis, who undertake lobbying work. Apparently, it was not seen as necessary to legislate for in-house lobbyists, as their involvement would be disclosed in the departments' quarterly returns of meetings.[34] Notably, this excluded David Cameron when he was lobbying intensively for Greensill Capital.[35]

In the event of a breach, a notice may be given by the Registrar to a person to provide the relevant information, and it is an offence not to comply with such a notice. It is not known that there has ever been any such prosecution. Even if a breach is found, the sanction of £7,500 is unlikely to be a big deterrent for a major lobbying firm.

There is discontent with the Act within the lobbying industry itself. Iain Anderson said to me: 'The present statutory system is flawed. I have to declare under the Act whereas others do not have to do so. It creates a distorted lens. We need a level playing field.'[36]

The Registrar of Consultant Lobbyists

Step forwards the official who has to police this rickety and complex structure. Harry Rich is the Registrar of Consultant Lobbyists, and he has at present about 150 registrants to be concerned with. He is engaged to work in this role for between thirty and forty days a year and also runs a business coaching executives. His responsibilities include:

* setting up and managing the statutory Register of Consultant Lobbyists;
* making sure that the industry is following the requirement to register;
* publishing detailed guidance for the industry about lobbyists' duties.

He told me he seeks to proceed informally and also tries to achieve consensus with the industry he regulates, with the aim of overall transparency. He finds that public affairs people (the larger operators) do generally cooperate with him.[37] He has, however, only three staff, which is actually a recent increase from the 1.8 full-time equivalents in previous years. The organisation has ordered just six statutory requests for information about potential unlicensed lobbying activity in the UK since the law came into operation in 2015.

Ian Gregory, chief executive of Abzed Political and Media Relations and a former journalist, told me:

> The law says lobbying firms must register if they communicate directly with ministers or Permanent Secretaries. Yet in this the regulator has been given a meaningless line to police. I don't need to speak to ministers – it is much more powerful to have my clients communicate with them, and for my team to secure newspaper front pages and build backbench support. Yet none of these trigger the need to register. That is why Mr Rich only has a small proportion of independent lobbyists on his books – and of course none of the in-house ones, whom the law ignores.[38]

I would give the Registrar 4 out of 10 on my score card but recognise he has been dealt a bad run of cards by Parliament.

Outside regulation: MPs and All-Party Parliamentary Groups

There are two other areas of regulation involving lobbying that we should review before looking at potential reforms: the first is the lobbying of government by MPs and the second the thorny issue of All-Party Parliamentary Groups.[39]

Restrictions on lobbying by MPs

Lobbying is now mainly carried on by outsiders operating on politicians and civil servants, but this has not always been so. It was a lucrative sideline for MPs themselves for decades.[40] Martin Smith, a lobbyist who formerly worked for the National Consumer Council, was surprised to find that 'in competing for business we were actually competing against some MPs who were running small lobbying businesses from within the Palace of Westminster'.[41]

The valuable restrictions now placed on MPs are that they are not allowed to speak in the Commons, make approaches to ministers, vote or initiate Parliamentary proceedings in return for direct payment, whether in cash or kind.[42] MPs may engage in lobbying only if it is 'six months after the reward or consideration was received'. They are, however, allowed to participate in Parliamentary proceedings and conversations with ministers that would financially benefit their client as long as they did not start the interaction, the interest is declared and it is not for the sole benefit of their client. The *Guardian* showed in 2020 that 20% of staff members of MPs and peers have lobbying or outside interests. This is still too much, and MPs still break the rules, as happened with Owen Paterson.[43]

Steve Brine, Chair of the Commons Health and Social Care Committee, was investigated over allegations that he lobbied the NHS and ministers on behalf of Remedium, a recruitment firm that employed him and found guilty but no action was taken by the Parliamentary Commissioner for Standards beyond an apology and a promise not to repeat his conduct in future.[44] Scott Benton, Conservative MP for Blackpool South, lost the whip when he told undercover press reporters that he could 'call in favours' from colleagues and gain 'easy access' to ministers when queuing for votes in Parliament, although the Registrar decided to take no action.[45] The Standards Committee subsequently recommended a 35-day suspension from the House of Commons.

All-Party Parliamentary Groups

A lobbyists' wet dream is the All-Party Parliamentary Groups (APPGs), which are composed of backbench Members of the House of Commons, the House of Lords or in some cases of both Houses of Parliament. They are informal, bicameral, cross-party groups on topics of mutual interest that vary widely between them,[46] and they are supported by some twenty separate lobbying companies.[47] The Parliamentary and Scientific Committee was the first such group, created in 1939 to help the war effort.[48]

Open Democracy, a pressure group, estimated that APPGs have received around £25 million worth of benefits from outside bodies since 2018, of which more than half was provided by private sector organisations.[49]

As of 2022 there were 744 active APPGs covering all manner of subjects. The number has grown exponentially in recent years and is still rising.[50] There are indeed now more APPGs than there are Members of Parliament, and some are little more than fronts for lobbyists. Some MPs are very active across many such groups.[51] At least six APPGs are linked to crypto currency companies, while at least two Gulf countries have financially supported them.[52]

There is only minimal regulation of this area. The Parliamentary Commissioner for Standards maintains the register of APPGs. In order to use the prestigious title, a group must be open to all Members of both Houses, regardless of party affiliation.[53] APPGs are either country based, such as the APPG on Saudi Arabia, or subject based, for example the APPG on Breast Cancer. They are not, however, official Parliamentary bodies, as many outsiders naturally assume that they are, and the rules provide that Groups must avoid presenting themselves in a way that leads to their being confused with Select Committees,[54] which are in fact official committees of the House. This is easier said than done.

The case for APPGs is a reflection of that for lobbyists more generally. They provide:

- a forum for cross-party interaction that is not controlled by the whips and between Parliamentarians and academics, business people, the third sector and other interested parties;
- a time and space for policy discussion and debate;
- a means for Parliamentarians to set the policy agenda, which is normally dictated by the front benches.

As Marisa Heath, who runs an APPG, told the House of Commons Committee on Standards on the issue:

> A good APPG should be ears on the ground; it should be listening to what is happening outside Westminster, picking up on trends, and starting the process that moves into policy. Someone who sits in the middle, who is able to engage with

all the outside bodies, should be those ears on the ground, and should be able to pick up on all the things that are happening. It is really useful to have that person who is informed and engaged with the sector that the APPG is representing, so that they are able to say to the politicians – the members of the group – 'This is what is going on out there; this is what we might need to look at'.[55]

Mark Harper MP (now the Secretary of State for Transport) explained to me: 'APPGs in principle perform a very useful function. It is, however, important that people know who is funding them.'[56]

There have been several reviews of the improper access that APPGs may provide, which led to Parliamentary rules being formulated in 2015. They include the following requirements:

- the Chair to be accountable to the Commons for compliance with Parliamentary rules;
- some internal elections for APPG officers;
- regular meetings – at least two a year, including an annual general meeting;
- a quorum of five MPs for each meeting;
- compliance with rules on registering financial benefits.

The Groups should be transparent about their nature, membership and funding. If a report or other publication has been compiled or funded by any external individual or organisation, this should be made clear.[57]

The current rules also require that support (either financial or in-kind) to an APPG of over £1,500 a year from a single source must be declared. More common, however, is provision of indirect support from outside in the form of administrative and secretarial assistance. The provision of secretariats for such Groups is itself a submerged form of lobbying. So Humanists UK acts as the secretariat for the All-Party Parliamentary Humanist Group. What may be seen as its 'opposition', the APPG on Christianity, is administered by a staff member from the Bible Society.

The Registrar also retains discretion to remove a Group from the Register unless and until it complies with these conditions for registration,[58] but this has rarely happened. The Parliamentary Commissioner for Standards may investigate allegations that a Group has broken the rules of the House.

So, these useful rules do not go far enough. Many APPGs still work well beneath the radar of public scrutiny. The House of Commons Speakers' Working Group noted that in its survey of MPs, 48% agreed with the proposition that APPGs were prone to be manipulated by public affairs and lobby groups.[59] The Speaker himself told the latest review by the Committee on

Standards 'about his concerns that APPGs are being abused by lobbyists by gaining sponsors for a Group and then arranging for those sponsorship funds to be used to pay them to act as the secretariat'.[60]

Sir David Natzler, the former Chief Clerk in the House of Commons, however, expresses some caution about their regulation:

> There is nothing wrong in principle with having such interest groups and indeed it does create a means of connection between the Parliamentary community and civil society, but I do not quite see why Parliament is expected to find space for such meetings and give them the special legitimacy which goes with the word 'Parliamentary'.[61]

He did not think that the transparency rules needed changing, but said that there must be an energetic investigative mind to put the information that is already available to good use. Rod Clayton of Weber Shandwick told me: 'APPGs can be very useful in driving policy debate internally, but I think that generally, for the purpose of driving broad external communications, most APPGs are of marginal utility'.[62]

Ian Gregory thought an important indirect 'benefit' was that 'Some APPGs do vital work in making Cinderella issues visible. Yet APPGs also help Downing Street by providing displacement therapy for former ministers.' He also predicted that if APPGs were formally banned they would spring up in another form, as they are politically useful.[63]

There is clearly a balance to be struck here. Sir Chris Bryant MP, Chair of the Committee on Standards, at a Committee hearing in January 2022 said: 'All-Party Parliamentary Groups play a crucial role in the work of Parliament and our democracy, but they cannot be a back-door means of peddling influence around the corridors of power without scrutiny'. Elizabeth David-Barrett, Professor of Governance and Integrity and Director at the Centre for the Study of Corruption at the University of Sussex, is more direct: 'APPGs are a key source of lobbying corruption'.[64] The Committee on Standards' 2022 report on APPGs said: 'The danger is that an APPG could all too easily become a parliamentary front for an external commercial entity. That would be wholly inappropriate.'[65] Clearly, these bodies should be genuinely led by Parliamentarians and not by external organisations.

The inherent dangers are demonstrated in the case of a Ms Lee, who was influential in setting up the Chinese in Britain APPG. Unusually, the security services issued an alert expressing their concern about her activities.[66] She had funded the Parliamentary staff of the Chair of that Group to the tune of approximately half a million pounds over a period of years, and directly financed the APPG, as well as paying for the then Chair to go on a trip to China for four days.[67] There may be other undetected Ms Lees.

The same 2022 report, however, generally gave APPGs a clean bill of health and concluded: 'We do not wish to give APPGs an incentive to de-register which would bring about a reduction rather than an increase in transparency'.[68] The present Committee on Standards agreed with this general thrust. It went on to decide, however, that 'APPGs must not be a vehicle by which paid external interests can achieve a level of access and influence not available to others'.

There should be disclosure of how each piece of work of an APPG is funded. At present no 'in kind' contributions by lobbyists need be disclosed. There should also be a special 'gatekeeper', who would have to approve the setting up of new APPGs. This might be the Chairman of Ways and Means of the House of Commons, or a special committee of MPs, similar to the Committee on Standards. The gatekeeper would apply set criteria, including avoidance of overlap, cross-party support, a statement of purpose and a state-ment of how it will be Member-led and avoid undue influence by any external organisation.[69]

General reform of lobbying: the Boardman Review

Moving on to the more general issue of lobbying reform, the Boardman Review in July 2021, which examined the Greensill Capital affair, was an excellent opportunity for review and reform in the area of regulation, but, overall, it was another missed chance, possibly because of lobbying by the lobbyists. Boardman's premise in his *Review* was that, generally, most lobbying was a rather good thing, since 'it can provide decision makers with insights and data and enables Government to understand the impact of public policy on those it may affect'. He did, however, go on to say that 'lobbying can also lead to undue influence in policy-making, unfair competition and regulatory capture which can be harmful or contrary to the public interest'.[70]

To conclude that, in terms of lobbying, 'the current system and those op-erating within it worked well' is, to say the least, a surprising conclusion when he was specifically reviewing the problems of incessant lobbying uncovered by the Greensill affair.[71] Boardman only goes so far as to say that lobbyists should provide more information as to who is ultimately paying for their work, to whom in government they are speaking and the content of their discussions. He recommended that the exemption for lobbying where that was 'incidental' to other activities should be removed or severely restricted. Lobbyists would be required to conform to a statutory code of conduct setting minimum standards. These are valuable recommendations as far as they go but would not allay concerns about the lobbying industry if it is not properly regulated within a full statutory structure and one where the Registrar has real power.

The overall issue is one of transparency. As Duncan Hames, Director of Policy for Transparency International UK, puts it:

> When private interests meet with public decision makers, there is a risk that decisions that should be made in the public interest become corrupted. We see transparency in lobbying as an antidote to this risk, which brings in its wake accountability.[72]

John Penrose MP, who is the former Anti-Corruption Tsar,[73] called for an overhaul of lobbying rules on the basis that the 'future of our democracy is at stake'. He said that 'it was too difficult to link up who ministers have met with, who the lobbyists are working for, with who is donating money to which political party'. Transparency International UK summed up what is needed as follows:

> Success will only come, in time, through the cumulative effect of a package of measures which is urgently needed to:
> a. deliver a culture of openness around lobbying
> b. secure maximum transparency where specific activities seek to influence public office holders
> c. provide greater clarity on the standards expected of public office holders
> d. reassure the public that an ethical approach to lobbying is understood and actively being applied by all those who are involved in lobbying.[74]

It said that details of lobbying should be revealed every four weeks rather than, as of now, quarterly.[75]

Further statutory restrictions are essential, and these reforms should be at the top of the agenda:

• The definition of what a lobbyist is should be extended. All of them should register with the ORCL, even if this means the catching in the net of some folks whom many would not obviously identify as lobbyists.[76] The CSPL has from time to time rejected this on the basis that it 'would create the danger of giving the impression, which would no doubt be fostered by lobbyists themselves, that the only way to approach successfully Members or Ministers was by making use of a registered lobbyist. This would set up an undesirable hurdle, real or imagined, in the way of access'.[77] This argument is difficult to accept because it could be made clear by the Registrar and others that there was no exclusive route in.

- All meetings with lobbyists as defined should be declared wherever they take place. Duncan Hames told me: 'In practice, declarations are administered by departmental private offices, which only have access to the diaries that they run for ministers, and information they hold from arranging or attending these meetings. It seems nothing else gets declared.'[78]
- Rigid enforcement of the rules should be stepped up. As the CSPL has said, 'The lack of any meaningful sanctions for a breach of the rules is no longer sustainable'.[79]
- To improve the quality of transparency data, the government should ensure a sufficient level of detail is provided on the subject matter of *all* lobbying meetings and any policy matters which are discussed.[80]
- Government departments and ACOBA should have power to issue a statutorily backed lobbying ban for ex-ministers for a period of up to five years where they deem it appropriate.[81]
- Those on the lobbying register should have to declare the date, recipient and subject matter of their lobbying, in order to make it easier to cross-reference the Register with departmental releases of transparency data.[82]
- Secondments to government departments of those who may be seen to be lobbying should be stopped. The Commons PAC report in 2013 gave examples of employees from the four big accounting companies who 'go back to their firms and advise their clients on how they can use those laws to reduce the amount of tax being paid'.[83] This is pernicious but it is now deeply embedded in the system (and the Labour Party in opposition has also accepted such secondments).
- Instant messaging applications, virtual meetings, phone calls and emails should be included in this category when the representations to government are serious, premeditated and credible, or are given substantive consideration by ministers, special advisers or senior civil servants.[84] Any lobbying of ministers through informal or alternative channels, such as WhatsApp or Zoom, should be reported to civil servants.[85]

Dealing with this area will require serious political will. The sad fact is what Iain Anderson considered:

> Typically, political parties talk a good game on ethics whilst in opposition but are nervous about pushing the agenda forwards on coming into office. I want to go for maximum transparency and would go further than Nigel Boardman in his

report. You only stop this whirlygoround of cleaning things up by transparency, by showing exactly who is meeting whom.[86]

As a footnote, it does not require professionals to gain lobbying access. Possibly the finest lobbyist in recent years was Carrie Johnson, who was in-house, so to speak, at Number 10. There is clear evidence of Carrie's impact on government policies, as seen within days of her relationship with Boris Johnson starting, in relation to (of all things) the banning of electronic collars for pets. On 7 February 2018 Carrie was photographed with her future husband at the Black and White Ball,[87] a fixture on the Conservative Party fundraising calendar. Two days later, the Conservative Animal Welfare Foundation, of which Carrie had been a patron since 2017, promoted a campaign to ban e-collars.[88] On 20 February 2018, Boris announced his support for a ban.[89] Within six days, Carrie's ex-boyfriend, Harry Cole, then deputy political editor at the *Daily Mail*, reported that the Department for Environment, Food and Rural Affairs would ban e-collars,[90] and on 11 March 2018 this came about.[91] A High Court judge, however, decided in a judicial review that the Department had no 'evidential basis' to explain why between 5 February and 21 February 2018 it changed from permitting e-collars to deciding that they should be banned.[92] That is lobbying without payment.

Chapter 11

The Civil Service Commission: a few issues of decline and a few insidious features

'Integrity' is putting the obligations of public service above your own personal interests; 'honesty' is being truthful and open; 'objectivity' is basing your advice and decisions on rigorous analysis of the evidence; and 'impartiality' is acting solely according to the merits of the case and serving equally well Governments of different political persuasions.

Civil Service Code, 2010

It is a priceless gift that we have an impartial non-corrupt civil service.

Giles Radice[1]

In September 2022 Liz Truss was elected leader of the Conservative Party. She chose as Chancellor her old friend Kwasi Kwarteng, who lived on the same street in Greenwich and shared her radical view about the need for economic growth above all else and for immediate tax cuts. When they were new MPs they both contributed to the book *Britannia Unchained: Global Lessons for Growth and Prosperity*.[2] Within days of Truss's election, Kwarteng strode into the Treasury building and unceremoniously sacked the Permanent Secretary, Sir Tom Scholar. It was like a mafia greeting but with less blood on the carpet. This was in fact quite a good day to bury bad news surrounding the sacking, because it coincided with the Queen's death. Dave Penman, the General Secretary of the First Division Association, called it part of 'an ideological purge of permanent secretaries'.[3]

This dismissal opened up the possibility that the most senior civil servants could be subject to some kind of ideological purity test rather than assessed on the basis of their competence and willingness to serve, which is the principle of merit that has survived since the Northcote–Trevelyan Reforms of the Victorian era.[4] Scholar was no slouch or *ingénue*; he had steered the nation through the COVID-19 emergency and had successfully piloted the furlough scheme. Some thought that he was one of the most outstanding civil servants of his generation. Without him, the Truss government stumbled into a disaster of a mini-budget that had to be painfully undone piece by piece and became her chief legacy.[5] Soon afterwards, Truss and Kwarteng themselves were history. At forty-nine days, Truss was the shortest serving PM in UK history.

The brutality of Scholar's sacking may have been linked with Truss's attack on Treasury 'orthodoxy' and 'abacus economics' during her fraught leadership campaign against Rishi Sunak for the Tory leadership, but we do not know. No details about the reason for the dismissal came from the lips of Kwarteng.[6] Maybe it was thought that the Permanent Secretary was not sufficiently supportive of Brexit.[7]

Political support from a civil servant has never in the UK been a qualification for holding public office and should not be. Rather, civil servants have been expected to swivel on a sixpence and loyally turn from a government of one political hue to another. Scholar's defenestration was criticised by two former Heads of the Civil Service, Lord Kerslake and Lord (Gus) O'Donnell. Lord Butler, the former Cabinet Secretary, said on BBC Radio 4 that 'they are behaving improperly towards the civil service. It will weaken them but it will also corrupt our system because one of the great advantages of having an independent, loyal civil service will be compromised.'[8]

This was part of a pattern of prizing and rewarding political loyalty developed during the Johnson/Truss period. Lord Hogan-Howe was in 2022 the preferred candidate of Boris Johnson's Number 10 for the top post at the National Crime Agency (NCA), even though as Commissioner of the Metropolitan Police between 2011 and 2017 he had presided over the disastrous Operation Midland investigation into a supposed VIP paedophile ring. This had ruined the lives of several prominent and blameless public figures, including Lords Brittan and Bramall. Strong support for Hogan-Howe from Number 10 was trailed in many newspaper pieces. The Home Office would only comment that 'a fair and open recruitment campaign is under way'.[9]

What made Hogan-Howe stand out for Number 10 was that, unusually for a senior police officer, he had endorsed Johnson (with whom he had worked when the latter was London Mayor) for the Conservative leadership in a sophisticated campaign video. The appointment process was restarted by Downing Street after the two candidates who were called for interview, Neil Basu and Graeme Biggar, interim Director General at the National Crime Agency, were told they were not to be appointed.

Perhaps complete impartiality of the civil service is unachievable. The British civil service is in fact one of only a few in the developed world not to be politicised in its upper reaches. It is a prize worth hanging on to. Andy Haldane,[10] a former senior official at the Bank of England and now chief executive of the Royal Society of Arts, told me: 'We are generally blessed with our civil service; it is a well of expertise and goodwill.' An alternative view was, however, put to me by Michael Gove:

> There is a tendency in the civil service to recruit in their own image, to be suspicious of public opinion. You don't want a bureaucracy that is self-satisfied, more interested in itself than the people it serves.[11]

What is clear is that civil servants are likely to be less keen to speak the necessary truth to power after Scholar's defenestration. Serious criticism of the civil service was voiced by Dominic Raab when he resigned as Secretary of State for Justice.[12] Sir David Normington, the former Commissioner for Public Appointments and Civil Service Commissioner, put it in this way:

> It is fundamental to the way the UK government works that civil servants are impartial. They are there to give objective and frank advice, but then to implement the policies of the government of the day. The sacking of Tom Scholar strikes at these basic tenets of that relationship. It suggests that senior civil servants are only safe in their post if they agree with the government and that they cannot be trusted to do what the government asks.[13]

This period of demoralisation for the civil service coincided with Simon Case running the shop as Cabinet Secretary (though it started earlier).[14] Case is the youngest ever holder of that position, and it is generally speculated that he was chosen at an early stage of his career so he would be beholden to the political masters who had placed him in the role, and especially to Boris Johnson. There was widespread discontent about his appointment (he had never run a government department) and then over his tepid response to the COVID partying culture at Number 10. A key question is whether he was as energetic in seeking to protect Scholar's position as his predecessors might have been. A source told me that 'Simon Case is not a natural leader. He has not run a department but was part of the Johnson set.' Some of the emails he wrote that were disclosed in the lockdown files obtained by the *Daily Telegraph* in March 2023 suggest a contempt for the public too.[15]

What I found in my interviews (many of them with civil servants who wanted to remain anonymous) was uniformly very low morale with low self-confidence.[16] Some pin the blame on the constant denigration of the profession by people like Francis Maude[17] (now brought back as an adviser on the civil service).

The civil service is intended to be, and for many years has been, an important check on ministers – read any ministerial diary or memoir for some vivid examples. The (Robert) Armstrong memorandum of 1985 summarises the constitutional doctrine:

> Civil servants are servants of the Crown. For all practical purposes the Crown in this context means as it is represented by the Government of the day.... The Civil Service as such has no constitutional personality or responsibility separate from the duly constituted Government of the day.

Civil servants derive their power from their grip on detail and their perceived roles as experts (although in practice they rotate so quickly that they often do not have time to develop expertise in a particular sector before they are moved on to other jobs). They have been described as 'the hidden wiring of the constitution' and should be its vital support structure.

However, part of the overall populist agenda is an attack on expertise.[18] This was expressed most clearly in Michael Gove's well-known remark, voiced in the midst of the fraught Brexit referendum campaign, that 'the people of this country have had enough of experts'.[19] It is part of the reason the civil service is no longer accorded the same degree of respect.

Around 500,000 of those employed by the state qualify as civil servants.[20] It is a fundamental principle of the constitution that civil servants are appointed on the basis of merit, and the protection of this principle is presided over by the Civil Service Commissioners.[21] One of the great constitutional reforms of the Victorian period following the Northcote–Trevelyan Report of 1854 was to end patronage within the service,[22] because that system had led to the appointment of 'men of a very slender ability and perhaps of questionable character to situations of considerable emolument'.

It is a simplification, but generally accurate, to say that between 1854 and the 1960s we saw centralising forces in the civil service, but in 1980s the clock was turned back and there was a deliberate reversal into executive agencies at arm's length from departments. There was increasing delegation from the centre of many management responsibilities, and this has taken the responsibility away from civil servants to public appointments (and the private sector).[23] Today's civil service is virtually unrecognisable from the traditional body of policy developers of before, so much delivery has in effect been contracted out.[24]

The Civil Service Commission

The Civil Service Commission's primary job is to safeguard an impartial and effective civil service and to ensure appointments are made on merit. The Commission's existence and role were enshrined in legislation in 2010.[25] The Commissioners are independent of government. They regulate the appointment of the most senior civil servants and determine complaints about whether there has been a breach of the Civil Service Code.[26] Appointments within the Senior Civil Service (SCS) require the Commission's written approval.

On the recommendation of the CSPL, made in 2003, the First Civil Service Commissioner is appointed by the government after consultation with the leaders of the main opposition parties. The Commission's powers and responsibilities are laid down in the CRGA.[27] The post is subject to pre-appointment hearings in the House of Commons.

It was somewhat of a surprise that the Johnson government chose as the First Civil Service Commissioner the former Labour MP and now crossbench peer Gisela Stuart in March 2022. She was politically close to Boris Johnson, having been on the stump with him during the Brexit referendum campaign.

I cannot cover the whole field of the civil service and standards; instead, I isolate some aspects that feed into the narrative of my subject of declining standards. At the heart of this is a concern that the crucial impartiality of the civil service is being gradually undermined. This is not necessarily achieved by a full-frontal attack (although at times it has felt that way), but there are a number of insidious features that are necessary to consider.

1. Undermining civil service impartiality

Ministers are required to account for the actions of the executive to Parliament. Civil servants are accountable to their minister.[28] The relationship between civil servant and politician has worked well in the past, to the extent that officials and ministers thought of themselves as involved generally in the same overall project. It helped that they often went through the same schools and universities. The Civil Service Code, which forms part of civil servants' contract of employment, identifies the values that civil servants are expected to uphold.[29]

There will, however, always be tension in this symbiotic relationship. In evidence to the CSPL for its ninth report, Dr Tony Wright MP, Chair of the Public Administration and Constitutional Affairs Committee (PACAC), identified what he called 'a culture clash': 'You have civil servants who are

… very attached to formal procedures. Then you have politicians … who see themselves as "can do" people who have got to sort things out.… It is not surprising that there are tensions that arise out of that.' PACAC, however, described the interchange between ministers and officials as the 'fulcrum of Whitehall effectiveness'. Its 2018 report on the subject also spoke about that relationship as one of 'unrequited love'.

The downward spiral in morale comes amid the removal of a handful of key senior figures (some in quite egregious circumstances) and the voluntary departure of a significant number who do not want to work in the current political culture. Treating civil servants as a hostile 'blob' that seeks to undermine the government, as many Conservative ministers (but not Rishi Sunak) do, is likely to be as foolhardy as it is counterproductive.[30]

There is, however, an opposing narrative, that the civil service no longer provides quality service. I heard this critique not only from the political right. An experienced minister, Helen Goodman, who was the Labour MP for Bishop Auckland and served as a minister at the Department for Work and Pensions and as Deputy Leader of the House of Commons, told me: 'Many senior civil servants are not as good as they think they are. They are overconfident. Their life experience is limited and they can be naive about the realities of life beyond Whitehall.' There probably never was a golden time for the operation of the civil service. Decades ago, Thomas Balogh, an adviser to Harold Wilson, directed a blistering attack on 'the myth of a perfectly working government machine' in his essay 'The apotheosis of the dilettante'.[31]

Some civil servants are too cautious, perhaps because fewer good people are being attracted. Individuals are often agile and willing to come up with realistic solutions rather than process-driven treacle, but the system as a whole pulls them back. There is also a natural feeling that the generalism at the heart of the service is no longer fit for purpose in a modern, complicated world that needs expertise (an argument which has been going on for a very long time). I heard from several sources that the civil service was 'driven by process over outcomes' and bedevilled by the constant movement within and between departments.

This claim receives some support from Dame Kate Bingham, who was the head of the COVID Vaccine Taskforce and argued in a speech delivered at the University of Oxford in November 2021 that the country would have faced months of delay in getting vaccines if the process had been left to normal governmental machinery. The government's Chief Scientific Adviser, Sir Patrick Vallance, had intervened to put it outside normal civil service channels. Bingham also criticised the lack of science graduates in the civil service.[32]

This echoes the critique of Dominic Cummings, effectively Johnson's Chief of Staff, who colourfully said that besides the brilliant few in the civil service, 'there were the confident public-school bluffers and the Oxbridge humanities graduates spitting drivel about identity and diversity'. He berated Permanent Secretaries for lacking any proper understanding of maths, data management and the skills to manage major projects such as HS2.[33] Cummings' ambition (if such it can be called) was to build up political appointments of 'weirdos and misfits', as an advertisement under his tutelage sought. It called for applications from 'some true wild cards, artists, people who never went to university and fought their way out of an appalling hellhole'. This misfired when his first appointment turned out to have racist views and resigned before he took up the post. The principle of the bright 'generalist' should be history, he opined, and there should be 'genuine cognitive diversity' within the Whitehall system.

The alternative argument was put by Sir Jonathan Phillips, former Permanent Secretary at the Northern Ireland Office and Master of Keble College, Oxford, who said to me: 'There is a need for some very high-level generalist skills in serving ministers directly (not least in relation to their Parliamentary roles) but there is a desirability of improving (in some cases substantially) specific skills in relation to e.g. procurement/project management'.[34] The think tank Reform, in its 2022 publication *Reimagining Whitehall*, says that 'There is a need for government that both espouses and models long-term thinking on strategic, national-scale challenges, fosters cognitively diverse expertise, and incorporates a practical understanding of the realities of implementation and delivery'.[35] Leaks of Lord Francis Maude's forthcoming report on civil service governance and accountability in October 2023 suggested he would be calling for ministers to have more say in the appointment of Permanent Secretaries.[36]

There is also the persistent critique that civil servants rarely pay for their failures. For example, Sir Philip Barton, Under-Secretary at the Foreign Office, was seriously criticised by the Foreign Affairs Select Committee for his role (or lack of it, as he was on holiday) during the chaotic withdrawal from Afghanistan in the summer of 2021, but he did not resign nor did anyone prise him from office.[37] The symbiosis referred to above can be seen from the practical reality, which is that if he had gone, the spotlight would have fallen on Dominic Raab (the Foreign Secretary), who himself, as was well publicised at the time, remained on holiday.[38]

Everyone will have their own private list of policy blunders for which no one has paid with their job, but mine includes: the poll tax, the mis-selling of personal pensions, the Child Support Agency, the Millennium

Dome, individual learning accounts, the Assets Recovery Agency, many IT projects, the London Underground public–private partnership and identity cards. Anthony King and Ivor Crewe, in their great work *The Blunders of Our Governments*, concluded that '[British governments] screw up more often than most people seem to realise. Governments of all parties appear equally blunder-prone (but paradoxically) in spite of government's incessant blundering, the United Kingdom is in many ways a well-governed country.'[39]

Someone who is in a position to know told me that the problems arise for two main reasons:

• Pay – most Treasury civil servants are not able to buy a house on their civil service pay.
• Demoralisation – they are constantly attacked by politicians and this is compounded by social media.

It may also have something to do with the method of recruitment. The Social Mobility Commission, in research commissioned together with the LSE, found that the class composition of the civil service has barely changed since 1967. Their favoured behaviour was 'studied neutrality', which helps people reach top roles; they had an accent based on received pronunciation and they were 'emotionally detached and understated in self-presentation'.[40]

In his important Ditchley Lecture, Michael Gove sought to place this problem within a wider picture. He said: 'Now our age is not the 1930s. But it is an age of morbid symptoms. The model that the current generation of political leaders inherited has been crumbling.'[41] The root was a deep sense of disenchantment on the part of many citizens with a political system they feel has failed them. The context was of wider crises of authority in other institutions such as those 'in the church consequent upon abuse revelations, in Parliament following the expenses scandal and in the UK media after phone-tapping allegations [which] all unsettled faith in existing leadership'.

2. Spadocracy

The prestige of the independent civil service has over time also been undermined by the growth of the numbers and the role of special advisers (first introduced under Harold Wilson). They are temporary civil servants but not subject to the requirement that applies to permanent officials, to be objective and impartial.[42] Their role has been much expanded, often at the cost of the permanent civil service.

SpAds (as they are affectionately or otherwise generally known) have become powerful figures, but they do not have the accountability of either ministers or civil servants, nor are they selected on the merit principle. Some ministers now have several SpAds (even the Attorney General has one[43]) and they may spend more time with them than with civil servants. The interaction between them and the civil service can generate considerable friction.[44]

A paradigm shift occurred when Tony Blair gave Alastair Campbell and Jonathan Powell as his senior SpAds the right to give directions to civil servants by way of amendment to the relevant Order in Council[45] (repealed under the Brown government). This was in some ways symbolic only; many such advisers still do perform a quasi-executive role. Also, in the Treasury from that point on, Ed Balls and Ed Miliband were probably more powerful than any permanent official. Sir Bernard Jenkin MP, the Chair of the House of Commons Liaison Committee and former Chair of the Public Administration Select Committee, thinks the Blair innovation was a grave mistake and has led to the development of what he calls the 'spadocracy'. He told me over a coffee at Portcullis House that

> It was far from helpful to give Alastair Campbell the power to issue instructions to civil servants, as though he was a quasi-minister. We now have a spadocracy that considers itself in many ways to be more important than senior civil servants.[46] To be a SpAd is heady stuff for young graduates, who have worked within political parties. Some SpAds now have *de facto* leadership roles; some are very talented and expert in particular subject areas, but some are merely political operatives.[47]

The spadocracy is an important element in the civil service's 'loss of mojo', also known as the loss of the sense of being trusted by ministers.

Fast forward thirteen years and Nick Timothy and Fiona Hill were installed in the Home Office, playing a similar role and acting as Theresa May's shock troops or enforcers. Some say they were able to get officials they did not rate sent to 'internal Siberia'.[48] Under Johnson, centralisation of control went further, as Cummings told SpAds that he, rather than their Secretaries of State, was now their line manager (and they had to stay late on Fridays), although he did not last long in his post.

SpAds can, if given the power to do so by a major political figure, reach deep into the machine of the Department in a way that a Secretary of State hardly ever has the time for, given constituency, Parliamentary and other commitments. That power is not balanced by accountability. In the worst cases, SpAds have formed a protective shield around their minister, vetting the advice coming from their civil servants and even putting a black spot against the names of those whose advice they do not like.

Jenkin identified the problem:

> There are now triangular relationships at the top of many departments, with the Permanent Secretary and the special advisers competing for the Secretary of State's trust and attention.[49]

It is worth noting that one of the drivers of this trend is apparent frustration on the part of politicians at what they see as the unresponsiveness of the civil service: how long it takes to get things done, how often levers of change do not appear to work and things go wrong,[50] as forcibly expressed by Dominic Raab in his resignation letter.[51] That can result in frustration at the civil service, or at other institutions like the NHS, including a perceived lack of accountability.

Lord Wasserman, who was for twenty-seven years a civil servant in the Home Office, emphasises how useful SpAds can be for getting things done, 'as they are close to the ministers and can have a word in their ear'. But he added that 'there was a closer personal relationship between ministers and civil servants before SpAds came on the scene. This is a shame because good civil servants enjoy working closely with ministers in developing their policies and seek opportunities to do so.'[52]

A retired civil servant told me that SpAds 'can also do useful things, such as liaising with the press, which civil servants cannot easily do. In my time at four ministries a large majority (though not all) of my dealings with SpAds of all three political parties (I worked for Conservative, Labour and Lib Dem ministers) were positive.' Tim Durrant, now of the IfG and previously a civil servant for five years, offered me this balanced view:

> SpAds are beneficial to ministers as they help to spread a very busy workload and to civil servants so they are not expected to play a political role. But that does not mean they should just be friends of friends of the minister – it may be helpful to appoint subject-matter experts rather than party faithful. SpAds need to know what their minister thinks, but they should not necessarily follow them around, as they can more usefully contribute by informing civil servants and others of their boss's priorities; and they should have more guidance about what the role involves as protection for both sides.[53]

Number 10 itself is a hodgepodge of officials and political operatives. The role of special advisers in Number 10 has evolved, and it is sometimes difficult to detect who is a civil servant and who is on the political operation there. This is problematic, as it undermines both ministerial accountability to Parliament and collective responsibility on the part of the Cabinet.[54] Ministers should be fully accountable for the actions of their special advisers,[55] but this line of accountability has become blurred.

There are also recent examples where individuals have been hired as contractors to fulfil what appear to be roles as SpAds, and under Liz Truss's short-lived administration even her Chief of Staff was hired through a company. There is little information about how many of these there might be or what they are doing.[56] One unusually prominent role to be performed by a SpAd was when Lord Frost (a diplomat and head of the Scotch Whisky Association from 2013 to 2016) actually led negotiations with the European Commission as a SpAd in 2019, only becoming a minister after some eighteen months. There should be some merit-assessment for SpAds and pre-appointment hearings in Parliament for senior Prime Ministerial SpAds, because of the power they wield in some cases.

3. Warehouse clearance

The relations between ministers and senior officials are often tense but may turn toxic (as was the case with Sir Philip Rutnam and Priti Patel at the Home Office[57]). But past sporadic fallings-out are nothing compared with the wholesale warehouse clearance that took place in the early stages of the Johnson government (partly covered above). What is probably the most insidious feature is the potential subversion of the senior civil service and the undermining of the long-standing principle of merit.

As Johnson's first Chief of Staff in 2019, Dominic Cummings, was determined to be seen as a revolutionary, but was less sure about what revolution he wanted to wreak. He certainly brought havoc (and fear) to parts of the civil service (he promised a 'hard rain' would fall) and under his watch many senior civil servants 'left'.

In February 2020, a 'hit list' that was leaked to the media (it is not clear by whom) identified three Whitehall departments whose heads the government was apparently seeking to remove.[58] This appeared to be remarkably prescient and well informed, as each of the heads duly departed. Sir Philip Rutnam, Permanent Secretary at the Home Office, and Sir Simon McDonald[59] at the Foreign Office, both resigned in somewhat acrimonious circumstances.

The Permanent Secretary at the Ministry of Justice, Richard Heaton, in August 2020 resigned rather than be retired or transferred, and Jonathan Slater at the Department for Education was forced to resign by Boris Johnson in the same month, with the PM citing a 'need for fresh official leadership' following a row about A-level results.[60] This was an especially notorious de-fenestration (which no doubt had a chilling effect on others' willingness to be direct with ministers), because the minister responsible for the A-levels fiasco, Gavin Williamson, retained his post. Williamson also presided over a series of other disasters before eventually being dismissed in the September 2021 reshuffle, and then received a knighthood for his 'services', which even the Number 10 Press Office did not feel able to justify.[61] Slater told me he was never given the reason for his dismissal, even though it is a statutory require-ment as an employee.[62] It is probably too much of a coincidence that Clare Moriarty left the Department for Environment, Food and Rural Affairs on the same day as did Heaton. Sir Olly Robbins, who led the European negotia-tions for Theresa May, was also 'let go'.

In 2020, in addition to eight departmental Permanent Secretaries leaving one way or another, the head of the Government Legal Department and the Cabinet Secretary all went. Early on under a new government, some turnover of senior officials is to be expected, but this went far beyond what previous ex-perience suggested would happen and appeared to presage a changing of the civil service guard each time there was a change of government, as happens in the USA. The message to others is palpable, although it could be said that the system reasserted itself in that when Permanent Secretaries were eased out they were in all cases replaced by civil service lifers and not by outsiders.[63]

Another precedent was set when Mark (now Lord) Sedwill was forced to resign before the end of his term as Cabinet Secretary (he served from June 2018 to September 2020). His supposed failings have again never been made clear to the public. Was he insufficiently supportive of Brexit? Was he just seen as insufficiently loyal? Was it just because he had been appointed by Johnson's predecessor (and adversary) Theresa May? This removal is likely to deter future Cabinet Secretaries from standing up for the civil service (and Case's record in this respect is poor). So far, Sedwill has not broken his silence, save in the most vanilla terms.

All of this turnover creates costs. Large settlements have been paid, includ-ing (reportedly) £340,000 plus costs to Sir Philip Rutnam, the Permanent Secretary at the Home Office who complained about Priti Patel's 'bullying' and was the first Permanent Secretary ever actually to bring a claim in an employ-ment tribunal. It was reported that Scholar received a £457,000 settlement.[64]

Some, however, are positive about ministers appointing their Permanent Secretaries. The argument is that Permanent Secretaries and other senior officials are cosseted because they do not talk much to the public and think the country runs far more smoothly than it does. Top civil servants, on this view, are innately small 'c' conservative. They can frustrate ministers through delay.[65] They are also policy focused, rather than being good at delivery. I favour the existing system.

4. Ministerial Directions

Another indicative feature of poor relationships is the increasing use of Ministerial Directions to direct civil servants.[66] This use indicates that the politicians are not accepting the advice of civil servants. In August 2019, Sonia Khan, the Brexit-supporting special adviser to the then Chancellor, Savid Javid, was marched out of Downing Street with a police escort.[67] This case brought to public attention the little-known issue of these Directions. It came about because Boris Johnson specifically instructed the former Chief Executive of the Civil Service and Permanent Secretary of the Cabinet Office, Sir John Manzoni, not to settle her case, even though Manzoni – and in all likelihood his legal advisers – thought that doing so would be better value for money for the taxpayer. The instructions from the Prime Minister included this curious sentence: 'The legal position is clear that the Prime Minister may withdraw consent for the appointment of any Special Adviser'. That is indeed clearly so, but it is equally apparent that this does not override the legal protections Khan had in law. The case was eventually settled in December 2020 for a five-figure sum, and that agreement was surely significantly timed, just before Dominic Cummings was asked to leave his position as (*de facto*) Chief of Staff to Boris Johnson. The likelihood is that it would have been a lower burden on the public purse if settled earlier.[68]

A Ministerial Direction also serves as a form of protection for civil servants, as it enables them to speak truth to power.[69] They are formal instructions from ministers telling their department to proceed with a spending proposal, despite an objection from the Permanent Secretary. This present structure has been functioning since 2011 and is based on the proposition that the Permanent Secretary of each department is also the 'accounting officer' for that department – a general practice that actually goes back to the nineteenth century.[70] The Permanent Secretary is the person whom Parliament (through the Public Accounts Committee) calls to account for how the department spends its money, and this emphasises that officials are accountable to the legislature and not just to their minister. Francis Maude described them as a 'constitutional safety valve'.[71]

Civil servants have a duty to seek a Ministerial Direction if they think a spending proposal breaches any of the following criteria set out by the Treasury:[72]

- Regularity – the proposal is beyond the department's legal powers or agreed spending budgets.
- Propriety – it does not meet 'high standards of public conduct', such as appropriate governance or Parliamentary expectations.
- Value for money – something else, or doing nothing, would be cheaper and better.
- Feasibility – there is doubt about the proposal being 'implemented accurately, sustainably or to the intended timetable'.

After informal discussions, the Permanent Secretary writes to the Secretary of State expressing concerns, seeking a Direction. It would instruct the civil service to implement the decision so that they do not have a choice in the matter but the formal accountability for the decision is pushed up to the minister.[73]

A minister in fact has to weigh up more than can be expressed just in terms of the actual cash. A good example was the Transport Minister's decision to require potential north of England rail franchisees to invest in 120 new vehicles. Officials not unreasonably thought this large expenditure went beyond what was necessary, and therefore might cost more than a pure 'value for money' franchise. However, as the Secretary of State wrote in the Direction: 'I believe there are wider issues to consider which I accept fall outside the remit of the Accounting Officer but that I consider material … uncomfortable and low quality [trains are] incompatible with our vision for economic growth and prosperity in the north'.[74]

A 2016 NAO report, however, asserted that accounting officers 'appear to lack confidence to challenge Ministers where they have concerns about the feasibility or value for money of new policies or decisions, not least because standing up to Ministers is seen as damaging to a civil servant's career prospects'.[75] Sir Amyas Morse, the Comptroller and Auditor General, in evidence to PACAC given in November 2017, emphasised that 'The issue is that accounting officers have a clear responsibility to obtain value for money, but they also have conflicting responsibilities to support their Ministers and carry through their policy'.[76]

Martin Stanley, the editor of the Understanding Government set of websites (which includes one specifically on the civil service) and a former civil servant, was positive about the mechanism: 'Ministerial Directions are a very useful device and are good ways of resolving differences with civil servants.[77] In times of harmony between civil servants and ministers who are prepared to accept civil service advice, however, there should be few such Directions.

The vast majority of the eighty-nine Ministerial Directions issued between 1990 and 2023 were on value-for-money grounds.[78] Generally, they are requested at the rate of two or three a year. Two of them were issued on notoriously wasteful projects, Kids Company and the London Garden Bridge (one of Johnson's big ideas[79]). No fewer than fourteen were set out in respect of the coronavirus pandemic. One would expect more to be issued during a crisis, but this number is nevertheless high. It indicates that Directions are no longer seen as the nuclear option.

The effectiveness of the system can be seen in the case of the government joining a consortium bid of $500 million in respect of One Web, a satellite company in Chapter 11 bankruptcy in the USA. The then-acting Permanent Secretary of the Department for Business, Energy and Industrial Strategy wrote to the then Secretary of State, Alok Sharma, to this effect:

> Having reflected carefully on the information provided, I have concluded that whilst there may be a commercial case for investing alongside other commercial investors if you accept advisors' assessment of One Web's business plan projections, as a standalone high-risk investment with a possibility that the entirety of the investment is lost and no wider benefits accrued, I cannot satisfy myself that this investment meets the requirements of Value for Money as set out in Managing Public Money.[80]

Sharma duly gave the Direction to go ahead with the bid. It will be instructive to follow the fate of that company and to see whether Sharma (or anyone else) is held to account if it is a disaster, though he has long moved on.

Another example where questions of propriety have arisen, but no Direction was sought or issued, is the Towns Fund – a scheme apparently designed to boost economic growth in certain areas – where two ministers put forward each other's constituencies for payments at the last minute when they were not on the list that had been drawn up by civil servants.[81] Other cases where Directions were not sought when it seems obvious they should have been were the National Programme for IT in the NHS (£10 billion), the FiReControl project (£469 million) and Universal Credit.[82]

The Home Secretary, Priti Patel, issued a Direction in April 2022 in connection with her controversial and expensive new policy to transfer asylum seekers to Rwanda so as to deter Channel crossings in flimsy boats. The Direction was needed because her Permanent Secretary said he did 'not believe sufficient evidence can be obtained to demonstrate that the policy will have a deterrent effect significant enough to make the policy value for money'.[83]

Conclusion

Other current issues of concern in the civil service include blurred accountabilities between civil servants and ministers and low levels of recruitment from outside government. Excessive turnover of roles leading to reduced expertise can also have a major impact on ministers, as knowledge is lost and the quality of the advice given is adversely affected.[84] An example of this was the introduction of Universal Credit, which over five years had six senior responsible owners.

A loss of faith among politicians and the public in the civil service opens the door for a dilution of the civil service's impartiality that would lead to even more short-term policy decisions, a less skilled workforce and a creeping corruption of public life. Martin Stanley summed it up for me: 'Ministers in recent years have treated senior officials badly and they have as a defence mechanism tended to become risk-averse and courtier like. There is less keenness to say truth to power.' That also has long-term consequences for the rule of law, which we will consider in the penultimate chapter.

We should not inexorably move to a system such as exists in the USA, where senior civil servants change with the political party of the government, especially without realising we are doing so. However, in the light of recent experience, we need further institutional protection for the Senior Civil Service, such as used to exist in local government as a result of the Waddington Review. This ensured senior officers could not be dismissed without the imprimatur of an independent outside person (known as a designated independent person, or DIP). The DIP scheme provided protection from political interference.[85] It was abolished in England in 2015, though it survived in Wales till 2020.

The benefits of SpAds may be recognised, but there should be more rigorous vetting of suitability for appointment and some sort of merit test. Further, the head of the Civil Service Commission should not be a political figure, as is Gisela Stuart. We should recognise that when there are blunders, civil servants should occasionally pay for them (as occurs in any other walk of life), but the procedures should be transparent, open and fair.

Part III

Cross-cutting issues

Chapter 12

MPs for hire:
second jobs in the spotlight

You might think that being an MP is a full-time occupation. Some, however, take the view that one job is not enough. When Dudley Fishburn arrived as the Conservative MP for Kensington after having won a byelection in 1988, he was told by other MPs that he must add a proper job, to help with his bank account as well as to raise his intellectual sights.[1] That is no doubt what Owen Paterson thought he was doing with the healthcare company Randox. In 2015, Paterson's work as MP for North Shropshire (a constituency he had held since 1997) took a lucrative turn as he moonlighted in second jobs, in particular as a part-time consultant for Randox at a rate that by 2019 had reached £8,333 a month.[2]

Randox is a clinical diagnostics company,[3] and Paterson told the Advisory Committee on Business Appointments (ACOBA) in advance of taking up the role that it 'may involve discussions with ministers'. His monthly commitment was sixteen hours. He also worked for Lynn's Country Foods, a company specialising in liquid seasoning and 'Naked Bacon' (marketed as a healthy alternative to traditional bacon), based in County Down, for which he was paid £12,000 per year.[4] These sums well exceeded his salary as an MP.

The beginning of the end of Boris Johnson as Prime Minister can be dated to his attempt to save his good friend Owen. The plan was hatched in the grandeur of a dinner at the male-only Garrick Club, populated primarily by *Telegraph* journalists. Paterson had a seemingly impregnable majority and was a committed Brexiteer. It looked likely that he would comfortably continue in Parliament until he decided it was time to retire. He had served as Secretary of State for Northern Ireland from 2010 to 2012 and held the top job at the Department of Environment, Food and Rural Affairs thereafter to 2014. Team Johnson saw him very much as 'one of us'. This is a story of lobbying and Parliamentary rule breaking, and yet also of 'the system' reasserting itself after a damaging few days.

Paid advocacy by MPs has been banned in one form or other since 1695. Paterson's advocacy, which was referred to the Committee on Standards, consisted in his making three approaches to the Food Standards Agency relating to Randox and the testing of antibiotics in milk, four feelers to ministers at the Department for International Development about Randox and blood-testing technology, and seven again to the Food Standards Agency on behalf of Lynn's Country Foods. The last fell within his former ministerial bailiwick.

On 26 October 2021, the Committee on Standards (made up of his peers), on the basis of a report by the Parliamentary Commissioner for Standards, decided he should be suspended from the House for thirty days because of an 'egregious case of paid advocacy' which had 'brought the House into disrepute'.[5] Indeed, it judged that 'no previous case of paid advocacy has seen so many breaches of such a clear pattern of confusion between the private and public interest'. He also broke the rules by using his Parliamentary office on twenty-five separate occasions for business meetings with clients, as well as using his Parliamentary stationery for this consultancy work and failing to declare his interests in some meetings.

Paterson did not take the judgement lying down (nor would his friends), believing that it did not comply with natural justice.[6] He has subsequently taken this point to the European Court of Human Rights. The sensitivity of this penalty was that it could have triggered a recall petition, whereby 10% of a constituency's voters may force an MP to face a byelection in their seat.

A motion to carry out the recommendations of the Committee and suspend Paterson was put to Parliament in the normal way, but what followed was anything but. For the first time in history, the Commons blocked the recommendations of the report of a Committee into the conduct of a MP. An amendment was tabled to delay consideration of Paterson's suspension and to set up a new committee to investigate the whole disciplinary process for MPs. This body would have a Conservative majority and Chair. The government supported the amendment and issued a three-line whip to support it. The amendment passed 250–232, with thirteen Conservative MPs voting against and ninety-seven absent or abstaining.[7]

The amended motion was then passed by a twenty-seven-vote majority. The new Committee, to be chaired by a former Tory minister, would give MPs a right of appeal similar to employees. It could decide to reconsider the case against Paterson and how the standards rules should be revised to be 'compatible with natural justice'. The Commissioner for Standards would be redundant.

There was a widespread outcry. This smacked of the government changing the rules retrospectively and making a heavy-handed response that appeared designed to protect a friend; it seemed to say again boldly that if you are on Team Johnson the normal ethical rules do not apply. The Chair of the CSPL, in a speech to the IfG, called the move 'an extraordinary proposal … deeply at odds with the best traditions of British democracy' and said that it was a 'very serious and damaging moment for Parliament and public standards in this country'.[8]

The idea of the new Committee gained few friends. Opposition parties were not willing to participate. Stung by the outcry, the government did a reverse ferret and announced that a vote *would* still take place on whether Paterson should be suspended. On 5 November 2021, however, before this happened, Paterson announced his resignation from Parliament because of what he said was the 'indescribable nightmare' of the investigation. After a further debate, Parliament passed a motion accepting the findings of the original report. In the subsequent byelection in North Shropshire, the Tories lost one of their strongest majorities to the Lib Dems.[9]

Second jobs in the spotlight

This incident shone a spotlight on the difficult question of second (and third and fourth, etc.) jobs for MPs. Ian Hislop, editor of *Private Eye*, subsequently told the Committee on Standards that the public were being taken for fools: 'I think we have to admit that the system failed in that Owen Paterson had obviously no idea that he was breaking the code and a large number of his fellow MPs decided they had no idea either'.[10]

The Code of Conduct of the House of Commons presently prescribes no limitations on the kinds of employment in which MPs can engage or what their salary may be from those roles, save that they should not act as 'paid advocates' for their employers. Since the 2009–2010 Parliamentary session, however, Members have had to report the precise amount of each payment they receive, describe the nature of their work and provide the name and address of the employer, although sometimes the details are put rather obscurely.[11]

We are talking big money here. Political scientist Simon Weschle surveyed the private-sector earnings of 845 MPs between 2010 and 2016 and estimated the total for all MPs to be between £4.6 and £6.7 million per year. He also noted the figure exhibited a slight upward trend. Interestingly, the sum was lower in the two election years he studied (2010 and 2015).[12] From the

2019 general election up to the end of 2022, Conservative MPs received the vast sum of £15.2 million from second jobs. Labour was well behind, at £1.2 million, and the Lib Dems further still, at £171,000. Perhaps surprisingly, the biggest earner in that period was Theresa May, who gained a princely £2.5 million, mainly from speeches for such organisations as JP Morgan and the private equity firm Apax Partners.[13]

In due course, the Commons Committee on Standards made recommendations, including introducing a requirement for MPs to secure a written contract for any outside job they take, and more timely transparency around ministerial declarations of interest, to bring them into line with the rules for backbench MPs. Neither recommendation has been implemented. On 16 March 2022, plans to cap MPs' earnings from second jobs were quietly dropped by the House of Commons on the basis this would be 'impractical'. Two months later the House of Commons banned MPs from providing paid Parliamentary advice, consultancy or strategy services and not just lobbying. But further than that it would not go, which may seem self-interested on their part or realistic, depending on your point of view.

Are there good jobs and bad jobs?

MPs have often worked on the side as doctors or lawyers. Few would say that those sorts of roles should be banned (unless they detract from their Parliamentary duties). But as Helen Goodman, the former Labour MP for Bishop Auckland, told me, it is 'difficult to draw the line between good and bad second jobs for MPs. Keeping a farm is not likely to produce a conflict of interest.'[14] The journalist Michael Crick agreed, opining that a 'ban on second jobs would be very difficult to police. For example, how could you ban book reviews?'[15]

The proposition that there are good jobs and not so good second jobs for MPs is intriguing. As many as a fifth of MPs in fact have a second job – that is, one that pays regular wages; two-fifths declare income from some form of extra-Parliamentary work.[16]

The case of Sir Geoffrey

The media coverage of Paterson drew renewed attention to the outsized extra-curricular activities of Sir Geoffrey Cox, who had long carried on a lucrative career at the Bar alongside his Parliamentary duties. In recent years he has earned £900,000 per annum as a consultant to Withers, lawyers to the global rich, which includes work in offshore tax havens.[17] There was some limited evidence that these activities detracted from his Parliamentary role. For example, Cox lobbied in Parliament against imposing tougher financial regulation on the Cayman Islands, a UK dependency, and argued against amendment to the Sanctions and Anti-Money Laundering Bill debated in Parliament in May 2018, which greatly affected offshore tax havens.

Cox spoke only three times in the Commons in the 2020–2021 Parliamentary session, and all of his speeches were delivered on the same day, 13 September 2020. During that period he was representing the British Virgin Islands (BVI) authorities, apparently with the approval of the Chief Whip. Cox was found to have missed at least twelve Parliamentary votes because of a trip to the BVI for one of his paid roles[18]. He was spotted by a *Times* journalist while carrying out a Zoom hearing on a BVI corruption inquiry from his Parliamentary office and was noticed to be voting by proxy from BVI during part of the pandemic lockdown. The Parliamentary Commissioner for Standards decided that the rules on the use of Parliamentary offices should be enforced with a 'sense of proportion' and did not pursue this. It is reasonable to infer from this that others were doing the same thing.[19] Cox's response to criticism is that he regularly works seventy hours a week and always ensures that his casework for constituents is up to date.

Angela Rayner, as deputy leader of the Labour Party, described Cox's behaviour as 'an egregious, brazen breach of the rules' and said 'you can be an MP serving your constituents or a barrister working for a tax haven. You can't be both, and Boris Johnson needs to make his mind up which one Geoffrey Cox will be.'[20] Evidently, Cox's West Devon constituents do not agree in the slightest with Rayner. He has a massive majority that has kept rising. Curiously, his defensive press statement used his name in the third person, saying 'Sir Geoffrey's view is that it is up to the electors of Torridge & West Devon whether or not they vote' for someone who 'still practises as a barrister'. Michael Crick agrees, and told me: 'Is it not appropriate to leave [the issue of what is acceptable] to the voters as Geoffrey Cox suggests? There is, however, more that could be done on revealing hours and contracts.'

One reason for allowing MPs to carry on legal practice is that it helps to fulfil the demanding role of a law officer, which Cox had held as Attorney General, and the Attorney General still leads the advocacy for the government in important cases. It might also help to have people in the Commons who are used to a professional environment and a rigorous code of ethics.

A YouGov poll found that 63% of the public believe no such outside work by MPs should be allowed at all. It is, however, necessary not to put good people off becoming MPs. While it is true the voters can decide, in fact many MPs do not take these roles until they are elected and then do not exactly advertise to their constituents what they are doing in addition to working as MPs, or at least how much time the jobs take.

More sophisticated is the CSPL's suggestion of 'an objective means of setting reasonable limits' on outside earnings. Ideas put forward following the Paterson scandal included a limit on the time to be spent on, or a ceiling on earnings from, second jobs.

Conclusions

Voters should know exactly what their MPs are doing and precisely how much time they are spending on activities above and beyond their Parliamentary duties. Most people would now be horrified by the statement made by Sir Patrick McNair-Wilson, MP for New Forest, to the *Lymington Times* on 1 July 1989: 'the public do not have an automatic right to know what their MPs get up to'. In the old days, people would come to the Commons in the afternoon after practising at the Bar or in the City in the morning, and this was part of the reason Parliament worked such funny hours, starting at 2 p.m. most days.

I agree with Ian Hislop, who has called for a requirement to record the reason for any MP who takes on an outside interest or accepts a gift or hospitality. The MP would need to make clear how doing so forms part of the role. I would, however, go further and impose a ban on all second jobs for MPs save for a restricted list of 'good jobs' and on application to the Speaker's Council on a case-by-case basis. Being an MP should be recognised as a full-time occupation (as it surely is if done properly). There are only a few jobs that can appropriately be combined with being an MP – for example, very part-time care services, writing and farming – these should be listed and within the discretion of the Speaker's Council. MPs have more than enough to do representing their constituents.

This should be linked with a one-time increase in remuneration, a point developed in the final chapter. We have already discussed the revolving door of jobs, which overlaps with this. Now we turn to where ministers were moonlighting in recommending friends for PPE contracts.

Chapter 13

Anatomy of a recent scandal: PPE

Dodgy contracts, privileged access, jobs for their mates, this is the return of Tory sleaze.

Sir Keir Starmer at Prime Minister's Questions, 14 April 2021

It is an important question to ask why do standards matter? Trust in institutions is very important. Where there is a higher level of trust wellbeing is likely to be greater. Lack of trust is likely to be corrosive in institutions.

Gus O'Donnell[1]

Demand for personal protective equipment (PPE) increased exponentially in England from March 2020 because of the COVID pandemic. The government needed to acquire masks and gowns, goggles, tracing apps and lots besides, and it needed them very, very quickly. The Department of Health and Social Care spent more than £13 billion on PPE during the period. What, you might ask, could be more natural than ministers turning to their friends and overlooking pesky procurement processes that were getting in the way? Only 1% of the £17.3 billion spent on COVID contracts was awarded through competitive tendering.[2] There was, it is true, insufficient time to follow *all* of the normal procurement procedures that are designed to protect the public purse. This should not have been an excuse for lack of any competition *at all*. Transparency International UK calculated that £2 billion of the pandemic contracts went to those with links to senior Tories.[3]

Many of the chums (otherwise known as 'Covid oligarchs'), however, did not perform well – by not delivering at all, by supplying unsuitable or substandard items, by failing to meet deadlines or by hugely overcharging. The government could have approached major manufacturers and importers of textiles and other relevant items and asked them urgently to switch or ramp up production in order to meet the urgent needs.

These circumstances raise serious issues for standards in our public life and whether the relevant regulators were fit for purpose. The NAO found that hundreds of millions had been wasted on unusable equipment and supplies that had passed their expiry date.[4] This shed light on issues in public procurement that had been bubbling up for some time. Lord Wood of Anfield, a former academic who served as an adviser to Ed Miliband, told me that 'Informal methods of procurement are rife now; COVID simply magnified the issues in terms of PPE contracts'.[5] On 3 March 2022, Sir John Bell, Regius Professor of Medicine at the University of Oxford and a key player in the government's response to the pandemic, criticised the profiteering by firms during the pandemic in a speech he made to the Royal Society. He concluded that 'the behaviour of some companies was completely unacceptable and disgraceful'.[6]

What appeared to be a wartime requisition drive to the outside was a story of lobbying, lack of proper documentation, denial of involvement by people in particular companies and poor public practice, and just possibly corruption.[7] It shone a light on the chumocracy at work (and at play). Dominic Cummings was characteristically direct in one of his emails, which said 'someone please ensure they have 530k within 24 hours from now and report back to me it's been sent. No procurement, no lawyers, no meetings, no delay please – just send immediately.'[8]

Exhibit 1 is PPE Medpro, a company which secured a government contract worth £80.85 million to supply 210 million facemasks. Shortly after that, it received another contract worth £122 million to supply the NHS with masks and surgical gowns.[9] Yet the company was set up only weeks before this outstanding success. People naturally wanted to know who was behind this obscure vehicle, which was awarded the two government contracts in May and June 2020. Anthony Page was its only public face, as he was apparently on paper the sole owner and principal director of both the Isle of Man and UK versions of PPE Medpro. It turned out that he had been for a long time a wealth-management expert employed by Douglas Barrowman's Knox House Trust, an Isle of Man group.[10]

And that is the key, because there were reasons why Barrowman might wish to keep secret his involvement, and that of his *much* more famous wife. For she was Lady Mone, who ran the lingerie company Ultimo before becoming a Conservative peer in 2015, ennobled by David Cameron. At length, in May 2022, *The Times* reported that Barrowman did indeed have an interest in Medpro. Leaked WhatsApp messages appear to show Mone herself discussing details of the gowns and the Department of Health and Social Care's purchase orders, although she, through her solicitors, denied any involvement in the company. It was she, however, who referred the company to Michael Gove personally, then to the Cabinet Office minister and to Lord Agnew.[11] She is alleged to have shouted down the phone at officials to ensure contracts were awarded to LFI Diagnostics, another company with which she was involved.[12] There was a complaint by the Labour peer Lord Foulkes to the Lords Parliamentary Commissioner for Standards about her conduct under several sections of the House of Lords Code of Conduct, including taking 'financial inducement as an incentive or reward for exercising parliamentary influence'.

When asked by the *Guardian* why she did not include PPE Medpro in her register of financial interests for the House, Mone's lawyer replied that 'she did not benefit financially and was not connected to PPE Medpro in any capacity'. Documents leaked to the newspaper suggest that this is not the full story and, further, that in September 2020 at least £65 million in 'profits' was transferred to one of Barrowman's Isle of Man trusts. Lady Mone admitted in December 2023 that her family stood to gain from involvement in PPE Medpro.[13]

The NAO is the institutional hero of the general PPE tale, because it brought it to light by meticulous work over many months. But, as in other scandals, no one in government was really held to account, even though many health and other workers died because PPE was either missing or inadequate.

Other unlikely entrepreneurs who had never been involved in healthcare products stampeded to join in, earning millions of pounds. Unknown firms won deals worth hundreds of millions for COVID testing without competition or effective scrutiny.[14] Some of the successful companies were linked to ministers, and these chums got a special hotline all of their own. A young friend of mine who was working at the Department of Health in a junior capacity during the crisis registered her disgust with me at the time it was happening, and further revelations were made in the lockdown files published by the *Daily Telegraph* in March 2023. Even if these contracts were not in fact dodgy, the whole exercise did not pass the smell test, as important as it is vague.

Subsequently, the NAO conducted a searing investigation and concluded:

> we cannot give assurance that the Government has adequately mitigated the increased risks arising from emergency procurement or applied appropriate commercial practices in all cases. While we recognise that these were exceptional circumstances, there are standards that the public sector will always need to apply if it is to maintain public trust.[15]

But this was far too late and entailed no sanctions.

Procurement by public bodies in the UK, such as government departments and their agencies, NHS organisations and local authorities, is subject to the complex regime set out in the Public Contracts Regulations 2015 and related instruments. These rules seek to ensure that, in procuring goods, services and works, public bodies adhere to fair and reasonable timetables and procedures, and, most importantly, that they encourage open competition.[16] Such organisations should document their procurement decisions fully and ensure that conflicts of interest are managed.

The NAO found a lack of the transparency that should be at the heart of the regulatory framework. It looked at over 1,000 coronavirus contracts worth £18 billion between January and July 2020: the details of only about a quarter of them were published within the statutory ninety-day limit, and over half had still not been made public at the time of the NAO's March 2022 report.[17] Of those, £10.5 billion was awarded without competition at all.

This is problematic on several levels. As Jolyon Maugham KC, the founder of the Good Law Project (GLP), which has brought cases regarding the award of PPE contracts, told the *Guardian*, 'if you ditch process, you're going to have corruption. That's just inevitable.'[18]

It was John Penrose, the Conservative MP and Anti-Corruption Tsar (and husband of Dido Harding[19]), who said that 'covid has been a salient reminder of how important it is that we maintain our strong standards and protections in public procurement'.[20] The PAC concluded that 'suppliers and intermediaries are likely to have made excessive profits providing substandard PPE'.[21] Dame Meg Hillier, the Chair of the PAC, when announcing the publication of its report, stated that 'the complete collapse of some of the most well-established civil service practices beggars belief'.[22]

The NAO proved what was long suspected, that suppliers in the 'VIP track' had a ten times greater success rate in being awarded contracts.[23] And it was a VIP lane to which only those who were close to the 'right' people in government need apply. Suppliers that came through these routes were awarded no less than £6 billion out of the £7.9 billion total of testing contracts awarded between May 2020 and March 2021.[24] The NAO identified corruption risks in seventy-three UK government contracts.

The VIP track

Many of the VIPs got into this track by donating to the Conservative Party or just being lucky enough to be buddies of the relevant ministers or NHS officials and/or by being 'very important'.

One official said, in emails which were disclosed in a legal claim subsequently brought by GLP, that 'we are currently drowning in VIP requests and "high priority" contacts that despite all of our work and best efforts do not either hold the correct certification or do not pass due diligence'.[25] This represents a slew of illegalities or at least widespread bending of the rules. We will consider just two that were broken wholesale. Regulation 18 of the Public Contracts Regulations 2015 is headed 'Principles of procurement' and provides: 'Contracting authorities shall treat economic operators equally and without discrimination and shall act in a transparent and proportionate manner'. The Ministerial Code also emphasises that ministers 'must ensure that no conflict arises, or appears to arise, between their public duties and their private interests', and that they 'should not act or take decisions in order to gain financial or other material benefits for themselves, their family, or their friends'.[26]

The principles should be tightened further. As Gareth Davies, the Comptroller and Auditor General, told the PAC on 10 January 2023, peers and MPs should declare any link to those they recommend for contracts, even in an emergency such as COVID procurement.

You can usually tell that there is some sort of a scandal if there is an attempt at cover-up and when answers given to pertinent questions are as clear as mud. In November 2020, the government informed the NAO of forty-seven contracts that were in that privileged track. In November 2021, it found that fifty companies were given the VIP treatment and that, of these, no less than eighteen had been nominated by Conservative politicians. This figure was, however, revised in February 2022 to fifty-one, after GLP obtained a leaked database revealing that sixty-eight companies were referred to as VIPs. The Health Secretary was also hauled over the legal coals in the High Court for failing to publish details of these PPE contracts in sufficient time.[27]

Ministers and advisers were (shall we say) traffic wardens in this important lane for business.[28] These are just a few examples:

- The then Transport Secretary, Grant Shapps, was named as the 'source of referral' for the VIP firm EyeSpace Eyewear. The previously unheard of company landed a £1.4 million deal to provide goggles.
- The GLP names Lord Leigh twice as a source of referral (for Maxima Markets and Skinnydip). He has donated over £100,000 to the Tory Party.[29]
- Alex Bourne, once the landlord of a pub that was close to the then Health Secretary Matt Hancock's home, landed part of a £40 million contract to provide medical equipment without having any experience in that area of supply. Hancock described the story as 'a fabrication pushed by the Labour Party'. He may have been thinking of the fact his Department signed a

contract not with Bourne but with a company called Alpha Laboratories, which was, however, subcontracted to Bourne's company Hinpack, which usually made plastic cups and takeaway boxes for the catering industry. Bourne joked in a text to the Health Secretary that he (Bourne) had 'never heard' of his famous friend, even though a photo came to light of Hancock pulling pints in Bourne's pub.[30]

- Priti Patel, then Home Secretary, was close to a Mr Samir Jassal, a council-lor in Kent, who also worked for Patel as an unpaid adviser. He represented Pharmaceuticals Direct Limited (PDL), which received a £28.8 million contract for surgical masks.[31] This was unreported and was won without competition six days after Patel contacted procurement officials.
- The Paper Drinking Straw Co. Ltd landed a £20 million contract to provide surgical masks after being referred by the Tory donor Stuart Marks. Marks has donated more than £100,000 to the Conservatives according to the latest Electoral Commission data.

The NAO subsequently found there was no evidence that ministers were *directly* involved in awarding contracts. The watchdog, however, barked loudly about the lack of documentation, which made it impossible to know why some companies gained supply deals.[32]

Many of the stories I heard about the VIP lane featured Lord Bethell, who apparently used his private email accounts for thousands of messages relating to COVID contracts.[33] He is a former part-owner of the Ministry of Sound nightclub and is probably the only super-DJ employer to have held a hereditary peerage. And there was a really big kerfuffle about his phone, which emerged in disclosure in the GLP case on PPE procurement.[34] The Government Legal Service sent letters to the effect that after Lord Bethell confirmed he had sent the texts and messages from his own phone relating to a PPE contract, he could not produce them because the phone had been 'lost'. But, a few days later, his lordship indicated instead that his phone was 'broken' or 'defective'. Finally, in a meeting with lawyers, he said that too was wrong, and he had given the phone to a member of his family to use.

The unholy trinity: closeness to government, lack of transparency and poor delivery

Between January 2020 and December 2021, the Department of Health and Social Care and Public Health England (PHE) awarded twenty-two contracts to Randox Laboratories Ltd, or its strategic partner Qnostics Ltd, with a maximum value of £776.9 million. Randox was one of the biggest players of COVID bingo and seemed to be the biggest winner of the game. It also sponsors the Grand National horse race.[35]

The NAO carried out a separate inquiry into the relationship between the Department and Randox. It could not provide assurance that procurement standards had been met, not least because the Department of Health and Social Care had 'no documentation of the negotiations'. Minutes were kept of only two of the eight meetings that took place between ministers and Randox in 2020–2021.[36]

The story has the added piquancy that Randox engaged Owen Paterson as a lobbyist for it, which got him into a whole heap of trouble, documented elsewhere.[37] The NAO summary says:

> The speed of action required at the beginning of the pandemic to build high-volume testing capacity necessitated the use of emergency procurement without competitive tendering. However, the Department did not document key decisions adequately, disclose ministerial meetings with Randox fully or keep full records of ministerial discussions involving Randox.

The PAC in 2022 concluded that it was 'impossible to have confidence' the contracts 'were awarded properly'. The NAO said that 'The gaps in the audit trail mean that it is not possible to provide positive assurance in the normal way, but we have not seen any evidence that the government's contracts with Randox were awarded improperly'.[38]

This relationship also did not pass the 'smell test'. There were other questionable elements. Matt Hancock attended a private dinner and stayed overnight at a country estate owned by Randox's managing director. None of these events was recorded in the Department's transparency returns relating to hospitality or ministers' external meetings.[39] Perhaps the computers just rejected the word Randox.

Naturally, the subsequent verdict of the PAC was scathing:

> The potential for conflicts of interest was obvious, but the Department neglected to explicitly consider conflicts of interest in its awarding of contracts to Randox.... The role of the Department's ministers in approving the contract was also confused and unclear.... Randox struggled to deliver the expected level of testing capacity against its first contract, which did not set out any performance measures. Yet the Department still awarded Randox a contract extension worth £328 million seven months later, again without competition.[40]

A £253 million contract went to Ayanda Capital on or around 29 April 2020. This was a firm with zero experience in the field, which was charging almost twice as much as the market rate, but which was again controlled by Conservative Party donors. The company in fact described itself as a family investment firm that specialises in 'currency trading, offshore property, private equity and trade financing'. Maybe the attraction was that property and private equity can also be abbreviated to PPE! Closeness to government was part of the mix here too. Its involvement in this supply operation was brokered by someone who until recently had been an adviser to the then International Trade Secretary Liz Truss – Andrew Mills, an Ayanda 'associate'.[41]

Tellingly, a civil servant wrote of Ayanda Capital and the quality of its PPE that 'the bar seems to have been lowered on this one'. There was no competitive tender. This contract itself was not published until 4 September 2020, which was (not coincidentally) shortly before the response was due to the claimants' pre-action protocol letter in the legal claim brought by GLP. A massive £50 million worth of the facemasks were never used because of doubts over whether they provided 'adequate fixing' around the face. Ayanda said that the Department of Health and Social Care and the NHS ordered but then changed its requirement for masks.

There were other egregious examples of closeness to government, lack of transparency and poor delivery (and sometimes this less than holy trinity put together). Globus Shetland, a business that had donated £400,000 to the Conservative Party since 2016, received £94 million of PPE contracts. Another donor, David Meller of Meller Designs, gained over £160 million in PPE deals. Meller's companies normally design and manufacture fashion and beauty products.[42]

Pestfix had never before supplied medical PPE, yet it was favoured with contracts to a total value of approximately £313 million. The award of two contracts to Clandeboye Agencies Limited for the supply of gowns with a total value of £108 million on or around 28 April 2020 also aroused interest and mystification. The company had previously supplied only confectionery products.

Parliamentarians

The conduct of various Parliamentarians came under the spotlight. The House of Lords Committee on Standards launched an investigation into Lord Chadlington for breaching financial conduct rules relating to the award of £50 million worth of government contracts: one for £23.9 million for supply of coveralls and another for £26.1 million for hand sanitiser. Abkar Khan, the Lords Commissioner for Standards, however, decided that there should be no disciplinary action, as his lordship had not *directly* approached the government on behalf of SG Recruitment, part of a group of which he was a director and shareholder; instead, he had given the company's chief executive David Sumner the email address of Lord Feldman of Elstree, a former Chair of the Conservative Party who worked in an unpaid role for Lord Bethell, a health minister from March to May 2020.[43] Three days later, SG was awarded the first government contract. The second contract was granted on 28 May 2020.

Conclusion

The procurement rules could not be much clearer (although they are detailed), but it is the enforcement of them that was weak, and still no one seems to be held accountable when things go wrong, which clearly reduces public confidence. Recommendation 4 of the NAO's report should be adopted: that 'Government should provide additional guidance to clarify the role of ministers in procurement processes, including contract discussions and approvals'.[44] The urgency is obvious. What is not explicable is the award of contracts to chums.

Chapter 14

Greensill: 'no rules were broken'

... a screaming, glaring conflict of interest

Darren Tierney, Director-General of Propriety and Ethics at
the Cabinet Office, in evidence to the Public Administration
and Constitutional Affairs Committee, 26 April 2021

Perceptions of conflicts of interest corrode trust in politics and politicians, and the Greensill scandal did so in spades and at many different levels. It is a story of weak governance, lax oversight and the mingling of the public and private sectors in a way that was bound to lead to manifold conflicts of interest. It also overlaps with the issues of ministerial jobs after leaving government, which has already been considered. It demonstrates the lobbying potential of ex-Prime Ministers and how the chumocracy works or, on another view, it shows that it ultimately does *not* work. It clearly demonstrates the need for further regulation of the vast lobbying industry.

It also brought into sharp focus the overlapping jurisdictions in the area of investigation and judgement (as can be seen in several recent scandals),[1] because Greensill's failure in March 2021 triggered several reviews, bouts of evidence taking and investigations.[2] On 16 April 2021, Boris Johnson commissioned Nigel Boardman, a Slaughter and May commercial lawyer,[3] to examine the development and use in government of supply chain finance by Greensill Capital. The Treasury Select Committee also held oral evidence sessions, and published a report on the lessons to be drawn from Greensill. The Public Accounts Committee took evidence on broadly the same issues on 22 April, 13 May and 22 July 2021.[4]

The Greensill scandal indeed provided a great opportunity for reform in a whole series of areas. At the heart of Boardman's conclusions was that 'the Government should establish an effective method for ensuring compliance with governance processes', such as is well known in the private sector, but his recommendations are insufficient to allay public concern in this contentious area.[5]

Greensill Capital started life in 2011 when the eponymous Lex (who came from the village of Bundaberg, Australia) left his employment at Citigroup. He had previously operated at Morgan Stanley and there had worked with Jeremy Heywood, who had been had been Principal Private Secretary to Tony Blair and was taking a break from the public sector. Lex, a charismatic and persuasive salesman,[6] who also grandly claimed to have advised the White House, produced a scheme for early payments that he was keen to sell into government. The basic operation is that a bank inserts itself between a company and its suppliers, offering to pay their bills immediately and taking a fee.[7] His claim was no less than that he was democratising for the masses access to sophisticated forms of finance.

The general problem of small suppliers waiting to be paid by government had been recognised long before. Gordon Brown introduced a policy to pay those who supplied government within five days, but this was often honoured in the breach rather than the observance. Greensill's scheme was not straightforward. Brendan Pellow, Director of Government Banking, was picked up in one of the emails obtained by the *Sunday Times* as warning that the Greensill plan could pile 'risks' and 'administrative costs' on the taxpayer.[8]

A key problem was that although Greensill lived the life of the super-rich, with private planes and lavish expenses, and the company had gained no less than $1.5 billion in funding from Softbank's Vision Fund 1, Greensill Capital was in fact not profitable. So, the company went into the cognate business of loaning money. Here there was another snag: the loans were made to a collection of Greensill's friends, family and assorted acquaintances, and this did not net a big return either.

David Cameron's involvement

The easy-going Australian, however, gained unique access to the heart of government. He was appointed as an unpaid adviser on supply chain finance to David Cameron's government.[9] In 2013 he moved on to become a Crown Representative, a post he held until 2016.[10] He had a desk at Number 10, with a security pass to match. Apparently, there was no contract of any sort to set out his obligations and how obvious conflicts of interest (between his private and public personas) were to be avoided. The role was unremunerated but expenses were paid. He distributed a business card describing himself as a 'Senior Adviser in the Prime Minister's Office' and possessed a Downing

Street email address (a nice feature to use in pitches to clients).[11] He was placed in the Economic and Domestic Affairs Secretariat of the Cabinet Office, although the line of authority (and authorisation) is still opaque even after multiple investigations.

His purported closeness to power in Number 10 may to some degree have been a puff on Greensill's part, as Cameron claims to have met Greensill only twice while Prime Minister. Boardman's *Review* described the use of 'the *soi disant* title of "Adviser to the Prime Minister" on the Greensill website'. Michael Gove told me that he 'was surprised at how Greensill, after his original appointment [as a Crown Representative] was signed off by Francis Maude, went up and up' in the official hierarchy.[12] Extraordinarily he appeared to be in a position to make or at least influence the making of government policy on early payment, even though he had an obvious commercial interest. This is lobbying from the inside. It is extraordinary that a presentation on supply chain finance for a round table[13] with the government's major private sector suppliers which was chaired by Cameron as Prime Minister was largely written by Greensill and was 'not balanced', as Boardman found.

In December 2012, Greensill wrote to Paul Kirby of the Number 10 Policy Unit confirming what had been agreed, which was to 'move forward on the supply chain finance agenda per the PM's direction and my requested support … monitor and report to him [the PM] on the adoption of supply chain finance by UK corporates'.[14] Six weeks after becoming Cabinet Secretary, Heywood (an evangelist for innovation in government) was chairing a meeting with the big banks to discuss Greensill's ideas and how they could operate in government. Particularly striking is this email from Heywood (described by Theresa May as 'the greatest public servant of our times') to those beneath him in rank: 'Lex and I have been working on this stuff on and off for five years. It is a HUGE frustration that HMG continues to leave free money on the table in this way….' On the contrary, Boardman concludes that 'it is very unlikely that supply chain finance has a role in direct government commercial activity'.[15]

It is also clear that many civil servants had real doubts about the whole supply chain finance proposition as providing a boon for government and the public and about the degree of access Greensill obtained. For example, Catherine Zeng, a Treasury official, warned others in an email to 'rein him in – stop him approaching departments unilaterally'. Boardman's *Review* concluded that 'Mr Greensill's role in government had the consequence of providing him with a marketing platform for Greensill Capital's business with the private sector'.[16] In the PACAC *Interim Report* on the affair, Darren Tierney conceded that it appeared to be a 'glaring' conflict of interest for Greensill to be 'employed' by the Cabinet Office and to go on to win government contracts for his company.[17] As Boardman said in his own report, 'This seems an exceptional level of access and institutional endorsement for somebody hired as an unremunerated consultant'.[18] Greensill was awarded a CBE, and Liz Truss appointed him to a role on the G7 Council. He was riding high but was too close to the sun, as it turned out.

Cameron, the Conservative Party leader from 2005 to 2016, had joined Greensill's operation in 2018 with the offer of lucrative share options.[19] He attended Greensill board meetings, despite not being a member.[20] His role was to introduce Greensill to the great and the good. After his resignation as PM he opened many doors that would otherwise have remained closed, not least in the Middle East.[21] For example, in 2019 Cameron took Greensill for a private drink with Matt Hancock, then Secretary of State for Health, with a view to the introduction of a Greensill payment scheme for NHS staff; the meeting was not minuted, as it should have been.[22] Cameron was unexpectedly recalled to government in November 2023 as Foreign Secretary.

A real blue-chip line-up was by then batting for the genial Aussie. This proves again how easy it is for an outsider to gain the imprimatur of the English establishment (think Beaverbrook, Robert Maxwell, Conrad Black, etc.) and how lobbying is carried out at the highest level, wholly without regulation and without much transparency either. As an example, Lord Prior, a minister under Cameron and then the Chair of NHS England, fixed up a meeting for Greensill with the NHS's chief financial officer, Julian Kelly, and its chief executive, Sir Simon Stevens. Other cheerleaders for Greensill included Lord Blunkett, Lord Hogan-Howe,[23] former head of the Metropolitan Police, and Dame Louise Casey, the homelessness tsar.

This would have just been another tale of a company with serious influence in the heart of government and potential conflicts of interests, likely confined to the business pages, if the affair had not come to wide public attention. This happened because Cameron lobbied very, very hard for access for Greenhill's company to the coronavirus support schemes and for government-backed loans under the Covid Corporate Financing Facility (CCFF). The latter was designed to help large companies through the rough economic rigours of the COVID pandemic.[24] The former Prime Minister told civil servants in incessant emails (many to those he had worked with in government) that 'it was nuts to exclude him [Greensill] from the scheme'. This was a lobbyfest *par excellence*, but in fact it did not achieve its aim. Again, you could say that in the end the system operated as it should.

Cameron sent multiple texts to Rishi Sunak, then Chancellor of the Exchequer, and to two other Treasury ministers, John Glen and Jesse Norman, lobbying hard for Greensill to have access to the schemes from which he was excluded. In one response, made on 23 April 2021, Sunak said he hoped to find a way for Greensill to qualify for the largest available government-backed loans under CCFF, yet he told MPs later that Cameron's communications had zero effect on him, even though Cameron had sent twenty-five text messages and twelve WhatsApp messages, and had made eleven phone calls and sent eight emails to him. Sunak also said he had only spent a small amount of time on them and in fact replied to only two.

The contents of some of the communications were indeed jaw dropping. In one, Cameron said: 'Rishi, David Cameron here. Can I have a very quick word at some point. HMT [i.e. the Treasury] are refusing to extend CCFF to include supply chain finance.... There is a simple misunderstanding that I can explain. Thanks DC.' Sunak told Cameron he had 'pushed the team' to see whether it was 'possible for Greensill to qualify for support' and to explore 'an alternative with the Bank that might work'. In one week of March 2021 he messaged Tom Scholar, the Treasury's Permanent Secretary, almost daily.[25]

The former Prime Minister also reached out to Sir Jon Cunliffe, a Deputy Governor of the Bank of England (who had been a senior Treasury official while Cameron was Prime Minister), saying 'please include in the CCFF the ability to purchase bonds issued in respect of supply chain finance'. Cameron complained about the 'incredibly frustrating' situation, as the company was, as he put it, denied access to financial support by the Treasury. He emailed the Number 10 adviser Sheridan Westlake after the Treasury had finally rejected the company's attempts to gain access to the scheme. Matthew Gould, who had worked as Director of Cybersecurity in the Cabinet Office under Cameron, was a further recipient of several emails; the former PM wanted Gould, then head of NHSX (the digital arm of the NHS), to speed up the progress of an early-payment scheme.

Overall, Cameron sent fifty-six texts to ministers. He pronounced in one that 'It can be a win-win with large companies and small suppliers both benefitting from this innovative scheme'. This lobbying by an ex-PM was well beyond the acceptable. Indeed, William Wragg, the Conservative Chair of PACAC, described it as 'tasteless, slapdash, unbecoming'. He used this phrase during a four-hour grilling of Cameron over Zoom by two Parliamentary Select Committees sitting together. Siobhain McDonagh, a Labour MP, said there that Cameron had demeaned himself by 'whatsapping his way around

Whitehall'. Cameron countered that he needed to make his case speedily amidst the COVID crisis. Gordon Brown told me in a written answer to my questions that 'This is both unethical and an abuse of the current Ministerial Code and wholly unacceptable'.[26]

The failure of this lobbying merry-go-round led inexorably to the spectacular collapse of Greensill Capital in March 2021. The immediate reason for the failure of Greensill was the decision of Tokio Marine, its principal insurance provider, not to renew its cover.[27] Greensill's company at one time was valued at $7 billion, but it crashed and burned, and, in the slipstream, badly singed the reputation of David Cameron.

Cameron subsequently accepted that his approaches to government officials should, as an ex-Prime Minister, have been made through 'the most formal of channels, so there can be no room for misinterpretation'. Cameron said 'I have reflected on this at length. There are important lessons to be learnt.' The effect of this statement was, however, diminished, because it was issued on 11 April 2021, some weeks after the scandal broke.[28]

Exposing anomalies in the system

The system fought back; it did not just buckle under this relentless lobbying by a former PM. Cameron was correct to say there really were no rules broken here, but it is the scope of those rules and their interpretation that need reconsideration. One wrinkle related to the anomalies is the system for regulating ministers (including Prime Ministers) after they leave office. Cameron was *employed* by Greensill, rather than contracted to the company as a consultant, so that he was not required to register his lobbying activity with the Office of the Registrar of Consultant Lobbyists (ORCL), the body established in 2014 during his first term as Prime Minister.[29] As we have seen, the ORCL was given a limited remit by the Cameron government. He did not have to tell ACOBA about the role either, because it was more than two years since he had left office.[30]

The Boardman Review[31]

According to the *Sunday Times*, Boris Johnson was telling everybody who would listen during the height of the Greensill furore that 'We've got to clean the Augean stables', which in his mind involved exposing Cameron. This may have been fuelled by his rivalry with Cameron over the years, starting, one assumes, at Eton.

Nigel Boardman was seen by Number 10 as the very man for the task of pronouncing on the aftermath of the Greensill affair. He had recently completed a review of the Cabinet Office's use of the COVID-19-related emergency procurement provisions, and some thought he had been rather too kind to the government (more favourable indeed than the NAO was subsequently). Boardman was also paid £20,000 per annum as a non-executive at the Department for Business, Energy and Industrial Strategy.

Prime Minister Johnson said Boardman would have *carte blanche* and 'maximum possible access' to the relevant staff and documents for the purpose of his *Review*. Even so, in the Introduction to that *Part 1* of his *Review* (published in July 2021), somewhat defensively, Boardman says he did not have time for a 'forensic interrogation of every detail of the issues' and that he had only established the 'facts as far as possible'.

All parties would no doubt agree with the first words of Boardman's *Review*: 'Mr Greensill had a privileged – and sometimes extraordinarily privileged – relationship with Government', and the concern that this happened must attach to politicians as much as civil servants. Further, on the appointment of Greensill to the heart of government, Boardman rightly says 'the process should be more clearly delineated and requires greater transparency to maintain public confidence'.

The civil servants are, however, in the 141 pages of *Part 1* of his *Review*, treated as the primary villains. Boardman's laser-like focus was trained on the deceased Lord Heywood.[32] Heywood had worked alongside Greensill at Morgan Stanley and was identified as having sanctioned the appointment of Greensill to the role of Crown Representative and special adviser, when it seems that it may have been Lord Maude as Minister for the Cabinet Office who, crucially, approved it.

There are some important recommendations in the *Part 2* of Boardman's *Review*.

Managing conflicts of interest pre-appointment

To deal with the specifics of the Greensill case, Boardman recommended that the appointment letter for direct ministerial appointees such as Greensill should include the name of the appointing minister. Any individual who is brought in should abide by the Civil Service Code, including the Nolan Principles and provisions about security passes and IT access.[33] A civil servant should be nominated as the line manager for each such person who is so introduced. Where ministers and civil servants disagree on the appointability of a person (for example because of conflicts of interest) but the minister wishes to proceed, the relevant minister should give a written direction to this effect to the civil service, and it should be recorded in the departmental annual report.

Ad hocery

Part 1 of the Boardman *Review* demonstrated the problems caused by ministers making *ad hoc* appointments to ill-defined roles. These include the ever-expanding number of tsars and trade envoys with responsibilities that are often unclear, as well as having opaque (if any) appointment procedures.[34] The process for direct ministerial appointments is, Boardman says, 'poorly understood'. Boardman sees the need for greater transparency about those whom ministers and civil servants meet, with more regular and detailed publication of the information.

My conclusion on Boardman

Most of the recommendations concentrate on civil service processes. A weakness is the lack of suggested changes for ministers. Boardman also failed to make sufficient recommendations to deal with former ministers lobbying those who were once subordinate to them. The need for a clean-up of lobbying is an issue which we have already considered. As Lord Falconer told me, 'The problem about Greensill was the light it shone on gaining access at the highest level of government'.[35]

Yet it is not even clear the government is really behind Boardman's agenda. One's confidence is not increased by the fact that *Part 2* of the *Review* was published quietly during the height of a major government reshuffle in September 2021, even though it is dated 5 August 2021. Was this seen as a day to bury bad news or just a mess-up? We do not know. The government's long-awaited response to Boardman, not published until 20 July 2023 (some two years later), was tepid.[36]

Overlapping investigations

The multiple investigations into Greensill are not an efficient use of resources and could have led to different conclusions being reached in each case. This argues for an overarching investigation body of the sort referred to in the final chapter. The Public Administration and Constitutional Affairs Committee held days of hearings but was restrained by the fact Lex Greensill declined its invitation to give evidence before it. It was also prevented from hearing from Sue Gray. She had initially agreed to appear, but her appearance was subsequently blocked by the Chancellor of the Duchy of Lancaster, Michael Gove. This has left a number of significant questions outstanding.[37]

Part IV

Conclusion

Chapter 15

Conventions, the rule of law and declining standards: what happens when good chaps do not behave

Almost entirely, the functions and working of this intricate mechanism, perhaps the most perfect, efficient and disinterested the world has ever seen is the product of convention, tradition and administrative practice.

Lord Hailsham[1]

Here one comes upon an all-important English trait: the respect for constitutionalism and legality, the belief in 'the law' as something above the state and the individual, something which is cruel and stupid of course but at any rate *incorruptible*…. In moments of supreme crisis the whole nation can suddenly draw together and act upon a species of instinct, really a code of conduct which is understood by almost everyone, though never formulated.

George Orwell[2]

Our constitution evolves by no particular great theoretical elaboration of a concept; it evolves by practice. This is the way we have done things, rightly or wrongly, in this country.

Lord Bew[3]

Lord David Wolfson of Tredegar resigned on 14 April 2022 from his role as a minister at the Justice Ministry. His resignation letter was more notable than most. In fact, it was a collectors' item. The perceived infringement of the rule of law was at the heart of the concerns that led him to leave the Johnson government. The impetus for this missive was Johnson's failure to resign over the fixed penalty notices that had been issued to him by the police over partygate.[4] Wolfson's arrived some three months before the mass of ministerial resignation letters that precipitated the Prime Minister's ultimate fall from power. As an experienced barrister, Wolfson's primary concern was the infringement of the rule of law. The letter referenced the Somerset case, decided in 1772, where Lord Mansfield importantly said 'justice prevails though let heavens fall'. This is the essence of the complex (yet essentially simple) concept of the rule of law.

Wolfson said the PM's actions were 'inconsistent with the rule of law' and that it would be wrong for 'that conduct to pass with constitutional impunity'. He stressed that 'Justice may often be a matter of courts and procedures but the rule of law is something else – a constitutional principle which, at its root, means that everyone in a state, and indeed the state itself is subject to law'. Wolfson told me over breakfast seven months later why he wrote in those terms:

> The rule of law is threatened when those who make the law treat it as unimportant, when they explain things away. The higher you are, the more punctilious you should be. Comparing a fixed penalty notice in these circumstances to a parking ticket [as Johnson did] shows disdain. I was concerned by the scale, context and nature of these breaches.[5]

The rule of law is central to our constitution and goes beyond the law as it is applied day to day. But what *does* it mean? What, more broadly, is the constitutional basis for our governance and, most importantly for present purposes, what is there to stop corruption of our institutions and the downward spiral in public standards getting out of hand? Is it purely a legal process or is it based on understandings that are not legally enforceable, or is it a bit of both?

We need to trace the existing architecture before we can prescribe the rebuilding in the next chapter. We will now look at the separation of powers and the conventions that support this concept, before returning to the crucial question of the rule of law and its infringement.

Separation of powers

It is easy to trace the essential accountability of politicians to the electorate. The key legal concept of our unwritten constitution proceeds in this way (which could be scribbled on the back of a postage stamp but on which many books have been written):

- Civil servants are accountable to ministers.
- Ministers are accountable to Parliament.
- Members of Parliament are accountable to their constituents.[6]

As it was put by the judges in the case of *R* v. *Prime Minister*, 'the Government exists because it has the confidence of the House of Commons. It has no democratic legitimacy other than that.'[7] But there must be balances to protect public standards. Lord Wallace of Saltaire summed it up in a House of Lords debate on standards in public life: 'It is about limited government, checks and balances on executive power, the rule of law, transparency and respect for minorities as well as for the majority currently in power'.[8]

It clearly undermines confidence in democracy, the rule of law and indeed politics more generally when people think politicians do not have to account in this sense and that there is one law for one and another for others, as they did in partygate. Similarly, the controversy about Owen Paterson initially not being disciplined by Parliament over lobbying[9] appeared to represent a direct rejection of fundamental principles of the rule of law, such as not changing rules retrospectively.

The separation of powers and the rule of law are indeed closely linked. There is at the base of our UK political system a somewhat crude separation of powers between legislature, executive and the judiciary (although the three were formerly united in the person of the Lord Chancellor[10]), and there are many conventions that seek to protect this principle, some stronger and better recognised than others. The ethical watchdogs we have been reviewing perhaps form a distinct, fifth branch of government.[11]

Lord Mustill laid out the various features of those powers very clearly in *R* v. *Home Secretary ex p FBU*:

> Parliament has a legally unchallengeable right to make whatever law it thinks right. The executive carries on the administration of the country in accordance with the powers conferred upon it by law. The courts interpret the laws and see that they are obeyed.[12]

The role of Prime Minister is pivotal, yet this office is, surprisingly, largely based on conventions rather than hard law. The danger signal goes up if that person cannot be trusted to abide by constitutional niceties and to enforce them. That is so not least because the PM spans the executive and legislature. Judicial review is the method by which an overmighty executive may be held in check by the courts.

The doctrine of Parliamentary supremacy or 'sovereignty' (still the *general* principle of our constitution) holds that the monarch, Commons and Lords together have supreme law-making authority.[13] That authority is exercised differently from time to time. One Parliament cannot bind its successors, which can do something entirely different, save as to the manner and form of that legislation, as was the case with the now repealed Fixed Term Parliaments Act 2011. There is indeed no legal limit to what an Act of Parliament can accomplish, including the dismantling of established constitutional architecture and principles. This, of course, gives vast power to a government with a large majority, although it may still find it difficult to maintain control of its MPs if it overreaches itself.

This sovereignty is a construct of the judges with a bit of legislation thrown in for seasoning,[14] and was somewhat modified by the incorporation of the European Convention on Human Rights (ECHR) as enacted by the Human Rights Act 1998, which in effect created a new legal order and a minimum standard of legal rights.[15] The ECHR is not like most international treaties, which merely operate between states; rather, it creates obligations for citizens within its jurisdiction, including those of other states.[16]

Lord Reed, the current President of the Supreme Court, stated in evidence to the government-established Independent Review of Administrative Law that the constitution is based on two 'long-established constitutional principles of fundamental importance': firstly, that government power (including the prerogative) must be exercised in accordance with the law – a narrow meaning for the rule of law with which it is hard to quarrel – and secondly, that 'ultimate sovereign power rests with the Queen in Parliament'. Sir Vernon Bogdanor concludes that 'The old constitution was based upon the sovereignty of Parliament. The new constitution is based on the idea of a constitutional state based upon a separation of powers.'[17]

The separation of powers is not written down as a legal rule, but then not much that is constitutional is in the UK. We are one of the few states in the world to manage without a written constitution (Israel and New Zealand being others). Nick Barber, a legal scholar at the University of Oxford, makes this distinction:

> a small 'c' constitution … consists of those rules that constitute the state. All states must possess a small 'c' constitution. But not all need to possess a capital 'c' Constitution. The small 'c' constitution includes both legal and non-legal rules.[18]

By capital 'c' Constitution, he means the written model.

What passes for a British constitution is thus a largely mythical and fragile fabric. According to the political philosopher Keith Dowding, the gap this leaves 'is a narrative peopled with civil servants, politicians and judges blessed with a nature not typically human and a set of statements about "conventional behaviour" which does not describe how people typically act'.[19] This is popularised as the 'good chap' theory that has surfaced from time to time throughout this book. This is essentially the need for those involved in the system to behave properly. In the end, perhaps we cannot go further than J. A. G. Griffith of the London School of Economics and Political Science, who said decades ago that 'the constitution is what happens'?[20] However, this does mean, as Daniel Greenberg, the Parliamentary Commissioner for Standards, put it, that our constitution is 'supremely agile' and can react to changing circumstances.[21]

Conventions oil the wheels of the (formally non-existent) constitution. The regulatory expert Frank Vibert notes that 'This does not mean that constitutions are synonymous with the rule of law – the rule of law can exist without a constitution and constitutions vary widely in quality'.[22]

Lord Neuberger, the President of the Supreme Court at the time, made some pertinent comments on this in the important case of *R (Miller)* v. *Secretary of State for Exiting the European Union*. The claim was in respect of the appropriate method for the UK to leave the EU.[23] Neuberger said that, on the one hand, there *was*, and, on the other hand, *was not*, such a thing as a constitution, which is (you might think) a typically British compromise, or even quite a muddle. He put it this way:

> unlike most countries, the UK does not have a constitution in the sense of a single coherent code of fundamental law which prevails over all other sources of law. Our constitutional arrangements have developed over time in a pragmatic as much as a principled way, through a combination of statutes, events, conventions, academic writing and judicial decisions.[24]

The judge went on, 'The legal principles of the constitution are not confined to statutory rules, but include constitutional principles developed by the common law'.[25] There is indeed also a whole gradation or spectrum across items that may be thought to be constitutional.

What are conventions?

Many of these conventions that make this flexible method of governance work are in effect an answer to the simple question 'What is the right thing to do?' They describe what most of us feel would be acceptable to all persons operating in a liberal democracy, and they proceed from first democratic principles. But conventions can break down.

A restaurant may have a formal dress code or you may just be able to predict what to wear without anything being formally stated because of the nature of the place. You might say what you have here is a sartorial convention. You just know what to expect. This has some passing resemblance to a constitutional convention, in that it is the *conventional* behaviour to be expected of those participating. A convention of the constitution is this writ large, so in respect of Royal Assent to Acts of Parliament, it is expected that the monarch will sign into law all of the bills that have been passed by Commons and Lords and does not in fact exercise any discretion, which the sovereign theoretically retains the right to do.

But what is to stop the bad chaps taking over? What happens then? That is when serious and enforceable conventions are needed to restrain them.

The conventions of the constitution are generally informal understandings, some of which have crystalised over many centuries. For the great constitutional authority A. V. Dicey, writing in the 1880s as a Whig jurist, conventions were principally customary rules that determined the way discretionary or prerogative powers would be exercised.[26] They have an uncertainty and flexibility about them so they can mould to different political and social circumstances and alignments. They must be generally acknowledged as having a character of obligation to qualify. They should be upheld by all those working within the governmental system, as well as those outside. But they derive their authority only from the fact there would be a political price to pay if they were not followed.

There is at present no legal sanction for disobedience.[27] The only court is that of public opinion. As was vividly put in *R (Miller)* v. *Secretary of State (Miller No. 1)*, 'Judges therefore are neither the parents nor the guardians of political conventions; they are merely observers'. The Supreme Court went on to say, however, that courts 'can recognise the operation of a political convention in the context of deciding a legal question', but a court cannot 'give legal rulings on [a convention's] operation or scope, because those matters are determined within the political world'.[28] The Sewel Convention was in play in this case.[29] It limits the constitutional capacity of the Westminster Parliament to legislate on matters passed to devolved national institutions. Lord Neuberger said in the Supreme Court that this 'was adopted as a means of establishing cooperative relationships between the UK Parliament and the devolved institutions, where there were overlapping legislative competences'.[30] The judge went on: 'the policing of its scope [i.e. the convention] and the manner of its operation does not lie within the constitutional remit of the judiciary, which is to protect the rule of law'.

It is those 'good chaps' again who act as arbiters and who should blow the whistle if the rules and conventions are not observed, and this is often expected to be found in the person of the Prime Minister. When the consensus breaks down, conventions are not enough to maintain constitutional order and the rule of law.[31]

Without any covering shelter or the protection of something written on tablets of stone, the delicate system of conventions as checks and balances has to come into play and can easily break down.[32] The IfG rightly said that 'Relying on goodwill and acceptance of unwritten rules only works when people in public life are willing to accept implicit limits on what they can do. If informal norms are not recognised, there is little that can be done to respond.'[33] The Johnson government was, as we have seen, not one for obeying rules,[34] especially those with soft edges, leeway or any degree of wriggle room, and it seriously exposed the weakness of a purely conventions-based system. There should be real-world political consequences if they are not obeyed.

Our constitution is now under intense strain. That fragility means we need to protect conventions from those who mean them ill, as already illustrated in many examples, or take a radically different approach. Codification is needed, as has occurred to some extent in Australia.

The Ministerial Code

Some of the key conventions are collected together in some form in the Ministerial Code, which we have already encountered.[35] An example is that 'ministers who knowingly mislead Parliament will be expected to offer their resignation to the Prime Minister', to which we will turn in a moment.[36] The Code is issued under the auspices of the Prime Minister.

A central weakness (as with similar documents) is that it lacks a clear mechanism for independent enforcement. Enforcement is in the hands of the Prime Minister. A key provision is set out in paragraph 1.6: 'Ministers only remain in office for so long as they retain the confidence of the *Prime Minister*. He is the ultimate judge of the standards of behaviour expected of a Minister and the appropriate consequences of a breach of those standards' (my emphasis). If there is a wrong 'un as Prime Minister, the whole edifice can collapse. This lack of independence is one of the key issues that a new standards system needs to address. The Code should be laid before the House of Commons, or at least PACAC should have a role in giving it approval.

The Cabinet Manual is the closest we get to a conventions codification. It sets out rules and practices, although only relatively few of them. The first version was introduced by Gus O'Donnell as Cabinet Secretary in October 2011. It includes material on the monarchy, elections and government formation, the Cabinet, ministers, the civil service, devolved administrations, finances and public information. For example, it refers to the process in the instance of an inconclusive election result and for changing Prime Minister in the middle of a Parliament.

Particular conventions: misleading Parliament and individual ministerial responsibility

We need to discuss two important conventions that restrain the executive and are important in maintaining the ultimate accountability of government to the public. Firstly, it is no more than a convention of collective responsibility that a government defeated in the House of Commons should resign – but this has frayed; governments now do not resign even when defeated several times in Parliament, including in the case of Theresa May, when her government lost by 230 votes on its principal policy programme, Brexit. The principle is detailed in the Cabinet Manual.

Secondly, and linked like a Siamese twin, is what in the 1960s Lord Morrison called in his book *Government and Parliament* 'one of the fundamentals of our system of Government ... that some Minister of the Crown is responsible to Parliament and through Parliament to the public for every act of the executive'.[37] He was describing the key convention of individual ministerial responsibility. The traditional understanding is to pin the blame on the minister heading the department for *every* failure of departmental policy or administration within it.[38]

The gentlemanly approach adopted in the 1950s can be seen in the ministerial resignation of Thomas Dugdale over the so-called Crichel Down scandal, even though his own actions were not at the time being questioned.[39] There was also John Profumo's resignation in the 1960s over a sex scandal and the years he spent re-establishing his trashed reputation working for a poverty charity in the East End of London. This can be set against some of those who might have been expected to resign or be sacked for serious blunders or misbehaviour in recent times but remained in office. Just recall a few: Gavin Williamson and the A-level fiasco,[40] (later Dame) Priti Patel, Matt Hancock and the PPE fiasco, Johnson and his numerous evasions, including about Jennifer Arcuri and Number 10 wallpaper. The list goes on and on.[41]

Ministers should resign in certain circumstances of dishonesty, especially when they mislead Parliament, an area over which the Commons Committee on Standards has jurisdiction. The basic justification is that the House of Commons, in order effectively to fulfil its roles of scrutinising the work of government, passing legislation and facilitating debate, needs to work with *accurate* information – and to have the confidence that everything said in the House is correct. Scrutiny is ineffective unless ministers answer MPs' questions truthfully.

The convention was tested in the heated political circumstances of the Scott report on the supply of arms to Iraq, published in February 1996. Prime Minister John Major, prior to Lord Justice Scott reporting, had stressed the importance of ministers giving accurate and truthful information to Parliament if they wanted to remain in post. This proposition was, however, subtly changed later when he posited that any misleading of Parliament needed to be done 'knowingly' for the minister to be required to resign. This had the immediate effect of saving the political career of William Waldegrave, who was a Foreign Office minister at the time of the events and a close political ally of Major. Scott's final report accepted that Waldegrave and other ministers in fact had no 'duplicitous intention' and that, while Waldegrave was in a position to know that his letters were 'apt to mislead readers as to the true nature of the policy on export sales to Iraq',[42] he 'did not intend his letters to be misleading and did not regard them as such'. This apparently excepted from the compulsion to resign instances where the minister had been negligent or incompetent in what he or she said. The convention was thus 'reinterpreted' in what may be seen to be a nakedly political manner and it was, unusually for such, formalised and enhanced in a Resolution approved by the House of Commons on 19 March 1997.

But, with these interpretations being so essentially political, who is to decide whether a person has been deliberately misleading? It is certainly not the courts. If a minister misleads Parliament, the ultimate arbiter of her or his position as a minister (as opposed to an MP) under the Ministerial Code is the Prime Minister, and the PM remains the only person who can launch an inquiry into whether the minister broke the code.

The edifice falls if fault is found in the Prime Minister him- or herself, as was the case with Johnson in relation to COVID lockdown parties.[43] The House of Commons Public Administration Committee aptly summed up the position:

> the attempt to ensure Ministers are accountable by seeking their resignation may be an informal and highly political affair. It cannot be reduced to firm rules and conventions. Nevertheless … it remains an essential component of the control of government. It is in effect the final stage in a process of accountability.[44]

Martin Stanley, a former civil servant who is now a prolific commentator, says that 'You could not anticipate getting to this stage in terms of public standards. The system relies on ministers resigning if they have lied or misled. It seems that ministers are just not embarrassable any more.'[45] So, the convention as it stands is not enough.

A tale of four Home Secretaries

We can seek to apply this principle by telling the tale (or tragedy) of four Home Secretaries. This senior job seems especially insecure, in a department that many have described over the years variously as 'not fit for purpose' or as 'dysfunctional'.[46] We can, then, see how the convention has played out (or not) in four different successive sets of circumstances. Two of these ministers were criticised for operational matters and two for making misleading statements.

Kenneth Baker as Home Secretary in 1991, on the occasion of a series of escapes from Brixton Prison, refused to resign for what he described as 'operational failures' by officers in the Prison Department, and he was not forced to do so.

Thirteen years later, David Blunkett denied that his private office had intervened with the Immigration and Nationality Directorate (which the Department controlled) regarding an application by his lover's nanny for indefinite leave to remain in the UK; however, he did go, even though his inaccurate denial was made to the media and not in Parliament. This was because he was under political pressure from Number 10 to do so.

Charles Clarke resigned over the treatment of foreign prisoners in 2006 precisely because of what may be seen as 'operational failures' for which it could not be said he was personally responsible.

Amber Rudd in 2018 left office over inadvertently misleading statements she had made to the House of Commons Home Affairs Select Committee about the treatment of the Windrush generation of immigrants.[47] Rudd told MPs on 25 April 2018 that no targets had been set in the Home Office to remove illegal immigrants, when in fact some had been established. This was because under the 'hostile environment' policies of the government many immigrants were not able to provide documentation to prove their entitlement to reside in the UK. This meant many were denied access to the NHS and social services and some were even threatened with deportation. Rudd resigned, although many thought her resignation was unnecessary. She actually lost her job because of the political pressure that built up over time due to mistakes by officials. She did not knowingly lie but instead failed to keep herself fully informed of the position within her department.[48] We also saw in another chapter the contrasting case of her successor, Priti Patel, who did not resign even though she was condemned by the Independent Adviser on Ministers' Interests, Sir Alex Allan.

This quartet shows that the way the resignation convention plays out depends on the political circumstances and pressures at the time – and often most importantly on the interest taken by the media.[49]

Two other recent cases are of note, where ministers did not resign but this reflected the political weakness of the then PM, Theresa May. In 2017 David Davis as Brexit Secretary was rebuked by the Speaker for misleading MPs when he said no impact assessments had been made on the effects of Brexit on the British economy. And in 2018 Esther McVey as Secretary of State for Work and Pensions was publicly chided by the NAO for misrepresenting its report on Universal Credit.[50] There was no investigation in either case, even though these actions might have appeared to have been in breach of their respective duties under the Ministerial Code. The Prime Minister of the day did not think this necessary.

So we have seen both the key benefits of and the major problems with relying on conventions. They are inherently malleable and are moulded by the politics of the moment, but they are also unenforceable. An extreme example of this was when Jacob Rees-Mogg claimed a new Prime Minister coming in to replace a sitting Prime Minister (he was speaking when Boris Johnson was under pressure to resign over partygate) would need to gain a new mandate. Lord (Daniel) Finkelstein nicely called this a 'pot noodle constitutional doctrine', although that is not, as far as I am aware, a precise legal term of art.[51]

It was Gladstone who rightly said in 1879 that the British constitution 'presumes more boldly than any other the good sense and good faith of those who work it'.[52] The problem now is that the tacit understandings about how things are done are crumbling. The seriousness of the situation was emphasised by Lord Hennessy of Nympsfield, who described Johnson's reaction to being fined for breaking COVID regulations as evoking nothing less than a constitutional crisis because it put great strain on those conventions.[53] However, Lord Sedwill said: 'I'm a believer in conventions, because they are a more agile and flexible way of reflecting the underlying principles that are most important'.[54]

Given the squalls of recent years, there is a demonstrated need to codify the conventions in more detail so that everyone knows what the rules really are.

The rule of law

The downward spiral in standards can have an impact on respect for the rule of law, as Wolfson pointed out. Lord Patten of Barnes told me about his time in the Far East:[55]

> I had to spend some time trying to explain to my opposite number [in China] when I was Governor of Hong Kong that there was a difference between rule by law and rule of law. The latter governed the actions of ministers and not just those of citizens.

Accountability and adherence to conventions are aspects of the rule of law that are under threat and, although Johnson was probably a one-off, we must not allow complacency to take hold.

First, though, we must consider which of the many senses of that concept of rule of law is in play. The use of the term is promiscuous,[56] and the separate nuances of meaning depend on your standpoint and why you are considering it. It is ultimately more of a political construct and philosophy than a legal principle.

The legal scholar Brian Tamanaha calls the rule of law the 'preeminent legitimating political ideal in the world today'.[57] It is 'an overarching principle of constitutional law'.[58] People of goodwill can probably detect a threat to the rule of law when one comes to light.[59] The concept has even been adopted by statute, but, unhelpfully, without definition: section 1 of the Constitutional Reform Act 2005 states that the Act (which introduced, among other things, changes to the role of the Lord Chancellor) does not adversely affect '(a) the existing constitutional principle of the rule of law'. It is an ancient creed which can be traced as far back as Aristotle, who said 'It is better for the law to rule than one of the citizens ... so even guardians of the laws are obeying the laws'.[60]

I now take a rapid tour of the many stations of this cross:

- *Equal under the law.* Lord Bingham's important work *The Rule of Law* defines the central premise of the concept as, 'that all persons and authorities within the state, whether public or private, should be bound by and entitled to the benefit of laws publicly made, taking effect (generally) in the future and publicly administered in the courts'.[61] Overall, it comprises the control of politics by legal standards and the fair enforcement of the law for everyone. It is indeed at the heart of the human rights framework, especially the European Convention on Human Rights, and it closely interacts with it.[62] Bingham also saw as part of the concept that 'ministers and public officials at all levels must exercise the powers conferred on them reasonably, in good faith, for the purpose for which the powers were conferred and without exceeding the limits of such powers', and also to maintain proper public standards.[63] This is in addition the essence of the important role of judicial review in the legal system, which is also presently under threat. This was what was so insidious about partygate and why Wolfson was right to be concerned.

- *Access to the courts.* This is another crucial aspect of increasing importance. As Lord Reed said in the UNISON case regarding the imposition of fees for applications to employment tribunals (which was declared unlawful by the Supreme Court), 'The constitutional right of access to the courts is inherent in the rule of law'.[64]

- *Fairness or natural justice.* Others use the term to describe the bare irreducible minimum for legal regulation in a modern democratic society. As Lord Steyn said in 1997, 'the rule of law enforces minimum standards of fairness, both substantive and procedural'.[65] Part of this is that the nature and limits of encroachment on civil liberties should be clearly stated in advance of any action taken in the name of the state. Another sense of the concept is, as Frank Vibert put it, 'There should be conformity between the law on the books and the law in the real world and that laws should be publicly accessible and inapplicable retroactively'.[66]

- *An independent judiciary.* Lord Burnett emphasised yet another aspect in his Blackstone Lecture at Pembroke College, Oxford,[67] in 2022 when he said that the rule of law depends upon there being an independent judiciary with individual independence in their decision making and institutional independence. That is vital to ensure an effective system of adjudication and that the powerful – for example, governments, large corporations and trade unions – have no special advantage in the courts.

- *The ethical underpinning.* Genuine rule of law probably requires a common set of values to underpin it beyond the formality of a document, and these must include the key ethical principles such as those laid down in the Nolan Report.[68] When standards slip too much, public disrespect for the state presents a real and important threat to it.

A key aspect of the rule of law is that the government should claim no exemption from the rules that apply to all. The physician and preacher Thomas Fuller put it thus, in a much-cited quotation, 'be you never so high, the law is above you'.[69] That applies whether you are Prime Minister or a Secretary of State or even (dare I say it) a member of the Royal Family. No one should be above the law and everyone is subject to the courts. Magna Carta itself requires that the government should not be treated differently from ordinary citizens. The great constitutional scholar Professor A. V. Dicey many years ago said that all officials should be bound by the 'ordinary law of the land and amenable to the jurisdiction of the ordinary tribunals' and that 'the rule of law is imperilled where certain people are able to defy the law'.[70] Dicey made the important but basic point that, while the government has powers beyond those of ordinary citizens, every official, from the Prime Minister down to a constable or collector of taxes, is under the same responsibility for every act done without legal justification as any other citizen.[71] The rule of law 'excludes the idea of any exemption of officials or others from the duty of obedience to the law which governs other citizens or from the jurisdiction of the ordinary tribunals'.[72]

The rule of law is inevitably undermined where the government itself (or senior government officers) breaks it. There is then seen to be one law for those in power and another for everyone else. The Johnson years saw contempt for the rule of law; it was almost Trumpian in intensity. For example, his government proposed post-Brexit legislation that was clearly and admittedly in breach of international law. This feature returned in May 2022, when the government decided to repudiate the Northern Irish Protocol to which the UK was bound. The Internal Market Bill would break the binding agreement with the EU but only in 'a very specific and limited way', as the then Northern Ireland Secretary of State, Brandon Lewis, rather laconically said.[73] This was later withdrawn and was not part of the Northern Ireland Internal Market Act 2020, but Sir Jonathan Jones, the respected Head of the Government Legal Service, resigned in protest. Bizarrely, Lewis eventually became Secretary of State for Justice in September 2022, although only under the forty-nine-day premiership of Liz Truss.

This notion was put at risk time and again under the Johnson government, for example in the excusing of Dominic Cummings for breaching lockdown rules, in the proroguing of Parliament to avoid debates on Brexit that might not have gone as planned[74] and in the apparent immunity of ministers who had broken the Ministerial Code, such as Priti Patel. It is richly ironic that the only person who resigned over the bullying allegations against Patel was Sir Alex Allan as Independent Adviser on Ministers' Interests.[75]

The rule of law is under threat from declining standards in public life. We have a uniquely powerful prime ministerial constitutional model, but under Johnson it was beginning to look like the 'elective dictatorship' of which Lord

Hailsham, the Conservative Lord Chancellor, warned in his Hamlyn Lectures in the 1970s.[76]

The pressure group More in Common, in its pamphlet *Democratic Repair: What Britons Want from Their Democracy* (2022), describes this decline as having led to 'Increased disengagement, indifference, and resentment [which] has made democracy more vulnerable to the forces of extremism and division'. This may have long-term consequences. As Jonathan Freedland put it in the *Guardian*, 'It is the dismantling, bit by bit, block by block, of the apparatus that holds up a liberal democracy'.[77] The Harvard political scientists Steven Levitsky and Daniel Ziblatt ask pertinently in their excellent book *How Democracies Die*, 'How do elected authoritarians shatter the democratic institutions that are supposed to constrain them? Some do it in one fell swoop. But more often the assault on democracy begins slowly. For many citizens, it may, at first, be imperceptible.'[78]

Undermining of judges

The second area where the rule of law is infringed is where the government positively undermines the judiciary. Attacks on those who are empowered to pronounce on the law are a dangerous part of populism. Given the need for respect for courts, the rule of law is actively weakened by attacks on judges by politicians, especially when that is implicitly supported by the executive of the day. This has rarely been seen at any previous time in Britain. Any undermining of, or apparent vengeance against, the courts, whether the notorious 'Enemies of the People' headline in the *Daily Mail* after the first *Miller* judgement or the briefing by the Johnson Number 10 criticising the Supreme Court (particularly after its prorogation decision designed to achieve Brexit, in the Second *Miller* case) is corrosive of the protections of separation of powers that are part and parcel of the rule of law.

It is notable that this 'Enemies' headline was published in reaction to the courts ensuring the government could not use its power unlawfully to prevent Parliament carrying out its proper function, giving effect to the separation of powers.[79] The impact was much exacerbated by the fact that when the newspaper pronounced this, Liz Truss as the Justice Secretary (and as Lord Chancellor, the traditional protector of the judiciary[80]) did not support the judiciary. Instead, she maintained a rather undignified silence, which in itself undermined proper respect for the rule of law. The judges themselves cannot answer back because of their position, for fear of trespassing into the political arena.

Other Cabinet ministers rubbed it in further, talking of left-leaning or activist lawyers and attacking judges for 'exceeding their authority'.[81] In a speech to the IfG on 10 February 2022, Sir John Major warned of the dangers of these sorts of sentiment being expressed when he pointedly said that 'Public denunciation of judges and lawyers gives credence to the belief that the Government wishes to usher in a compliant judiciary'.[82] After the Second *Miller* decision the Johnson government mounted a campaign to undermine the judiciary's power to scrutinise government, although this ran out of steam when Dominic Raab was sacked from his role as Justice Secretary (although he soon returned to the same office, only to later have to resign).

The main legal bulwark against such despotism is judicial review, and it is a strong brick in the wall of the rule of law. The Administrative Division of the High Court deals with these applications. Judicial review keeps the administration honest and away from unlawful and improper activities. It goes some way to answering the age-old question of 'who guards the guards?' by ensuring that the public authorities responsible for overseeing accountability of government do so within the boundaries of their own lawful powers.[83] The protection of public standards is one of the reasons why judicial review as an ultimate legal sanction is so important. Perhaps it should be the cause of little surprise that this area was also subject to attack by the Johnson government. There were several attempts (ultimately unsuccessful) to reduce the scope of judicial review.

These are attacks on public standards, because this is part of what such actions protect. As David Davis, the former Conservative Cabinet minister, wrote in the *Guardian*, this would 'tip the scales of law in favour of the powerful'.[84]

Conclusion

Many features prized by the Nolan Report were undermined by populism in general and Johnson in particular, such that there is no longer a consensus view of what is ethical and what is not, on which our conventions can be built. It is doubtful any of the Nolan Principles were much referred to in Number 10 during the Johnson government or that the Nolan Report was ever open on the Prime Minister's desk.

So, what is the state we have reached? There has been a fraying of values on which the rule of law is based, but that is happening in stages, so it is more difficult to detect. This outcome is particularly anxiety-inducing, since it is hard to recognise. We saw during the Johnson era a normalisation of bad behaviour and of contempt for standards and for some conventions. This is dangerous.

We need to heed Lord Wolfson's warning about those who make the law treating it as unimportant. To reassert ethical values we require a new structure for ethics. What we should do about it practically is the primary subject of the next chapter.

Chapter 16

Conclusion: new timber to replace the rotten wood

A culture of high standards, where all public officials are encouraged to consider, discuss, and apply the Seven Principles of Public Life to their everyday work, will help ensure such situations do not lead to oversight, negligence, or errors of judgement.

CSPL, *Upholding Standards in Public Life: Final Report of the Standards Matter 2 Review*, November 2021, p. 25

It was extraordinary that Andrea Jenkyns, newly appointed by the Johnson caretaker government to the role of Education Secretary, clearly raised her middle finger to the crowds outside Downing Street in full view of TV cameras. But why were we not so surprised? Perhaps this coarseness was emblematic of what has become of our political culture, given that Johnson was quoted as saying 'f*** business'.[1] On the other side of the aisle, Angela Rayner as deputy leader of the Labour Party described the Tories as 'scum'.

As Theresa May put it, rigorous debate between political opponents is becoming more like confrontation between enemies. There was certainly not much middle ground in the arguments over Brexit, and there has not been much since. This diminishes the reputation of public life and gnaws away at respect for politics.

The standards landscape today is complex and confusing to most in the Westminster village, let alone those outside. The patchwork of codes and regulators surveyed in this book reflects the historical development of ethics regulation in the UK, where a scandal may prompt institutional innovation in one particular area, while others are reformed only incrementally over decades.[2] I have not even covered all the institutions that should guard ethics in government.[3] The 'system' has grown up in an unplanned way, although sometimes pragmatism is better than even the finest architectures – just not in this case.

Leadership is, for good reason, one of the most important of the seven Nolan Principles. What makes it more likely for ethical standards to go into a sharp downward spiral, and to lead to ever-declining levels of propriety, is to have a person at the top who does not live by the Seven Principles of Public Life and does not set an example for others to do so. We saw in the historical Introduction that there was no golden age to which we should look back with fond nostalgia, but the Johnson government in a short time, recklessly or probably negligently, threatened to demolish the delicate edifice of standards for those who hold high office.

There is now talk of a post-Nolan age, not least by the immediate past Chair of the CSPL, Lord Evans.[4] The constitution now is somewhat like the emperor's new clothes, and the old saying seems especially apposite: 'The British acquire their institutions by accident and lose them in a fit of absentmindedness.'[5] This set of circumstances requires a full reconsideration, a new broad canvas: no less than a new ethical social contract.

There are too many cheques and not enough balances in the system. Some of the standards under which it should operate appear to have been corrupted over the years. The thin tissue of trust is corroding,[6] and as they say of virginity, once lost, it is impossible to regain. Yet we should try.

Morality sometimes seems to have become divorced from politics. The standard of honesty required for solicitors by the professional body is that they may be 'trusted to the ends of the earth'.[7] Few politicians attain this standard (and indeed few lawyers). It is unsurprising that the 2021 review by the CSPL, *Standards Matter 2*, concluded that these arrangements were not functioning as well as they should. Hannah White, Director of the IfG, identified to me, as one of the factors in a decline in standards, that there is less emphasis on personal morality than there was,[8] and this goes beyond the political sphere. The *Economist* in 2022 pulled no punches in pronouncing that 'Every part of the British establishment has debased itself'.[9] And Britain used to be renowned for the solidity of its institutions.

With the decline in standards, the future of our democracy and the very rule of law is at risk. Standards should not be an optional afterthought, but instead should be central to public life. We must try now to stop the downward spiral in its tracks. We need ethical buoyancy, as Lord Evans puts it.[10] For this, rules are necessary but not sufficient, because it is as much about culture.[11] Dame Julie Mellor, who was the Parliamentary and Health Service Ombudsman (2012–2017) and held many other public appointments, says that 'Penalties are not the heart of the issue; sanctions on their own make people nervous and risk averse and do not create the best long-term solutions which change the system to facilitate the right behaviour and inhibit the worst behaviour'.[12]

Lord Patten (Chair of the Conservative Party under John Major) told me:

> Peter Hennessy's observation about the way public policy has been conducted (the 'good chaps theory'[13]) is spot on; in the absence of a written constitution and a very detailed set of rules it is vital how people conduct themselves. There is an assumption behind it that those involved can tell the difference between good and bad and that good will prevail.[14]

As Mark Harper, the former Conservative Chief Whip under David Cameron and now Transport Secretary, said: 'It is important that people in public life do the right thing and by far the majority do so. Some standards have, however, slipped over the last few decades.'[15] This is worth emphasis: most public servants are beyond reproach and most public appointments too.

As I write this, I ponder long over what Daniel Greenberg, who was an experienced Parliamentary Counsel and is now the Parliamentary Commissioner for Standards, described to me as the ethical dilemma:

> You can take a horse to the ethical water, but you cannot make it drink. You can make it more difficult for a horse not to drink by articulating statutory ethical criteria that it must consider, but that drags judges further into the policing of ethics than they want to go because it leads to them being forced to adjudicate on the application of necessarily open criteria, in a context about which they know less than the regulator.[16]

The judges have a vital role to play in any new settlement, as surveys show they still have the broad trust of the public,[17] but of course the more legalistic things are, the longer will be the delays. First, however, we should review the causes of the downward spiral.

Lord Patten focused on modern political career trajectories in giving a reason:

> Standards have declined over a period and this may be linked to the fact that we have a much more political class than when I started. Paradoxically, I suspect that as politics has been regarded as a career much like any other, the idea that it should be determined by a notion of professional standards has gone by the board.[18]

He was drawing attention to the tribe of professional politicians who have done little else in their lives than be politicians.

Secondly, there is a strong argument that the standards malaise is linked to something else that may be even more threatening: populist politics. The breakdown of relations can be traced back, at least to some extent, to the deep and long-drawn-out Brexit fracture. This created acrimonious scenes in Parliament and elsewhere, adding extra toxin to the mix. This fracture has undermined the standards that were traditionally inherent (and embedded) in the public sector or, at least, these sinking standards have created the perfect breeding ground for the populist bacillus. A group of politicians have arisen who want to rail against the establishment and its apparently cosy values in a Trumpian manner. Patten, a strong supporter of membership of the EU, told me that 'Brexit has poisoned our politics; we have seen a triumph of zealous ideology over consensual centrist notions and evidence and reason-based policy arguments'.[19]

The third feature is that the division is fuelled by Britain's binary electoral system. Tories were furious about Harold Wilson, Gannex and the 'lavender list' of peers,[20] or about Tony Blair and Bernie Ecclestone, and fooled themselves into thinking they would do better. Labour and Liberal Democrat people then turned on Cameron and Johnson in the same way. As soon as there is no immediate or at least short-term threat of a change of regime, the corruption and undermining gets worse.[21] This cycle needs to be broken.

The fourth feature is the quality of those who operate in public life.[22] Hannah White registered a specific concern:

Part of the issue was that neither of the 2017 nor 2019 elections were scheduled, so many candidates were selected without due diligence and not expecting to win and then they did. They were in some cases not well prepared for what their role would be in Parliament when other scandals emerged from their past lives.[23]

What to do?

We can now pull together the threads from the previous chapters to see what we should do. A good place to conclude is precisely where we started, with the Nolan Report. The Committee in the 1990s described the situation in this way:

We cannot say conclusively that standards of behaviour in public life have declined. We can say that conduct in public life is more rigorously scrutinised than it was in the past, that the standards which the public demands remain high, and that the great majority of people in public life meet those high standards. But there are weaknesses in the procedures for maintaining and enforcing those standards. As a result, people in public life are not always as clear as they should be about where the boundaries of acceptable conduct lie. This we regard as the principal reason for public disquiet. It calls for urgent remedial action.[24]

We need to create a climate in which what you can get away with is not the running theme, the predominant 'ideology'. This requires real-world deterrent sanctions. Johnson's period in office was the first time since Lloyd George when the very role of Prime Minister has raised issues of hard-core sleaze.[25] Our system of governance was, like the proverbial fish, rotting from the head down. The established conventions (and conventional wisdom) probably never anticipated that the PM himself would be the 'bad 'un'. This demonstrates that our constitutional norms post-Johnson need to be based on the fear or assumption that there may be a bad one at the top. As Aditya Chakrabortty wrote in the *Guardian*, 'Johnson has yanked down the stage set of the puppet show that passes for British democracy'.[26]

Several chapters have recorded that this precipitous decline in standards could easily get worse if nothing is done. The British state needs rewiring. Under-regulated politicians are tempted to behave badly, and Johnson showed what can happen. There have been advances, notably in the Parliamentary area (which is not the subject of this book).[27] As Michael Crick, an experienced journalist, told me: 'things have been tightened up in areas such as MPs' expenses through the IPSA and election expenses, which used to be a very difficult area'.[28] Tighter legal regulation and cultural change are necessary, but both need to be embedded in some material, tangible way. Duncan Hames, the Director of Policy for Transparency International and former Lib Dem MP for Chippenham, explains:

> Rules are important in establishing norms of behaviour, and cases of enforcement help incentivise adherence to both the rules and more positive norms, but it becomes impossible to enforce a rule if everyone is intent on breaking it.[29]

As the distinguished lawyer and former Attorney General Sir Geoffrey Cox KC told me, 'It is the values and not the legal enforcement which guarantee propriety',[30] and this is the theme of the CSPL review *Standards Matter 2*. This should be taken forward as much as possible by consensus.

Creating political space

The Johnson government showed itself unwilling to tackle the ethical issues and the decline in standards, to the extent of not responding with any positivity to what seemed to be relatively uncontroversial CSPL reports, so the question becomes why (and how) should parties take up this agenda, and how can it serve their electoral interests to do so in terms of positive proposals (as opposed to reacting to day-to-day events)?

The political space for a firm consensus for change would probably arise only where a government wants to draw a line under the past (as did the Wilson and Blair governments) or there was some threat to the political class that brings forth a consensus, as happened on MPs' expenses. The time was propitious following the defenestration of Johnson, but it did not come to pass, since Liz Truss, who was in effect the continuity candidate, proved the short-lived winner.

We need a new Nolan-style review to locate an ethical consensus in the form of a Speaker's conference or commission. The Speaker is a figure above politics who could convene the right mixture of politicians and outsiders. The review should consider how best to embed integrity and the balance between the need for tighter regulation and cultural change. It must assess what has gone wrong and seek to gain all-party agreement on the way ahead, so as to entrench high ethical standards, taking the issue away from the 'ya boo' politics of the here and now.

The US Supreme Court Justice Louis Brandeis famously said that 'Sunlight is the best disinfectant'. The best general approach overall is to let the light in (to adopt Leonard Cohen's phrase), but there needs to be a new institutional framework to coax this out.

The public also need to be motivated in this direction. As Lord Evans said, 'Standards issues only become political issues if they get into the public consciousness'. The various scandals considered in this book raise the more general and troubling issue of the overall accountability of government to the people. Even when there is avid media attention, a scandal and furore in the Westminster village may not register much on the voters' Richter scale. Mark Philp, Chair of the CSPL Research Board, commented to me: 'People do care about ethical standards. But it's not the only thing they care about.'[31] Public opinion is also fickle. Some were willing to forgive Johnson because he is a 'cheeky chappie' whom they would like to spend an evening with. There was a prevalent view among the public at one stage that while they knew Johnson was a rogue they thought he was *our* rogue, so the scandals were effectively 'priced in'. As we have seen, the tide turned for Johnson only with Paterson, partygate and Pincher, after which he became toxic to his party.

Popular opinion punishes those governments which seem to have lost the initiative and are considered to be sleazy overall. A strong case can be made that Macmillan's fall in 1963 came over Profumo and Major's over Hamilton.

It takes a while for this feeling to be embedded in the public consciousness. It may be that corruption kills you only when it is linked to governmental failure – those who are perceived to be winners have more leeway.

The new ethical settlement requires making politicians subject to more effective sanctions. An interesting sideline is provided by the *Report of the Citizens' Assembly on Democracy in the UK*.[32] The overarching question which members of that Assembly were asked to consider was, 'How should democracy in the UK work?' At the heart of recommendations 6.1, 6.2 and 6.3, made by a Citizens' Assembly composed of ninety-two people, was the expectation that improprieties and accusations that codes of conduct having been broken should be investigated by independent regulators, rather than at the discretion of the Prime Minister or by politicians, and that any sanctions proposed as the result of an independent investigation should be implemented.[33] The public really do believe that standards are important.[34]

Another important feature is the role of the media, mainstream and otherwise, and this is mixed. There is much more scrutiny of politicians in this era of rampant social media. This has had a big role in exposing what I have been looking at in this book, but also in obfuscating or normalising it, partly because everyone seems to exist in their own echo chamber composed of like-minded folks. As Michael Crick puts it, 'There is more scrutiny in this area than ever before from pressure groups, legal groups, Parliament and the media including social media. The media and public are less compliant.'[35] The highest-selling mainstream press is overwhelmingly Conservative, and this helped to maintain Johnson in office, downplaying some of the scandals.

So, if the press are not sufficiently scrutinising a decline in ethical standards, is there anyone filling the void? Some of the space has been taken up by campaigning lawyers. The Good Law Project, for example, has brought a series of legal actions over such matters as public appointments, the awarding of COVID contracts and Number 10 parties (not always successfully). Even the founder of the Project, however, does not consider this as the ideal way to go. Jolyon Maugham KC told me:

> I agree with those who say that self-regulation is a finer, sharper mechanism for ensuring good conduct than litigation. My point is, well, what do you do when self-regulation isn't happening? – and in that world there is certainly a place for the law to play a part.[36]

The new ethics regime will require in general a more legalistic approach than we have been used to, because our tour has shown the insufficiency of informal conventions.

There is a multiplier effect here when the party of government begins to think the opposition cannot beat it through the electoral system and it consequently becomes more shameless and/or careless. In our system, fear of losing office and disgrace are arguably the only true disinfectants. The longer or more securely a regime goes on, the greater the creeping culture of fear among civil servants and potential whistleblowers/regulators. Conversely, it is also possible that when a party realises it is probably going to lose the next election, the incentive to behave recedes. It was in this context that Lord Butler, the former Cabinet Secretary, complained to me that 'Ministers seem more interested in politics than in government'.[37] That was certainly an accurate description of Johnson.

Before coming to specific reforms, let us consider the effect of declining standards on key institutions and see whether the checks and balances on the executive are properly functioning.

Parliament and Cabinet

Parliament has not been a focus of this book but, as part of a reboot of standards, there is a need to tackle its increasing weakness,[38] and this goes well beyond the issue of sleaze. An important moment in this development was the Second *Miller* case, which concerned the prorogation of Parliament during the Brexit debates. This demonstrated a government that was determined to silence (or circumvent) Parliament over Brexit (to 'get Brexit done' in its ubiquitous slogan). The system worked because this mechanism was declared to be unlawful by a unanimous judgement of eleven members of the Supreme Court.[39]

Johnson's premiership saw a general contempt for Parliament born out of what many saw as a refusal by Parliament to accept the outcome of the Brexit referendum: for example, Dominic Cummings described non-compliant MPs as 'narcissistic and delusional' and speculated (presumably in jest) about bombing Parliament. He had already been held to be in contempt of Parliament before being appointed as *de facto* Chief of Staff by Johnson. This penalty was for not attending a Commons Culture, Media and Sport Select Committee hearing to which he was summoned. Cummings behaved like an unelected minister, Thomas Cromwell to Johnson's Henry VIII.

Linked to this is the long-term decline of Cabinet government. The days when matters were discussed in detail in Cabinet have gone,[40] with PMs instead deciding after consulting individual ministers (sometimes on the sofa) and then leaking and spinning the decisions before Cabinet even knows about them.

So, we urgently need a new arrangement, an overarching system, a new commitment to restore Nolan ethics – but to go further, to ensure as far as possible that they cannot be undermined again as they were during Johnson's tenure. This entails a new settlement designed to restore ethical values at the heart of government and tackle some of the symptoms. This should involve a reversion to a more sober culture, where standards are burnished, where there is more leadership by example and fewer apparent prizes (and promotions) for finding loopholes and breaking or twisting the rules.

Conventions and a written constitution

We need a 'soft' codification of the conventions considered in detail in the last chapter, although we should bear in mind what Hannah White warned: 'If you push at the boundaries of conventions you push for people to codify them; you should be careful what you wish for.'[41] Although the arguments on a written constitution are finely balanced (and beyond the scope of this book), overall I agree with Marcial Boo, the former Director of Strategy and Communications at the NAO and now the Chief Executive of the Equality and Human Rights Commission, that 'A written constitution is not the right answer for Britain, which has a gradualist approach to governance spanning centuries. Proposing a written constitution is anyway unachievable in present circumstances.'[42]

In the present era of toxic politics, it is unlikely that agreement could be reached on such a wide-ranging instrument anyway. The rigidity of a constitution also makes it difficult to change things and to react to differing political weather.

A statutory footing

The various ethical bodies should, however, all be placed on a firm statutory footing so that we have an ethical constitution. This is because, as Sir Chris Bryant MP, Chair of the Commons Committee on Standards, told me, 'We have very few checks and balances in the UK'.[43] Lord (Gus) O'Donnell, the Cabinet Secretary between 2005 and 2011 (under three different Prime Ministers), agrees.[44] Sir Geoffrey Cox KC, however, counsels that 'Cultural change is more important than making things statutory'.[45]

As Matthew Parris wrote in the *Spectator*, 'At present we flounder in a morass of variously external, internal, judicial, parliamentary and bureaucratic investigations, many of them leading to judgments that will immediately be dismissed as whitewashes or witch hunts by those who had wanted another outcome'.[46] As we have seen, there are too many bodies and they have too few powers.

Duncan Hames, the Director of Policy for Transparency International UK and the former Lib Dem MP for Chippenham, told me: 'The ethics bodies should be put on a statutory basis to avoid every so often the regulated party threatening to do away with them'.[47]

Statutory underpinning would, however, bring with it the increased likelihood of applications to the court for judicial review and the courts becoming more front and centre in matters of acute controversy, which many would consider unsatisfactory. Normally, judges are careful to keep out of politics. As Lady Hale, President of the Supreme Court, explained in the Second *Miller* litigation:

> although the courts cannot decide political questions, the fact that a legal dispute concerns the conduct of politicians, or arises from a matter of political controversy, has never been sufficient reason for the courts to refuse to consider it … almost all important decisions made by the executive have a political hue to them. Nevertheless, the courts have exercised a supervisory jurisdiction over the decisions of the executive.[48]

Judicial review is the best defence against an elective dictatorship. Far from being restricted (as was attempted by the Johnson government), it could usefully be expanded into areas such as the review of responses to the reports of the Independent Adviser on Ministers' Interests, which can at present be ignored, and policing of post-termination restrictions on taking employment on the part of civil servants and ministers, which at present have no enforcement mechanisms.

So, what would a new landscape look like? Let's start with the basics. Impressionistically (and there is probably no scientific way of assessing this), one can readily conclude that the best and brightest do not now go into politics or the civil service. There is a feeling of mediocrity and mendacity about some of those who do and rise to the top. There is no one presently in the Cabinet of the calibre (and hinterland) of Ken Clarke, Roy Jenkins, Willie Whitelaw or Kenneth Baker.

These are likely reasons for the lack of talent: pay, post-position provision and the *quid pro quo* of a restriction of second jobs. First, the pay of public servants greatly lags behind the private sector. Politicians are expected to maintain high standards while many of those with whom they went to university are cashing in at big banks, sometimes contributing to financial instability, and in some cases enabling tax avoidance and supporting kleptocrats.[49] Like-for-like roles are in receipt of much lesser remuneration packages in the public sector than in the private. It is in the overall public interest that good people come into the public service and then later in their career possibly move between the public and private sectors so they can bring different experiences to bear. This can be done successfully only with a general increase in public sector rewards.

The pay of MPs is well out of line with, for example, that of school heads and hospital consultants. There is also no provision for MPs to go up any scale on grounds of quality, seniority or active service, although the downside is that in the private sector there is generally less job security. As of 2023, the Prime Minister earns £164,951 (although he takes less), whereas other people in the wider public sphere are in the pay stratosphere, for example Mark Thurston, Chief Executive of High Speed Two Ltd (£676,000),[50] Andrew Haines, Chief Executive of Network Rail (£590,000), Jeremy Westlake, Chief Financial Officer of Network Rail (£420,000)[51] and David Peattie, Chief Executive of the Nuclear Decommissioning Authority (£400,000). Foreign leaders earn rather more: in 2021 Angela Merkel was paid the equivalent of £267,000 and President Biden £290,000. Another unusually extreme example is Nick Clegg, who as Deputy Prime Minister was paid £134,565, whereas when he became Vice President of Facebook (now Meta Platforms) he received, even at the start of that role, £2.7 million each year. Pay increases for politicians are of course always controversial but that is not an excuse for not recognising the disparity.

Former Prime Ministers should be generously provided for, as are Presidents in the USA.[52] The PM in the old days would almost certainly just expect a dignified retirement filled with sinecures and autobiography writing, since he (and it was always a he, until Margaret Thatcher) would be retiring in his sixties or seventies. A different set of challenges presents itself now that they retire typically in their forties or early fifties. The ten predecessors to Tony Blair were on average seventy-one when they left the Commons, whereas Blair was only fifty-four and Major fifty-eight. Cameron was just forty-nine. This need/desire for a further career was partly what lay behind Cameron's role in the Greensill scandal.[53] He was unexpectedly recalled as Foreign Secretary six years later.

This one-time increase in remuneration should be combined with draconian rules on outside interests for politicians, with real sanctions for the most serious breaches.[54] Being an MP should be recognised as a full-time occupation (as it surely is if done properly). There are only a few (good) jobs which can appropriately be combined with being a MP, for instance part-time writing, farming and working in the care services, and these should be listed and any others should be permitted only within the discretion of the Speaker's Council on application by MPs.

Lobbying

There should be complete transparency on lobbying, with a register of all such activities (and not just by consultant lobbyists or lobbying professionals).[55] This means that every discussion between a minister and a lobbyist should be recorded, with the nature of the issues discussed going into the public domain soon after they take place (even at party conferences and fund-raising events). Again, real sanctions must be imposed on the separate tribes of ministers and lobbyists who offend the rules.

There should also be a five-year cooling-off period during which former ministers and senior civil servants cannot engage in any lobbying activities in respect of their old departments. After that time, any information is likely to have lost its currency. This should be enshrined in legislation, and it should carry the ultimate sanction of an injunction to be issued by the High Court to enforce the cooling-off in the event of a breach. This would attach to the minister or civil servant involved and also the company or entity to which she or he moves on as a secondary party.

The Prime Minister

What the Johnson period has shown to be inappropriate is the centrality of the Prime Minister in the standards landscape, as initiator and judge, largely as a result of conventions and without statutory backing. To answer the question posed at the outset of this book, Johnson probably was a one-off, but we need to protect the system as far as we can against any other such occupant of Number 10.

The institutions that constrain Prime Ministers are inadequate. As Lord (Gus) O'Donnell put it to me:

> The 'system' relies on the Prime Minister of the day to implement ethics or public pressure may force him or her to. Leadership from the top is important. The system can reassert itself as it did after the Owen Paterson issue, but the PM can only be removed by (a) MPs of his own party or (b) an election.[56]

It was the former scenario that *eventually* played out in Johnson's case.

The Prime Minister must have the final say over who becomes a minister and (in general) who is dismissed from that role, but there should be a high hurdle, enshrined in law, for the PM to surmount if not abiding by a decision of the Independent Adviser on Ministers' Interests. The PM should give a detailed (and published) written determination justifying why she or he has not done so. This would be subject to scrutiny by PACAC or indeed by judicial review in the most egregious circumstances. The Administrative Court was willing to intervene in the case brought by the First Division Association regarding Priti Patel, and this might be developed further.[57]

Buttressing the Ministerial Code

Enforcement of the Ministerial Code itself should be strengthened. Ministers should swear an oath to abide by it when appointed. It should have the same legal basis as its companion codes for civil servants and special advisers. This does not mean that *all* of its content needs to gain the force of law. The Prime Minister should be required to publish the Code, and that it should include Nolan's Seven Principles of Public Life as overriding objectives.

Designing ethical bodies is not easy, but it is fair to say if one were starting now, one would not begin from precisely this spot. As Marcial Boo told me:

> We need to decide what sort of ethics watchdogs we want. Economic regula-tors, such as the FCA [Financial Conduct Authority] or the Competition and Markets Authority, can fine companies or withdraw licences. They may also set the economic terms of the market, as utility regulators do. These regulatory tools are less available to ethics regulators.[58]

Transparency International UK found there were more than sixty separate 'specialist enforcement, prevention, investigative and oversight agencies involved in the policing of offences directed against corrupt behaviour', although of course this focuses on criminal behaviour.[59] Yet the number of cases where questionable behaviour goes uninvestigated has in fact increased in the last few years. The Johnson period showed what can fall between the cracks.

It is an understatement to say, as the CSPL does, that 'The balance of evidence submitted to this review indicates to us that the existing standards framework is not functioning as well as it should'.[60] Jonathan Freedland, the *Guardian* columnist, told me: 'The ethical regulators are diffuse and obscure. No one body has clear moral authority and public visibility.'[61] The whole structure needs to be reviewed and reset.

Various authorities and committees designed to regulate public life in the years after the Nolan Inquiry and to maintain checks and balances in the system are now toothless. Some appear designed to be toothless, and perhaps are even necessarily toothless, given the central doctrine of the unwritten constitution as the Crown in Parliament as the sovereign power. You do not have to be a cynic to say it is in the interest of those regulated (i.e. MPs and others in positions of power and influence) for their regulators to be weak and divided. There is a need for outside guidance and adjudication if the conventions of the constitution (which under the new model would be codified) are under strain.

Model 1: an all-in body

One possibility is a single ethics commission to regulate ethical standards throughout government. This has been the preference of the Labour Party at some times. Lord Evans properly framed the question, and also the dangers, when I spoke to him in his office at Number 1 Horse Guards Road:

> The question on reform towards what an Office for Government Ethics might be is whether the sum would be greater than the parts or whether there are other unintended consequences. Standards bodies are not an alternative to elected democracy.[62]

This body could more easily go head to head with government if it needed to than a whole series of separate weaker regulators.

The convincing arguments put against this 'all-in model' (model 1) are, firstly, the overall problem of accountability and, secondly, how it would fit into our Parliamentary system. People to whom I spoke saw this significant downside in this arrangement. Duncan Hames said:

> The drawback of a single regulator is that there would be a single point of vulnerability. You could lose everything at once. If you have several different bodies the task involved in dismantling them would be more complex.[63]

This point was stressed to me by several interviewees on the Conservative side who emphasised accountability to the electorate. Nick Timothy, who served as Joint Chief of Staff to Theresa May as Prime Minister, told me:

> There is fragmentation and confusion as to who does what in terms of the various ethics bodies. There is a role for these bodies, but eventually it is the electorate who get to decide the fate of politicians and rightly so. Civil servants should not be the judge and jury on politicians.[64]

He did, however, see the need for a wider power of recall of MPs by their electorates. Lord Wolfson of Tredegar echoes this. He told me: 'What we ultimately need is not outside ethics advisers, however eminent, but a change of culture. In the final analysis, MPs and the electorate will take care of breaches of standards.'[65]

Sir Alistair Graham, a former civil service trade union leader and later Chair of the CSPL, presents a different opinion: 'An overarching Ethics Commission could have a more powerful enforcement arm and in this way a number of areas could be improved. It would need a firm legislative basis and it would need proper resources.'[66]

Michael Gove also was

> not sure about the merits of a single ethics regulator but they should be regularly reviewed as they grew up in an organic higgledy piggledy way. There should be a more coherent joined up approach, but it is unlikely we will achieve perfect symmetry. In politics, water usually finds its own level.[67]

Jim Gallagher, who served in the Number 10 Policy Unit, put it pithily: 'You cannot have a single guardian angel for every sin in public life'.[68] Such an Ethics Commission would accrue 'significant unelected power'.[69] Some, of course, would see this as a positive feature, because the problem at present is the weakness of the institutions, such that MPs and ministers feel they can thumb their nose at regulators. The democratic mandate could come from the approval of the Commissioners by Parliament and a requirement of representatives of each party to serve on the Commission.

Tony Blair told me:

> There is a case for a stronger ethics regulator, but whether amalgamation of existing bodies would have that effect is not necessarily a certainty. The question is always whether pooling specific focuses into one body makes each distinct area a lesser priority. I support any impartial body which ensures that ethics in public life are adhered to. The question is ensuring it is the most effective it can be.[70]

The second argument against this model is that such a Commission would still have to operate multiple codes, because they are applicable to different sets of people and separate circumstances.[71] A well-resourced Commission could, however, surely solve this conundrum and would be well placed to offer opinions on areas of overlap or dispute between codes; otherwise, things fall through the cracks or lead to multiple investigations of the same issues, as occurred in Greensill.[72]

Thirdly, it is objected that this proposal ignores the specialist nature of the various existing jurisdictions and we may finish with the same dissatisfaction felt as when the Commission for Racial Equality, the Equal Opportunities Commission and the Disability Rights Commission were merged to form the Equality and Human Rights Commission, that the specialisms which they had were effectively lost or particular expertise was submerged in the wider whole.

We need firstly to decide what regulation we want of ethics and recognise that 'Regulation has fed an appetite for more ethics intervention, without ever properly satisfying it'.[73] There are some straightforward changes that would help, such as training in ethics and integrity for new ministers.

Model 2: an overarching body

A variation on this theme (model 2) provides for an overall Ethics Commission that would not lead to the abolition of existing bodies but could in the case of each particular scandal determine (a) what body should be the lead investigator or (b) whether the Ethics Commission itself was in the best position to investigate. Jill Rutter of the IfG has described the concept as a National Audit Office for Behaviour.[74]

There is at present the risk of multiple bodies looking at the same issue. As it happened, the views of the various committees looking into Greensill cohered, but what if they had diverged markedly from each other? Indeed, the allegations about Number 10 refurbishment ('wallpapergate') were considered both by Lord Geidt as the Independent Adviser and by the Electoral Commission, with different results.[75] When Richard Sharp's appointment as Chair of the BBC was under scrutiny, there were reports by the Commons Culture, Media and Sport Select Committee, the CPA and the BBC itself.[76]

The key advantage of model 2 would be to avoid the hodge podge of several investigations and hearings being set up in an *ad hoc* manner.[77] It would also avoid what happened over parties during the COVID pandemic, so that one would not have the bizarre circumstance of the Cabinet Secretary being removed from investigating his own behaviour when it turned out his own office was involved in inviting people to the Christmas Party in Downing Street.

The overriding Ethics Regulator could determine what would be the lead inquiry, depending on the circumstances of the particular case, and stop others. It is wasteful for a series of overlapping inquiries to take place (and potentially inefficient and unfair to those who are placed under scrutiny), and the new regulator could determine that they be combined under a senior judge. Yet at the same time the specialist panels would retain their respective jurisdictions.

There would be a common pool of investigators, and the Commission would have the power to access any evidence they needed. There would also be clear sanctions for breaches of the Code that it operated, so that the Prime Minister would no longer be judge and jury over the conduct of ministers.

There is some precedent for something more joined up in Canada, where there is a Conflict of Interest and Ethics Commissioner who oversees both ministerial conflicts of interests and revolving-door legislation in relation to public office holders, with an enhanced regime for senior public office holders and a non-statutory code of conduct for MPs. The Commissioner is independent of the Canadian government and reports directly to Parliament. Australia is considering such a body too, at the Commonwealth level, in the form of an Anti-Corruption Commission; some such Commissions already exist in Australia at the state level.

In addition to the chairs of each of the ethics bodies as renamed, the First Civil Service Commissioner and the Government's Anti-Corruption Champion would sit on this Ethics Commission. The Parliamentary Commissioner for Standards is backed up by a strong Select Committee and the NAO by the Public Accounts Committee, and this should be the same for the new body, in this case probably with PACAC as such a guardian and supervisor.

What should happen to the ethics regulators if they stay independent while operating under this new body? They are at present under-resourced and this needs to change. Secondly, in most cases they do not possess legal powers. In fact, the only one with powers of any serious magnitude is the Electoral Commission.[78]

These are the characteristics of regulators that are important in terms of adjudication on ethical standards:

- independence, so that any adjudication is by disinterested persons;
- the right of those accused to be heard and to appeal from the initial decision;
- as little attendant bureaucracy as possible;
- that they are not centralised exclusively in the person of the Prime Minister as gatekeeper (although she or he may have to remain as the decision maker in some cases given the PM's role in appointing and dismissing ministers).

They should also fit within accepted constitutional principles, which makes for a tight squeeze.

I now review the role of each existing regulator in the new model 2, which I favour.

The Committee on Standards in Public Life

The CSPL should remain as an overarching think tank, convening body and policy exchange, and should regularly review the efficacy and scope of the other bodies. Its informal but essential role is to present a consensus viewpoint (including frontline politicians), and it can do a deep dive into particular issues. It may call upon expert analysis and evidence and has built up quite a following over the decades. The Chair can have a weighty role in the public debate.

In order to avoid the problems that a single Commission would bring with it, but to allow for better coordination, the CSPL could become the body that directs which organ should be involved in particular investigations rather than setting up another organisation. There is at present an informal network of regulators, but this should be put on a firmer footing. A list of retired High Court judges should be kept who could be brought in to supervise significant investigations as necessary.

There is an important distinction between this body and what I might call the casework agencies that deal with specific issues. The CSPL could itself take on a supervisory role for those other bodies as a meta-regulator. It should have statutory power to summon ministers and requisition documents.

ACOBA

ACOBA should be abolished in its present form and streamlined. The Advisory part of title of the Committee on Business Appointments should be jettisoned, to emphasise that it is a body now with legal powers of enforcement. The replacement statutory organisation should be given proper investigative powers and a protected budget. Salaries met directly from the Consolidated Fund, as 'standing services', are guaranteed against across-the-board budget cuts, and this signals the important constitutional independence from the executive; this is the case for example for the Electoral Commissioners (and older institutions, such as the Comptroller and Auditor General, as well as judges). This should be applied to the other ethical regulators operating within model 2.

The Committee should employ a fully independent staff so that they are no longer supported by seconded civil servants. The new COBA also needs power to obtain all relevant documents from ministers and civil servants and all of their subsequent employing companies or organisations after leaving office. This should be put on a statutory basis, to be enforced by an injunction in the event of breach and fines. Only then can they take a view of what they will actually be doing for the new employer. The aspirant employee should have the ability to appeal to the Upper Tribunal, which is an established quasi-court with various jurisdictions to which this will be added.

The Office of the Commissioner for Public Appointments

The scope of the rules enforced by the Commissioner leaves a dangerous penumbra of uncertainty, and the sanctions are very weak. The yawning gap at present concerns the absence from scrutiny of non-executive directors of government departments and the figures known as tsars. The appointment rules should have general application and these should be applied dynamically to all new roles, instead of maintaining the present closed list of those to whom the public appointment rules apply.

But more than that is required to restore confidence: a Public Appointments Commission to supervise all public appointments[79] and provide independent interview panels.[80] This would be on the model of the Judicial Appointments Commission (JAC), which has generally been a success.[81] The Commission puts forward for each role only one candidate to the Lord Chancellor, who then has a veto power (although this has never been used, so far as is known). Further, if the government reruns a competition for the same role it should publicly justify why it has done so.[82]

The Office of the Commissioner would comprise retired judges, senior civil servants and those who have worked in the NAO. It should have power to investigate public appointments as an appeal body from a revised Public Appointments Committee, which itself should also take over the work of the Commissioner for Public Appointments. It would investigate public appointment standards issues of its own motion, so that a holistic view might be taken of an issue, such as the appointment of Greensill to a Crown Representative position. There would instead be an independent experienced cadre of such investigators available to all the ethical bodies.

Ministers should be involved in public appointments only at the beginning and end of the process, not throughout as now, and if they reject the outcome of the independent process they should explain precisely why.

The new body should be given more legal powers, the rules it administers should be statutory and it should be able to order independent investigations into public appointments, with full powers to access documents, such as a court would have.[83]

It is just wrong from many points of view to seek ideological conformity in public appointments, not least because 'The whole point of having arms-length public bodies is that they are at one remove from central government and its board members are meant to exercise independent judgement'.[84] The CSPL is right to propose a limited ministerial role in the definition of selection criteria and short-listing stages, with no say over the final successful candidate, and that OCPA be transformed into a full commission for non-departmental public body appointments, like the Civil Service Commission. The government, however, rejected this proposal outright.[85]

We should more broadly return to the Nolan Principles; like many of the areas covered in this book, this is as much about culture as regulation and rules. I agree with Sir Vernon Bogdanor,[86] who thinks that 'Ministers could be required to defend their decisions on public appointments before a relevant Select Committee'. Sir Peter Riddell concurs.

The Commissioner has the power to commence any inquiries he or she wishes, but, unlike his or her Scottish counterpart, has no power to alert Parliament where there has been an abuse of the Code or to halt an appointment process. This is essential for credibility to return to the system.[87]

The Labour Party's Commission on the UK's Future, chaired by Gordon Brown, recommended that the Commissioner for Public Appointments and the Civil Service Commission 'should be merged into a single and more powerful appointments regulator which should ensure that all appointments, including appointments to public bodies, are made solely on merit. The members of this new strengthened regulator should be appointed only with the approval of both Houses of Parliament.'[88] This is a sound judgement.

The CSPL's conclusion in the *Standards Matter 2* review was that 'Though the public appointments system has generally worked well in recent years, it is highly dependent on informal mechanisms, including the willingness of ministers to act with restraint and the preparedness of the Commissioner to speak out against breaches of the letter or the spirit of the code'.[89] This rests on the 'good chaps' theory and needs to be redressed with more formal restraints. The CPA should be on a statutory footing and properly resourced.

The Independent Adviser on Ministers' Interests

In model 2 there should continue to be such an Adviser, but that person's nomination should be approved by Parliament. The Independent Adviser's function should have a statutory basis and operate more like the Parliamentary Commissioner for Standards, who possesses an independent power to investigate. The Independent Adviser should be dismissed only if a Select Committee agrees, as is the position for the head of the Office for Budgetary Responsibility.

Overall conclusion

There is a sense of decay in standards in the air. The cynical view that all politicians are liars and cheats needs to end. Very few in fact are. Even if the public do not care about standards, the Prime Minister should, as have occupants of the role before Johnson; that should be a job requirement.

So what, overall, do I take from this journey round the regulators and my attempt to look at what works and what we need? The first is that under Johnson the system went badly wrong, but it did come right in the end and eventually swallowed him up. It took a long time, and the excesses of the Johnson government should not be allowed so easily to happen again. One thinks of the three Ps in particular: Paterson, partygate and Pincher. It risks complacency to think that the system will always reassert itself (as indeed it would be simply to say that we have better standards in the UK than elsewhere). The reason I wanted to dissect the period in such detail is that it shows what can go wrong and that the existing guardrails are insufficient.

Secondly, we should make changes to each regulator and put them under an overarching body. We should also look again at each regulator about every seven years to check whether it is fit for purpose and in good working order.

Sir Alistair Graham, a former Chair of the CSPL, put it this way while Johnson retained office:

> There has never been a golden age of standards, but we appear to be living through a particularly grim period. The problem is that the practice of ignoring standards is being led from the top and this gives entirely the wrong message. I start from the principle that high standards lead to a more effective democracy and successful government. The country in recent times has experienced the disastrous period of the Johnson government where he has shown he could not care less about standards in public life. The key issue is leadership from the top together with politicians taking personal responsibility for their own standards.[90]

The taint of Johnson has got into the fabric of the political system. There is more lying in Parliament than ever before. Britain has not been well governed over the last few years. We can do better and we must.

I will leave the last word to the great German sociologist Max Weber:

Politics is not an ethical business. But there does nevertheless exist a certain minimum of shame and obligation to behave decently which cannot be violated with impunity even in politics.[91]

Appendix

Controversial public appointment cases (and two non-reappointment issues)

Relatively few public appointments come to public attention, but these are some of the strange to scandalous cases I have been able to untangle, often through unattributable sources.

Nimco Ali

A 'social activist' friend of Carrie Johnson, appointed in October 2020 to an ill-defined role as an adviser on tackling violence against women and girls via a direct appointment process without independent scrutiny.[1]

Dame Vera Baird

The Solicitor General under Gordon Brown was appointed Victims' Commissioner in June 2019 and resigned in September 2022, accusing government ministers of downgrading victims' interests. Instead of being reappointed, like her predecessor, she was told by Dominic Raab that the post would be open to competition and she did not apply.[2]

Channel 4

Uzma Hasan, a film producer, and Fru Hazlitt, a broadcasting executive and former managing director at ITV, Yahoo and GCap Media, were not reappointed to their posts on the board of Channel 4, without any misconduct or lack of capability on their part.[3] This decision was made against the express advice of both the board of the television company and of Ofcom. This left the board with seven white men and one disabled person, and the safest inference is that one major reason for the non-reappointments was their potential opposition to the sale of the broadcaster, mooted by the Johnson government.[4]

Department for Environment, Food and Rural Affairs

A minister in the Department appointed someone to a committee position for which they had not applied or been interviewed, despite an open competition being held. Although the Commissioner raised this with the Department, the minister went ahead with the appointment and declined to publish the required statement acknowledging that the Code had been breached.[5]

Robbie Gibb

Robbie Gibb was translated to the BBC governors by the Johnson government. He is one of the founders of the right-wing TV station GB News, a former BBC head of political programmes and former Communications Director at Downing Street. He is a former special adviser to Francis Maude and Michael Portillo.[6]

Nick Hardwick

Some have been forced out of public appointments by ministers when there is a crisis.[7] One of the extreme cases was the Chair of the Parole Board, Nick Hardwick, whose team had acted on legal advice regarding John Worboys, the taxi driver turned rapist whom they were going to release. This led to much opposition. The Board later received different legal advice. In the meantime, Hardwick was in effect sacked as Chair on 27 March 2018. Hardwick told me that David Gauke, the Justice Secretary, encouraged his 'resignation' by saying to him twice that 'he did not want to get "macho" with me', which he took as 'a threat'.[8] Mr Justice Mostyn subsequently said in a judicial review challenge:

> In my judgment it is not acceptable for the Secretary of State to pressurise the Chair of the Parole Board to resign because he is dissatisfied with the latter's conduct. This breaches the principle of judicial independence enshrined in the Act of Settlement 1701. If the Secretary of State considers that the Chair should be removed, then he should take formal steps to remove him pursuant to the terms of the Chair's appointment.[9]

Lightning struck twice, as Hardwick had been involved in another misapplication of the appointments principles when he had had to reapply for his role as Chief Inspector of Prisons after his three-year term finished. He found that the 'independent' members on the reappointment panel were both

Conservatives, Lord Henley, the Conservative peer and former minister, and Amanda Sater, an active member of the Conservative Party, who had stood for election to the Commons for the Conservatives and who has also acted as adviser on women to Grant Shapps as Chair of the Party.[10]

Aminul Hoque

Sir Charles Dunstone of Carphone Warehouse, a Conservative Party major donor, resigned as the chair of the Royal Museums Greenwich in February 2021 when the Johnson government refused to reappoint Aminul Hoque as a trustee whose academic work advocated 'decolonising' the curriculum. Hoque was Lecturer in Education Studies at Goldsmiths, University of London, and colleagues described him as 'devoted and conscientious'.[11] This rejection was linked with the culture wars agenda of Number 10.

Oluwole Kolade and NHS appointments

In March 2022 Oluwole Kolade became deputy chair of NHS England, having donated £859,342 to the Tory Party, to the Party's London mayoral candidate and to the Tory branch in Hitchin and Harpenden. He is a managing partner of Livingbridge, a private equity firm with major investments in private healthcare, which you might think was not the most obvious qualification for the NHS. In a parallel story, Simon Blagden became a member of the advisory board of the UK Health Security Agency. He and his companies have donated £376,000 to the Conservatives.

Murdoch MacLennan

The former *Telegraph* Chief Executive was appointed as Chair of the Office for the Internal Market without any obvious qualifications for the role. The *Telegraph* was the former employer of Johnson and remained loyal to him to the end.

Harry Mount

The editor of *The Oldie* was appointed to the House of Lords Appointments Commission by Johnson during the caretaker period after he resigned as PM. This broke the convention that a PM would not make controversial appointments in such a period. Mount's greatest literary work was entitled *The Wit and*

Wisdom of Boris Johnson, and he was a long time *Spectator* journalist. He resigned a month after his appointment.

Geeta Nargund

She was placed on the Human Fertilisation and Embryology Authority (HFEA) even though she is an advocate of what is termed 'natural' in-vitro fertilisation (IVF). The majority of the fertility sector do not support natural IVF nor do they practise it. This appointment therefore put the HFEA in a difficult position with the majority of the sector it regulates, as it looked as if they endorsed a clinical practice with which the sector largely disagrees.

Social Mobility Commission

Of seven Commissioners announced in September 2022 to the Social Mobility Commission, three had donor links to the Conservative Party and only one was a woman.

Dame Sara Thornton

The former Chief Constable of Thames Valley Police, she was subsequently appointed by Sajid Javid, when he was Home Secretary, as the Independent Anti-Slavery Commissioner from 2018.[12] The Commissioner posts normally last three years, and the assumption is that the holders will carry on in post if willing to do so. She was not, however, reappointed under the Johnson government but in 2021 was told that she could apply for her own post, an invitation she politely and understandably declined. She told me she found out when a friend of hers who was unaware of this called her to ask why her role was being advertised on the Conservative Home website. She said:

> I think that the Home Office was keen to comply with the Downing Street in-struction that appointments should be advertised. I suspect that I was regarded as having been outspoken on the Borders Bill.[13] But as the Anti-Slavery Commissioner I had a responsibility to comment on measures that would impact on victims of modern slavery.

Her successor, appointed some two years later, was a former Conservative special adviser.

Jenny Watson

She had a long line of public appointments but was associated with the Labour Party in the mind of the government and was not renewed in her role on the Financial Reporting Council, which had become quite political. She was also considered anti-Brexit.

Sir Vernon Ellis

Even the chairing of the bodies supervising honours has become more politicised. In 2015 Sir Vernon Ellis, a distinguished businessman who had held senior public appointments, and was Chair of the Arts and Media Honours Committee 2012–2015, pushed back on a senior honour being pushed hard for someone by Number 10. He was warned by the Cabinet Secretary that consequences would follow if this position was repeated and that the pragmatic course would be to accept it. The same candidate came up again six months later, with the same outcome and the consequence that Ellis's chairmanship was not renewed.[14] In 2022 John Booth, a Conservative Party donor close to Johnson's Number 10, was appointed to this post.

Abbreviations

ACOBA	Advisory Committee on Business Appointments
APPG	All-Party Parliamentary Group
C&AG	Comptroller and Auditor General
CCFF	Covid Corporate Financing Facility
CPA	Commissioner for Public Appointments
CRGA	Constitutional Reform and Governance Act 2010
CSPL	Committee on Standards in Public Life
ESSRC	Economic and Social Sciences Research Council
EU	European Union
FCDO	Foreign, Commonwealth and Development Office
GLP	Good Law Project
HoLAC	House of Lords Appointments Commission
IfG	Institute for Government
IPSA	Independent Parliamentary Standards Authority
MOD	Ministry of Defence
NAO	National Audit Office
NDPB	non-departmental public body
NED	non-executive director
NGO	non-government organisation
NHS	National Health Service
OCPA	Office of the Commissioner for Public Appointments
Ofcom	Office of Communications
Ofqual	Office of Qualifications and Examinations Regulation
Ofsted	Office for Standards in Education, Children's Services and Skills
ORCL	Office of the Registrar of Consultant Lobbyists
PAC	Public Accounts Committee
PACAC	Public Administration and Constitutional Affairs Committee of the House of Commons
PM	Prime Minister

PPE   personal protective equipment

PPERA   Political Parties, Elections and Referendums Act

quango   quasi-autonomous non-governmental organisation

SCS   Senior Civil Service

SpAd   special adviser

USPL   Committee on Standards in Public Life, *Upholding Standards in Public Life: Final Report of the Standards Matter 2 Review*, November 2021

Acknowledgements

I have had fantastic access and help throughout this project. In particular I would like to thank the following who all helped in different ways:

Sir Alex Allan
Mohamed Amersi
Iain Anderson
Howard Anglin
Jackie Ashley
Chris Ballinger
David Bennett
Tony Blair
Sir Vernon Bogdanor
Ivan Bolton
Marcial Boo
Emma Bowers
Gordon Brown
Sir Chris Bryant MP
Nick Butler
Lord Robin Butler
Lady Camilla Cavendish
Jack Churchill
Rod Clayton
Elizabeth Clough
David Conn
Dan Corry
Sir Geoffrey Cox
Emma Crewe

Sir Ivor Crewe
Michael Crick
Max Crofts
Elizabeth David-Barrett
Lady Ruth Deech
Danny Dorling
Pamela Dow
Tim Durrant
Richard Ekins
Sir Vernon Ellis
Lord Evans of Weardale
Lord Falconer
Stephen Fisher
Matthew Flinders
Michael Foster
Claire Foster-Gilbert
Jonathan Freedland
Ivor Gaber
Professor Jim Gallagher
Lord Geidt
Jonathan Gerlis
Joshua Getzler
Dame Helen Ghosh
Chris Gibson KC

Helen Goodman

Michael Gove MP

Sir Alistair Graham

Daniel Greenberg

Ian Gregory

Dominic Grieve

Andy Haldane

Sarah Hall

Duncan Hames

Nick Hardwick

Mark Harper MP

Susan Hawley

Jonathan Haydn-Williams

Lady Diane Hayter

Sarah Hearn

Lord Hennessy

Lady Susanne Heywood

Lord Jonathan Hill

Dame Meg Hillier MP

David Hine

Sir Tony Holland

Sir John Holmes

David Howarth

Will Hutton

Sir Bernard Jenkin MP

Richard Johnson

Fraser Kemp

Sir Ian Kennedy

Lord Bob Kerslake

Sir John Kingman

Richard Lambert

Anna Malkin

Michael Malone

Lord Francis Maude

Jolyon Maugham

Andrew Mell

Dame Julie Mellor

Jonathan Michie

Sir David Natzler

Linda Newbery

Sir David Normington

Lord Philip Norton of Louth

Matthew Oakeshott

Lord Gus O'Donnell

Claire Perry O'Neill

Sue Owen

Lord Patten of Barnes

Gillian Peel

Adam Perry

Mark Philp

Sir Jonathan Phillips

Lord Eric Pickles

David Prince

David Prout

John Pullinger

Harry Rich

Ed Richards

Steve Richards

Sir Peter Riddell

David Rose

Henry Russell

Sir Philip Rutnam

Jill Rutter

Charles Seaford

Gerald Shamash

Sir Paul Silk

Jonathan Slater

Ewan Smith

Martin Stanley

Chris Stones

Seth Thévoz

Dame Sara Thornton

Nick Timothy

Sir Edward Troup

Anne Twomey

Sarah Vaughan

Lord Gordon Wasserman

Hannah White

Lucy Wiseman

Lord David Wolfson of Tredegar

Clive Wolman

Lord Stewart Wood of Anfield

William Wragg

I recognise that not all of them will agree with my conclusions.

There were several others who helped me who wished to remain anonymous. Several others turned down the opportunity to participate.

I would also like to thank my PAs, Anna Malkin and Kate Roberts, and the fantastic team at Manchester University Press.

Most of all I thank my family for their support, Suzanne Franks and Emma, Hannah and Ben Bowers.

The book covers the period up to 9 January 2024. I hope more chapters do not have to be written!

Notes

Prologue

1 Delivered at the Edinburgh International Television Festival on 23 August 2022.
2 One can compare other backsliding democracies (e.g. South Africa, Poland, the US, indeed the US at various points in the mid-twentieth century) and say that guardian institutions are slowly and successfully nobbled before the real business begins.
3 There is a feeling of *noblesse oblige* behind this way of expressing it, but arguably the main cause of the rise of public standards in British politics was probably nineteenth-century Protestant puritanism coupled with the pressure coming from protests for representation from the poor.
4 *New Statesman*, 23 July 2021.
5 Attributed to Bayard Rustin, a Black Quaker leader in the Civil Rights Movement, and a phrase now widely used by Greta Thunberg, Extinction Rebellion and others.
6 Interviewed 30 May 2022.
7 See Chapter 4.
8 The 'good chaps' theory of UK government was coined by the constitutional historian Peter Hennessy. See Andrew Blick and Peter Hennessy, *Good Chaps No More? Safeguarding the Constitution in Stressful Times* (Constitution Society, 2019).
9 *Guardian*, 19 October 2023.
10 *Hansard*, vol. 814, 9 September 2021.
11 The argument is developed in Chapter 15.

1. Introduction

1 There is a case that Parliamentary shenanigans over Brexit in 2018 led to a drop in trust, which recovered after Brexit was delivered. See www.bsa.natcen.ac.uk/latest-report/british-social-attitudes-38/democracy.aspx (accessed 18 September 2023).
2 'Attlee on leadership', *New Statesman*, 14 May 2009.
3 Committee on Standards in Public Life (CSPL), *Upholding Standards in Public Life: Final Report of the Standards Matter 2 Review* (November 2021), para. 1.4 (henceforth *USPL*). Of course, many countries are democratic in name only.
4 Jonathan Rose and Paul Heywood, 'Political science approaches to integrity and corruption', *Human Affairs*, 23:2 (2013), 148–159, p. 149.
5 See for example Andrew Blick and Peter Hennessy, *Good Chaps No More? Safeguarding the*

Constitution in Stressful Times (Constitution Society, 2019). Nor are any other countries themselves beacons of ethical standards. Although not the highest-scoring globally, the UK usually performs relatively well in the Corruption Perception Index – a composite index based on expert assessments by country specialists and senior business people. As to individuals, in recent years Nicolas Sarkozy, the former President of France, has been sentenced to three years in jail for corruption; Silvio Berlusconi, the former Prime Minister of Italy, was convicted of tax fraud and sentenced to four years' imprisonment; Jacob Zuma, former President of South Africa, was in prison for contempt of court and facing trial for corruption; Donald Trump was impeached twice, and he and his company were subject to several civil and criminal actions. In 2018, the ex-President of Brazil, Lula da Silva, was sentenced to twelve years for corruption, although he had a second coming in the presidential election of 2022.

6 Jon Stone, 'Corruption experts warn Boris Johnson's government is worst since WWII', *Independent*, 29 January 2022, available at www.independent.co.uk/news/uk/politics/boris-johnson-corruption-b2002869.html (accessed 8 June 2023).

7 Transparency International, 'UK submission to the Committee on Standards in Public Life Standards Matter 2 consultation', p. 3, available at www.transparency.org.uk (accessed 8 June 2023).

8 Interestingly, those actually delivering public services, such as doctors, teachers, judges and local government officials, achieve much higher ratings in these polls. See www.ipsos.com/en-uk/ipsos-mori-veracity-index-2020-trust-in-professions (accessed 18 September 2023) and *USPL*, p. 7. Earlier, the Transparency International Corruption Perceptions Index 2012 report listed three particular problems in public life: prisons, sports betting and political parties. See https://www.transparency.org/en/cpi/2012 (accessed 24 October 2023).

9 As reported in *USPL*, para. 1.28.

10 This is reflected in similar figures in the USA. See Robert Putnam, *The Upswing* (Swift, 2020), p. 103.

11 Turnout rose steadily from 2001 until the 2016 Brexit referendum and has fallen slightly since.

12 Hansard Society, *Audit of Political Engagement 10*, 2019, ch. 3.

13 *USLP*, para. 1.29.

14 *Ibid.*, para. 1.32. See also *Future of Democracy in the UK*, Constitution Unit report, 23 November 2023, esp. ch. 3.

15 *Guardian*, 16 November 2022.

16 The speech, titled 'In democracy we trust?', was delivered to the influential think tank the Institute for Government on 10 February 2022. Ironically his government had engaged in political targeting of funds to local authorities too: see Hugh Ward and Peter John, 'Targeting benefits for electoral gain: constituency marginality and the distribution of grants to English local authorities', *Political Studies*, 47:1 (1999), 32–52.

17 Rose and Heywood, 'Political science approaches', p. 150.

18 *Guardian*, 19 July 2022.

19 Interviewed 21 September 2022.

20 Interviewed 12 December 2022.

21 See p. 14.

22 It is rumoured that this kitemark was sketched out by Professor Anthony King in the back of a taxi.

23 Committee on Standards in Public Life, *MPs, Ministers, Civil Servants, Executive Quangos*, Cm 2850, May 1995 (the Nolan Report, first report of the Nolan Committee).

24 *Ibid.*, p. 14.

25 House of Commons Committee on Standards, *Review of the Code of Conduct: Proposals for Consultation*, November 2021, para. 21.

26 Evidence to Committee on Standards 2, November 2021.

27 See Chapter 2.

2. A brief history of standards in public life

1 One other general lesson is that the more a government seeks to suppress a scandal the more likely it is to break as a story; it is often the cover-up that brings people down. In many cases, media investigations are pivotal in uncovering scandals.

2 C. R. Mayes, 'The sale of peerages in early Stuart England', *Journal of Modern History*, 29:1 (1957), 21–37; Lawrence Stone, *The Crisis of the Aristocracy 1558–1641* (Oxford University Press, 1965), ch. 3.

3 Alan Doig, *Corruption in Contemporary British Politics* (Penguin, 1984), p. 43.

4 Erskine May, para. 15.28.

5 G. R. Searle, *Corruption in British Politics 1885–1930* (Oxford University Press, 1987), p. 172.

6 Tom Cullen, *Maundy Gregory, Purveyor of Honours* (Bodley Head, 1974). Ironically, if Lloyd George had fallen, Britain would have lost a future war leader and the man who negotiated a huge loan from the USA for the war effort.

7 Searle, *Corruption*, p. 391. A Conservative Party pamphlet from July 1924 said: 'The corruption of our public life had reached a festering height which threatened the health of the whole nation. There was an air of Tammany in Westminster…. All that was morally bad in politics had gathered a courage and intensified an insolence which were carrying every successive barrier of decency and virtue before them.'

8 Isaacs, Masterman and Lloyd George sent the Master of Elibank, the Chief Whip, a telegram of congratulation on 'one of the most flagrant Honours Lists', bearing the ironic words 'all for merit' (Searle, *Corruption*, p. 150). Elibank's period saw a record number of peerages and baronetcies being created (*ibid.*). According to Tom Cullen, he had a 'list of from 300 to 400 worthies, all with their cheque books at the ready, whom he intended to recommend for peerages should it be found necessary to pack the Upper Chamber' (*Maundy Gregory*, p. 27).

9 Attlee was 'the nearest approach to a saint we are likely to see in this place' according to Richard Crossman MP. See John Bew, *Citizen Clem* (Riverrun, 2016), ch. 7.

10 In response to questioning by Hartley Shawcross before the Lynskey tribunal, Stanley said, 'You have caught me out telling the truth, Sir Hartley.'

11 This is not to be confused with the second committee with precisely the same title led by Lord Nolan two decades later.

12 See Nick Thomas Symonds, *Harold Wilson: The Winner* (Weidenfeld & Nicholson, 2022).

13 Crosland received a coffee pot worth £500. Poulson had a full-service architectural practice including design and quantity surveying. He was a devout Christian and travelled everywhere with a bible. He used the Labour MP Albert Roberts for contacts in Spain and Portugal and the Conservative MP John Cordle primarily for his connections in West Africa. Cordle wrote to Poulson, 'it was largely to the benefit of construction promotion that I took part in a debate in the House of Commons on the Gambia and pressed for HMG to award constructional contracts to British firms'. See Lewis Baston, *Sleaze: The State of Britain* (4 Books, 2000) p. 100. Local government was

not immune from scandal in later years, with the Westminster local authority 'homes for votes' scandal of the late 1980s of particular note.

14 The activities were carried on from 1963 but became public only about ten years later.

15 Poulson in fact said that 'Cordle's help to me was non-existent' and 'I considered I was conned' (Baston, *Sleaze*, p. 108). Cordle also owned the Church of England's newspaper.

16 The Poulson scandal was one basis for the acclaimed BBC TV drama *Our Friends in the North*, which had as its backdrop public life and events in northern England from the 1960s to the 1990s.

17 It was later reported that Major himself had had an affair with his fellow MP Edwina Currie before he became Prime Minister. There had also been extraordinary scandals involving Jeremy Thorpe, who was behind a murder plot on Norman Scott in 1975, and John Stonehouse, who in 1974 faked his own disappearance, but these were deeply personal. See John Hayes, *Stonehouse* (Robinson, 2021).

18 He launched it with a press conference where he said he was fighting with 'the sword of truth'.

19 Greer was said to preside over the 'most powerful lobbying group in the land' and had many politicians on his books. He was the son and grandson of Salvation Army officers.

20 Well covered in David Leigh and Ed Vulliamy's *Sleaze* (Fourth Estate, 1997). Ironically enough, Fayed said that he came to the UK from Egypt because he saw the UK as having a good reputation for probity.

21 The Chairman, Michael Grylls, the Vice Chair, Smith, and the Secretary, Neil Hamilton.

22 John Major, *The Autobiography* (Harper Collins, 2000), p. 576.

23 See Chapter 3.

24 Committee on Standards in Public Life, *MPs, Ministers, Civil Servants, Executive Quangos*, Cm 2850, May 1995 (the Nolan Report), p. 2.

25 Leigh and Vulliamy, *Sleaze*, p. xv.

26 As the CSPL recorded in its interim report, *Standards Matter 2: The Committee's Findings*, 14 June 2021: 'today, there is a more challenging environment for those committed to upholding ethical standards. The impact of social media, the coarsening of public debate and political polarisation have all contributed to increase the risk to public standards.'

27 *Ibid.*, para. 1.10.

28 See Chapter 5.

29 *USPL*, para. 16.

30 *Ibid.*, para. 17.

31 'Public' here encompasses all of those who are involved in the delivery of public services, not solely those appointed or elected to public office.

32 CSPL, *Standards Matter: A Review of Best Practice in Promoting Good Behaviour in Public Life*, Cm 8519, January 2013. See also CSPL, *Survey of Public Attitudes Towards Conduct in Public Life 2012*, September 2013.

33 *Ibid.*, ch. 3, para. 27.

34 *Ibid.*, ch. 3.

35 A survey of 250 such fringe bodies found that ten had been set up before 1900 and eighty-four before 1949. *Ibid.*, ch. 3, para. 3.

36 *Ibid.*, ch. 3, para. 33.

37 *On the Record*, BBC, 16 November 1997.

38 See Chapter 15.

39 It is unlikely that a minister would now have to resign in similar circumstances.

40 See Chapter 7. Those nominated for peerages were Chai Patel, Sir David Garrard and Barry Townsley.

41 Tony Blair, *A Journey* (Random House, 2010), p. 607.

42 Lord Levy, *A Question of Honour: Inside New Labour and the True Story of the Cash for Peerages Scandal* (Simon & Schuster, 2008).

43 *Ibid.*

44 Blair, *A Journey*, p. 608.

45 Blair had said he would resign if questioned under caution.

46 See Emma Crewe and Andrew Walker, *An Extraordinary Scandal* (Haus Publishing, 2019).

47 This did not contain any redactions, as would have happened in the official publication. David MacLean MP had unsuccessfully sought to exempt peers and MPs from the statutory provisions on freedom of information.

48 Although these were not actually claimed (according to Crewe and Walker in *An Extraordinary Scandal*), but rather listed as possible expenses. Nadhim Zahawi, later for a brief time Chancellor of the Exchequer, claimed £5,000 to heat his barn. It should be said that some MPs did not claim at all and some lived rather frugally.

49 There was one eccentrically discordant voice, who was soon silenced by his own party's leadership. Anthony Steen, Conservative MP for Totnes, told BBC Radio 4's *The World at One* (21 May 2009) that he personally 'didn't see what all the fuss is about', and suggested that the public were merely 'jealous' of his house, which he compared to Balmoral Castle, the Royal residence.

50 Criminal charges of false accounting were brought against Elliot Morley, David Chaytor and Jim Devine. This scandal also engulfed the House of Lords. Lord Bhatia was suspended from the House of Lords for eight months and told to repay £27,446. Baron Clarke of Hampstead, a Labour peer and former senior trade unionist, admitted that he had 'fiddled' his expenses to make up, he said, for not being paid a salary. Lord Hanningfield, a Conservative from a local authority background, was charged with two alleged offences of false accounting. In May 2011, he was found guilty on six counts, and was sentenced to nine months' imprisonment. The wealthy industrialist Baron Paul was suspended from the House of Lords for four months and ordered to pay back £41,982.

51 Interviewed 23 March 2022.

52 Of course, MPs' salaries are well above the average wage; see also Chapter 12. See Crewe and Walker, *An Extraordinary Scandal*, especially p. 19. It seems that the relatively low salary initially derived from Margaret Thatcher, who would not increase Parliamentary salaries.

53 In 2009 a 'cash for influence' scandal broke in the *Sunday Times* that concerned four Labour Party life peers (Lords Snape, Moonie, Taylor of Blackburn and Truscott) offering, in a series of covert interviews with journalists masquerading as lobbyists for an unnamed firm, to use their political influence to introduce amendments to legislation in return for payments of up to £120,000. The firm, the journalists said, wanted to set up a chain of shops in the UK and was seeking exemption from the then current laws on business rates.

54 It is notable that although MPs' expenses had dominated headlines, it seems to have had only a minor impact on the outcome of the 2010 general election. Andrew Eggers and Alexander Fisher carried out research on this for their *Political Science and Political*

Economy Working Paper (LSE 8/2011, London School of Economics, September 2011). While the authors did note a higher retirement rate among MPs who were caught up in the various expenses rule breaches and a lower vote share for those who claimed extravagant expenses that had little to do with MPs' official duties, they found, however, that there was no direct relationship between vote losses and the scale of the MP's venality.

55 Interviewed 23 March 2022.

56 BBC News, 11 May 2009. See about his own conduct in Crewe and Walker, *An Extraordinary Scandal*, p. 125.

57 Many argue this was in part because the former was for five years a coalition.

58 Although the focus of the book will not be on the media itself, such issues will inevitably impinge, especially the close link between newspapers like the *Sun*, *Daily Mail* and *Daily Telegraph* and Number 10, which help it to ignore these issues.

59 Interviewed 7 October 2022.

60 It was noticeable that the *Daily Mail*, a paper normally firmly supporting a Conservative government, ran a headline in 2021 that read 'Shameless MPs sink back to sleaze' (4 November).

61 The apogee of the links between politics and celebrity culture occurred when Matt Hancock took time away from being an MP to go to the Australian jungle for *I'm A Celebrity, Get Me Out of Here*. He subsequently engaged in an SAS-themed celebrity programme too.

62 Interviewed 7 December 2022.

63 Interviewed 7 February 2022.

64 Interviewed 23 March 2022.

3. Boris Johnson and the downward spiral

1 One fascinating feature is that he is a loner. A colleague said that, like Lord Palmerston, he does not have friends, only interests. See Sonia Purnell, *Just Boris: A Tale of Blond Ambition* (Aurum Press, 2012), p. 156.

2 Anne McElvoy, *Guardian*, 19 December 2021.

3 *New Statesman*, 4 November 2020.

4 *Guardian*, 15 October 2016.

5 In fact, Johnson first came up with this to describe his own journey towards Brexit in 2015. See Sebastian Payne, *The Fall of Boris Johnson* (Macmillan, 2022), p. 21.

6 *The Times*, 30 January 2022.

7 Purnell, *Just Boris*, p. 4.

8 Max Hastings, *The Times*, 6 February 2022.

9 Rory Stewart, *Times Literary Supplement*, 6 November 2020.

10 Lady Camilla Cavendish, *Financial Times*, 14 January 2022.

11 She said of Howard that there was 'something of the night about him'.

12 At Prime Minister's Questions on 24 July 2019 he attacked the 'doubters, the doomsters, the gloomsters – they are going to get it wrong again'.

13 Sebastian Payne, *Broken Heartlands* (Macmillan, 2021), p. 24. Andrew Gimson suggests that people warmed to Johnson because he was subversive and that his imperfections rendered him the underdog. Andrew Gimson, *Boris Johnson: The Rise and Fall of a Troublemaker at Number 10* (Simon & Schuster, 2022), p. 411.

14 Purnell, *Just Boris*, p. 174. Tom Bower, *Boris Johnson: The Gambler* (W. H. Allen, 2020),

p. 56. Guppy had been convicted of fraud after a journalist, Stuart Collier, exposed his crimes in the (now defunct) *News of the World* newspaper. It was Collier whom Guppy wanted to rough up. See also Payne, *The Fall of Boris Johnson*.

15 See Chapter 4.

16 See Chapter 15.

17 Ministerial Code as published on 26 April 2019.

18 Gimson, *Boris Johnson*, p. 262. Dominic Cummings said in his blog on 5 July 2021 that Johnson 'rewrites reality in his mind afresh according to the moment's demands. He lies – so blatantly, so naturally, so regularly that there is no real distinction possible with him as there is with normal people between truth and lies'.

19 For example, by Tom Bower, Sonia Purnell, Andrew Gimson and Peter Oborne (see the 'Select bibliography' at the end of this volume). For a dogged defence of Johnson see Chris Pincher, 'Beware of the Boris haters', *The Critic*, October 2022.

20 Referred to in a *Daily Mail* article of 12 April 2020 by Tom Bower.

21 Commons Committee on Standards, *Report*, 8 April 2019.

22 Peter Oborne, *The Assault on Truth* (Simon & Schuster, 2021), p. 9. Disraeli was also 'persistently careless with the truth' according to Douglas Hurd's biography of the flamboyant nineteenth-century politician. Douglas Hurd and Edward Young, *Disraeli, or The Two Lives* (Weidenfeld & Nicolson, 2013).

23 Oborne, *The Assault on Truth*, p. 14.

24 Sir Lindsay Hoyle, Speaker of the House of Commons, did not seek a correction from the PM for misleading the Commons about unemployment and crime figures.

25 *The Times*, leading article, 2 February 2022.

26 The Johnsons lived there rather than Number 10, as it has a bigger flat. This was indeed the position with successive Prime Ministers for twenty-five years until Rishi Sunak.

27 Lord Geidt's investigation is covered in Chapter 4.

28 Independent Adviser on Ministers' Interests, *Annual Report*, 6 May 2021, para. 23.

29 Email from Johnson to Brownlow, 29 November 2020.

30 Para. 23 of the Adviser's *Annual Report* says that 'The record shows that Lord Brownlow has pursued this task with energy and due regard for propriety throughout'.

31 An invoice shows £7,500 for sofas, £8,500 spent on lamps and £30,000 for the 'paint effect' in the hallway, as well as £3,675 on a nureyev trolly, whatever that may be.

32 This is what made the affair susceptible to the jurisdiction of the Electoral Commission (see Chapter 8).

33 The Conservative Party received a donation of £67,801.72 from Huntswood Associates Limited (Brownlow's company) in October 2020 – £52,801.72 of which was to cover the cost of three invoices relating to the refurbishment of Downing Street. Only £15,000 was reported as a donation in the Party's books. The Electoral Commission's investigation concluded that the full amount (i.e. £67,801.72) was in truth a donation and should have been reported to the Commission.

34 *Guardian*, 6 January 2022.

35 As *The Times* put it on 12 January 2022, in relation to Johnson's conduct over the refurbishment, 'he has a reliable indifference to standards of behaviour that most people would regard as axiomatic in their own lives, let alone in those occupying high office'.

36 On 8 November on the *Andrew Marr Programme* on BBC1, George Eustice (the Secretary of State for Environment, Food and Rural Affairs) claimed that Boris could not be investigated by the Parliamentary Commissioner for Standards over the redecoration

of his flat because this was a 'ministerial issue not an MP issue'. Dame Margaret Hodge also sought to refer the Prime Minister to the Parliamentary Commissioner for Standards, Kathryn Stone, but the latter decided to take no action on the referral.

37 See also the *Sunday Times*, 15 January 2023.

38 He also received £24,000 from the Bamford family to pay for his wedding to Carrie.

39 See further in Chapter 5.

40 Interviewed February 2022.

41 *Sunday Mirror*, 28 March 2021.

42 Para. 17.

43 See Adam Wagner, *Emergency State: How We Lost Our Freedoms in the Pandemic and Why It Matters* (Penguin, 2022). Further, the regulations proclaimed that 'workers should try to minimise all meetings and other gatherings' and 'only absolutely necessary participants should attend meetings and should maintain 2 m separation throughout'. The dating can be taken from para. 24 of Sue Gray's report: 'From 26 March 2020 the law in England required everyone to remain in their homes unless certain, very limited, exemptions applied. Restrictions were temporarily eased over the summer period in 2020 until most remaining national restrictions were removed on 4 July 2020. Restrictions were then reintroduced in gradations in the autumn culminating in the UK Government announcing from 5 November 2020 restrictions on movements and gatherings in England, essentially requiring people to stay at home. Restrictions on gatherings of two or more people applied in London through December 2020 and the first months of 2021. Indoor mixing of two or more households was not permitted again until 17 May 2021.'

44 Later it emerged that Johnson described one party as 'the most socially undistanced'; ITV podcast *Partygate: The Inside Story*, January 2023.

45 Martin Kettle in the *Guardian* of 9 December 2021 said: 'in less than a minute, the video captures all the shallow amateurism of modern politics; its absence of moral awareness, its capacity for abysmal judgment and its corrosive sense of entitlement, acted out against the backdrop of a wholly unnecessary flag draped in the briefing room…'. Stratton took the blame and resigned in a tearful recorded event outside her Islington home.

46 Press conference, 21 May 2020.

47 Cummings explicitly accused Johnson of lying about this event: Payne, *The Fall of Boris Johnson*, p. 52.

48 It is ironic that it took place in the same garden in which Cummings had made his cringeworthy defence of his own conduct in evading COVID rules by going to Barnard Castle about a year earlier.

49 Martin Reynolds (dubbed 'Party Marty') later sent a WhatsApp message welcoming the fact that 'we seem to have got away with' a restriction-busting gathering.

50 On 13 and 27 November 2020 there were gatherings in Number 10 Downing Street on the departure of a special adviser. On 10 December 2020 there was a party in the Department for Education ahead of the Christmas break. Senior officials and special advisers attended the event. Food and alcohol were available and it lasted for around an hour. On 15 December a Christmas quiz took place.

51 The Metropolitan Police statement said that 'as a result of information provided by the Cabinet Office investigation team, as well as assessments made by Metropolitan Police officers, they are investigating the events … with the exception of the gatherings on: 15 May 2020, 27 November 2020, 10 December 2020 and 15 December 2020'. The Cabinet Office in June 2023 referred several diary entries for Chequers which

appeared to show that gatherings had taken place there in breach of the Regulations but the police decided to take no action, for reasons which remain obscure.

52 There was some evidence about a party hosted on 19 June 2021 which was not covered in Sue Gray's report.

53 Oborne, *The Assault on Truth*, p. 163.

54 There were a series of denials. On 1 December 2021 he said 'All guidance was followed completely in No 10'; on 7 December 'I can tell you that the guidelines were followed at all times. I have satisfied myself that the guidelines were followed'; on 8 December after the appearance of the Allegra Stratton video, 'I have been repeatedly assured that the rules were not broken'; and on 13 December 'I can tell you once again that I certainly broke no rules'.

55 Rishi Sunak, who eventually replaced Johnson, also received a fine for attendance at a party.

56 She started as a civil servant in the 1970s but then ran the Cove Bar near Newry, County Down, for a few years before returning to work in the Cabinet Office under Tony Blair and Gordon Brown. In David Cameron's administration she rose to be director general of the propriety and ethics team in 2012. She then joined the Northern Ireland civil service and was later with the Department for Levelling Up. She subsequently left the civil service to become Keir Starmer's Chief of Staff, which was in itself a controversial appointment (see Chapter 6).

57 The report, formally entitled *Findings of Second Permanent Secretary's Investigation into Alleged Gatherings on Government Premises During Covid Restrictions*, appeared on 25 May 2022.

58 Some also asked how the matter had not been noticed by the police earlier, given that they were ever-present in Downing Street throughout this period. The general police answer to this question was that this was not their role. The Met had first said that they would refuse to investigate these parties on the basis they did not investigate offences retrospectively, which is patently absurd (although presumably they meant that it was not appropriate to probe events so long ago, especially when the potential punishment was only a fixed penalty notice).

59 Sue Gray described her role as follows at para. 13: 'My task was to establish a general understanding of the nature of the gatherings in scope. This was not intended to be an exhaustive process; nor was its purpose to determine individual wrongdoing or to produce a definitive, line by line narrative of each event. Rather the objective was to establish the broad facts of what took place at these gatherings, taking into account that some took place nearly two years ago.'

60 The report makes very little mention of Johnson himself and does not even say precisely whose leadership failed. The Scottish National Party's leader in the Commons, Ian Blackford, called the report 'a fact-finding exercise with no facts'.

61 General finding iii in the first report was: 'There were failures of leadership and judgment by different parts of Number 10 and the Cabinet Office at different times. Some of the events should not have been allowed to take place. Other events should not have been allowed to develop as they did.'

62 Johnson responded 'The revelations in Sue Gray's report shocked the public, and they shocked me', which will surprise some.

63 BBC Radio 4, *The World This Weekend*, 17 April 2022. Further, Robert Peston, the ITN political editor, said that this was 'perhaps the most important test of the robustness and efficacy of the checks and balances in the British constitution of my lifetime'.

64 John Major's speech to the IFG reported in the *Guardian*, 11 February 2022. He also said 'day after day the public were asked to believe the unbelievable'.

65 It was claimed by Laura Kuenssberg in a programme aired on the BBC in September 2023 that civil servants had considered warning the Queen about Johnson's unfitness.

66 See Chapter 14.

67 This describes the creation of successive chaotic distractions (causing situations to become confused) to get out of scrapes. Johnson metaphorically puts a dead cat on the table so that people are distracted from the real issue.

68 This was a phrase which had been used by Vince Cable in an article on 16 September 2017 in the *Independent*.

69 Mirza was followed out of the Number 10 door by Elena Narozanski, who had been in charge of the equalities brief in the Number 10 Policy Unit.

70 'Chris Pincher suspended as Tory MP after groping allegation', BBC News online, 1 July 2022, at www.bbc.co.uk/news/uk-politics-62014765 (accessed 12 June 2023).

71 In July 2023 he was suspended from the House of Commons.

72 The Speaker told the BBC that the revolving of ministers had reached 'bizarre' proportions and that 'we never knew who was going to be at the dispatch box'. See the *Guardian*, 27 December 2022.

73 Javid had previously resigned on 13 February 2020 as Chancellor, after Johnson said he would insist that Javid replace all of his advisers if he was to stay in the role.

74 He made similarly tasteless remarks when he resigned as an MP in June 2023, including describing the Committee on Standards as a 'kangaroo court'. Seven MPs and two Lords, close supporters of Johnson, were found guilty of undermining procedures of the House of Commons.

75 He likened himself to Cincinnatus returning to his plough; the fifth-century statesman left Rome for his farm only to be called in due course to return as a dictator.

76 Since leaving Downing Street Johnson has declared earnings of more than £5 million for speeches abroad, including in India, Portugal, Singapore and the US.

77 The Ministerial Code, para. 1.3, says that 'Ministers must not use government resources for Party political purposes'.

78 WhatsApp messages were lost in April 2021 amid security precautions when it was found that PM's phone number was listed on the internet, according to a statement by Sarah Harrison, Chief Operating Officer at the Cabinet Office.

79 *Guardian*, 22 June 2022.

80 Isabel Oakeshott and Michael Ashcroft, *Call Me Dave* (Biteback, 2016).

81 Interviewed 7 October 2022.

82 *Financial Times*, 23 May 2022.

83 BBC Radio 4, *The World This Weekend*, 17 April 2022.

4. The Independent Adviser on Ministers' Interests

1 This chapter concentrates on ministers. The Commons and Lords Committees on Standards have jurisdiction in relation to bullying and harassment in Parliament.

2 He had been Principal Private Secretary to the Chancellor and the Prime Minister, Chair of the Joint Intelligence Committee, Permanent Secretary at the Ministry of Justice and High Commissioner to Australia.

3 Her successor as Home Secretary, Suella Braverman, shares many of these characteristics.

4 She was dismissed by Liz Truss as Home Secretary in September 2022 and not reappointed by Rishi Sunak.

5 This was a feature of the Tolley report into the actions of Dominic Raab (see later in the chapter). Policy paper, *Investigation Report to the Prime Minister. Report of Formal*

Complaints about the Conduct of the Rt Hon Dominic Raab MP, Deputy Prime Minister, Lord Chancellor and Secretary of State for Justice, 21 April 2023.

6   *The Times* reported that this settlement included a payment of £340,000.

7   Correspondence on 21 November 2022.

8   In the court case that followed, the judges record that 'We were, however, told by counsel during the hearing and in a note following the hearing that a section of the report (said to contain the findings of the Cabinet Office) was provided to the Prime Minister as an annex to a submission made by the Cabinet Secretary on 31 July 2020. Neither that section of the report nor the submission itself were provided again to the Prime Minister when he took his decision on 18 November 2020 on what, if any, action to take in the light of the allegations that had been made.' *R (on application of FDA)* v. *The Prime Minister* [2021] EWHC 3279 (Admin.).

9   Sir Alex Allan told me that 'I could not interview Philip Rutnam because of strong legal advice that it would not be appropriate to do so since he was in the middle of a legal action.'

10 See Chapter 15.

11 *USPL.*

12 Under the Ministerial Code, all ministers are required upon appointment to each new role to complete a form giving information about their financial interests, including both assets and liabilities. Sir Alex Allan, the former Independent Adviser on Ministers' Interests, told me that 'Ministerial declaration of interests were generally well done'.

13 There are separate codes for the devolved administrations in Scotland, Wales and Northern Ireland. None are legally binding. They are differently policed.

14 Further, 'Public officers carry out their duties for the benefit of the public as a whole. If they neglect or misconduct themselves in the course of those duties this may lead to a breach or abuse of the public's trust.'

15 See Chapter 3 for partygate and Chapter 1 for the Seven Principles.

16 Green's situation is a particularly useful contrast. The report on his conduct was produced over the signature of Jeremy Heywood, then Cabinet Secretary. Green was required to resign as the First Secretary of State (in effect the Deputy Prime Minister) after admitting he had not told the full story about the presence of pornographic images on his House of Commons computer, which arose in an investigation dating back to 2008. This remains quite a confused case. The investigation found that Green's vehement denials after a Sunday newspaper reported that porn had been found were 'inaccurate and misleading'. There was then a separate investigation into allegations by the journalist Kate Maltby, who said in *The Times* on 1 November 2017 that Green had made an unwanted advance towards her during a social meeting in 2015, had suggested that a relationship with him might further her career, and later had sent her an inappropriate text message. This allegation was found to be 'plausible' by Sue Gray's report, but Gray said it was not possible to reach any definitive conclusion on the appropriateness of his behaviour. Green was asked to resign and did, but whether this was really necessary is doubted by many.

17 *R (on application of FDA)* v. *The Prime Minister.*

18 The claimant Association stressed that it was not asking the court to express any view on whether the Home Secretary did any of the things she was alleged to have done, nor as to what sanctions would be appropriate for her. Those, the Association accepted, would be matters for the ultimate decision of the Prime Minister if it succeeded in its claim and if the Prime Minister decided to reopen the matter.

19 He took evidence from sixty people. The *Investigation Report to the Prime Minister* was published on 24 April 2023.

20 He decided that Raab made 'unfairly personal criticism' of individuals, including telling one person their work was 'utterly useless' and 'woeful'.

21 His resignation letter of 21 April 2023 said that the report's 'two adverse findings are flawed and set a dangerous precedent for the conduct of good Government.... Ministers must be able to give direct critical feedback on briefings and submissions to senior officials, in order to set the standards and drive the reform the public expect of us.... In setting the threshold for bullying so low, this inquiry has set a dangerous precedent. It will encourage spurious complaints against Ministers, and have a chilling effect....' He told the inquiry the civil service had 'culture resistance' to some government policies. If he had not resigned he would probably have been dismissed.

22 Curiously he was given a second knighthood in 2014.

23 The failure to appoint for a long period stymied an inquiry into allegations of racism made by the former Transport Minister Nusrat Ghani MP against a ministerial colleague. This situation is unsatisfactory: see para. 81 of PACAC, *Propriety of Governance in Light of Greensill: An Interim Report*, Third Report of Session 2021–22, HC 59, 20 July 2021.

24 When the first one, Philip Mawer, was appointed, the Independent Adviser's investigatory remit was extended to include all breaches of the Ministerial Code and not just those relating to private interests.

25 Sir Alex also held investigations of the ministers Mark Field and Alun Cairns.

26 *Prospect*, June 2021, p. 8.

27 See Chapter 15.

28 Interviewed 12 January 2023.

29 Independent Adviser, Oral evidence to PACAC, 13 May 2021, response to Q24.

30 Independent Adviser on Ministers' Interests [Lord Geidt], *Annual Report*, May 2021, para. 6.

31 See Chapter 14.

32 Even the Johnson-supporting *Daily Mail* weighed in with a classic headline about the Prime Minister and his wallpaper, 'Pasted but not Hung', in describing Lord Geidt's first report on the subject. See p. 52 for the email trail.

33 There was also a complaint made under section 18 of the Members' Code to the Parliamentary Commissioner for Standards because he had not declared gifts over £300 as he should but she dismissed the complaint as being outside her jurisdiction.

34 Considered further in Chapter 16.

35 Electoral Commission, *Report of Investigation into the Conservative and Unionist Party – Recording and Reporting of Payments*, 9 December 2021

36 A donation is defined in the Act as 'any gift to the party of money or other property'. Under section 65(4) of the PPERA, the treasurer of a registered party commits an offence if, without reasonable excuse, she or he delivers a donation report to the Commission which does not comply with any requirements of the PPERA as regards the recording of donations in such a report.

37 The firm of solicitors Edwards Duthie Shamash acting for the Labour Party wrote to Lord Geidt on 4 January 2022 that 'the apparent failure' of the investigation to obtain the WhatsApp messages was 'more than unfortunate'. It also wrote to the Metropolitan Police suggesting that bribery may have been committed. Neither yielded anything.

38 Lord Geidt and John McDonnell to PACAC, 14 June 2022.

39 John Crace, 'Lord Geidt, the ultimate stooge, struggles to maintain the illusion of authority', *Guardian*, 14 June 2022.

40 The resignation letter went on in a courtly manner, 'A deliberate breach, or even an intention to do so, would be to suspend the provisions of the Code to suit a political end. This would make a mockery not only of respect for the Code but license the suspension of its provisions in governing the conduct of Her Majesty's Ministers. I can have no part in this.' Johnson had asked Geidt to consider the possibility of placing tariffs on steel, which would have broken the rules of the World Trade Organization (WTO), to which the UK was a party. Geidt explained this in his letter of resignation on 16 June 2022. Johnson's reply said it had been his intention to seek Geidt's 'advice on the national interest in protecting a crucial industry, which is protected in other European countries and would suffer material harm if we do not continue to apply such tariffs. This has in the past had cross-party support. It would be in line with our domestic law but might be seen to conflict with our obligations under the WTO.'

41 The Northern Ireland Act 1998 says that there must be a Ministerial Code and this must have certain provisions which can be changed only by cross-community agreement in the Northern Ireland Assembly.

42 Interviewed 7 July 2022. The reference to 'steel tariffs' relates to the Trade Remedies Authority issue mentioned above.

43 *USPL*, p. 9.

44 Interviewed 21 September 2022.

45 Recommendation 7 of *USPL*.

46 *USPL*.

47 This is developed further in Chapter 16.

48 *USPL*, paras 3.16, 3.17. As the CSPL said: 'Elements of the code that concern important governing processes, such as cabinet committees and ministerial management of the Civil Service, should be placed in the Cabinet Manual, where much of the relevant material is already duplicated' (para. 3.13). The Labour Party policy is that 'the code of conduct for ministers should be separated out from the day to day procedures for the operation of government, and set out in a code which is not determined by the Prime Minister of the day, but continuing and proposed to and approved by both Houses of Parliament'. Labour Party, *A New Britain: Renewing our Democracy and Rebuilding Our Economy*, 5 December 2022, p. 129.

49 See also *USPL*, para. 3.24.

5. The public appointments system and CPA

1 Interviewed 21 March 2022.

2 Interviewed 12 December 2022.

3 Some of this chapter appears in R. Johnson *et al.*, *Sceptical Perspectives* (Hart, 2023).

4 The OBE was awarded for services to education.

5 This included being an *ex officio* member of the Executive Committee of UK Research and Innovation.

6 Reported in *Financial Times*, 5 February 2022.

7 The *Financial Times* on 4 February 2022 reported 'One ally of Kwarteng said the minister was worried about Michie's previous political affiliations and about whether the ESRC would be politically impartial under his leadership and what sort of research it might fund'.

8 Number 10 had already objected to Sir Andrew Dilnot, who is Warden of Nuffield College, Oxford, another distinguished economist and not party political, sitting on the appointment panel.

9 *Research Fortnight*, 10 February 2022, available at www.researchprofessionalnews. com/rr-news-uk-views-of-the-uk-2022-2-kwarteng-s-esrc-intervention-crosses-a-line (accessed 27 July 2023).

10 Interviewed 18 November 2022.

11 Interviewed 24 March 2022.

12 For example, Lord Brownlow at the Royal Albert Hall; he was also involved in wallpapergate – see Chapter 3.

13 Richard Brooks, 'Defiant British Museum appoints Mary Beard as trustee', *Guardian*, 28 March 2020.

14 Of course, from time to time a friend of the minister may be the most appropriate appointment, but that should not be the reason for the appointment or one of them.

15 He subsequently chaired the British Transport Police Authority, and was himself turned down for a second term in the role by the *Labour* government.

16 The role played by SpAds is analysed below.

17 Interviewed 2 November 2022.

18 As Elizabeth David-Barrett of the University of Sussex Centre for the Study of Corruption commented to me on 30 January 2021: 'The public appointments system demonstrates a rewarding loyalty, buying loyalty culture. There is an element of state capture about it.'

19 For example, a well-placed Tory donor has shown me that on 12 August 2019 Jacqueline Neagle, executive assistant in the Treasurer's Department at Conservative headquarters, wrote to donors: 'It is important Conservatives rebalance the representation at the head of important public bodies'.

20 OCPA, *Report*, November 2020.

21 Interviewed 12 January 2023.

22 Sir Peter Riddell, Pre-valedictory speech, May 2021.

23 *Who's Accountable? Relationships Between Government and Arm's-Length Bodies*, Government Response to the Committee's First Report of Session 2014–15, March 2015.

24 Baroness Donaghy described the process as having been 'Grimstoned' in the debate on standards in public life on Thursday 9 September 2021 (*Hansard*, vol. 814). The pre-Grimstone public appointments process is detailed in the Commissioner for Public Appointments, *Code of Practice for Ministerial Appointments to Public Bodies*, August 2009.

25 The relevant agencies may be called parastatals, indirect public administrative bodies, bureaux, or commissions.

26 The Public Appointments Order in Council 2019.

27 See Chapters 1 and 2.

28 As Dame Rennie Fritchie, the then CPA, herself explained in evidence to the CSPL on 18 May 2004, 'If I remember why my office was set up in the first place, it was set up to ensure that cronyism was not the order of the day, and it was set up to ensure people who were appointed were fit for appointment'.

29 CSPL, *10th Report*, para. 2.10.

30 Interviewed 7 July 2022.

31 Interviewed 20 March 2022. He was Conservative Chief Whip and is now Transport Secretary.

32 As seen in the Michie case.

33 See CSPL, *10th Report*, para. 2.76.

34 Each candidate is different and has different skills and experience, so the questioning should reflect that. As one experienced appointee told me, often there is nothing asked about intelligence, commitment, personality, eloquence and so on. Another person experienced in the area told me that selection is based less on personal qualities and qualifications but more on the ability to 'talk the current business babble', as she put it. She went on: 'This fluent business babble disguises any real commitment and experience'.

35 Interviewed 15 February 2022.

36 As the 2020/2021 OCPA *Annual Report* says, 'The Commissioner has continued to make it clear that ministers have ample opportunities to shape the appointments process within the Code, and that the decision on whom to appoint is always for them to make while advisory assessment panels, with an independent element, have the critical role in assessing appointability'.

37 See also OCPA, *Adjudication on the Chairmanship of the Charity Commission*, March 2022. This post is discussed below. See *Guardian*, 3 January 2018.

38 Cabinet Office, *Governance Code for Public Appointments* (2016), clause 3.2.

39 See the case of Jonathan Michie above.

40 The 2020/2021 *Annual Report* of the OCPA reported that sixty-seven people were either appointed without competition or extended in their interim positions following consultation with the Commissioner.

41 Nolan Committee's *Recommendations*, p. 5.

42 By comparison, 900 new appointments and 651 reappointments were made in the 2019/2020 financial year.

43 The Commissioner oversees the appointments, which are made to over 300 public bodies by ministers in Whitehall and another fifty-six by the Welsh government. There are some apparent anomalies of coverage that are created by the split between the non-executive roles policed by the CPA and executive jobs, which are outside his or her remit. As an example, the CPA does not regulate the Governor and Deputy Governor of the Bank of England because they are executives, but it does cover the Court of the Bank, namely the non-executives who form what elsewhere would be seen as a board of directors.

44 CPA, 2020/2021 *Annual Report*, p. 2.

45 Sir David Normington said in a letter to *The Times* of 14 February 2023 that this reduced the CPA to a 'commentator whose advice is easily discounted'.

46 Interviewed 5 February 2022.

47 There are family connections to the Tory Party. Shawcross' daughter is a former special adviser to George Osborne, is currently a non-executive director of the DWP and is married to Lord Wolfson, a Conservative life peer. Shawcross said laconically to the PACAC hearing that was held to confirm his appointment on 16 September 2021 that he could not rule out discussing around the dinner table with these members of his family matters which touched on his role.

48 Riddell said in the OCPA's 2020/2021 *Annual Report* that 'it is quite reasonable for ministers to suggest names and also to reject the advice of an advisory assessment panel and to order the re-running of a competition. But what is against the spirit of the Code is to seek to influence the work of an assessment panel by leaking the names of preferred candidates beforehand which can be, and has been, a deterrent and discouragement to other potential applicants from putting their names forward.' In his *Annual Report* for 2019/2020, he noted that telling the press 'someone is a favoured candidate for a post – or has been effectively lined-up – is damaging, not only by appearing to

pre-judge the outcome of an open competition but also by discouraging other strong and credible candidates from applying.'

49 Sunak was Chancellor at the time of appointment.

50 The BBC Director General, Tim Davie, is a former Conservative councillor, and Robbie Gibb, who is on the board of governors, was a communications director in Downing Street under Theresa May. Curiously, Gibb is the sole shareholder of the *Jewish Chronicle*, which has been running a series of attacks on the BBC. This is not confined to the Conservatives: under New Labour Gavyn Davies was made Chair of the BBC, while his wife Sue Nye ran the personal side of Gordon Brown's office.

51 The PM and Culture Secretary receive advice from a BBC appointments panel of four people, who must run a 'fair and open' competition.

52 The BBC Radio 4 *Today* programme, 22 November 2021. Dowden was later sacked as the Culture Minister by Johnson primarily it seems for not pushing Dacre's candidacy with sufficient vigour.

53 Lord Puttnam, in his Shirley Williams Memorial Lecture, 15 October 2021, said 'when the PM actively – and repeatedly – intervenes to manipulate an ideological ally into the chairmanship of Ofcom, every alarm bell should start to ring signalling the absolute nonsense that's being made of the regulator's independence'. He also commented it should not be 'in the hands of anyone with a discordantly ideological turn of mind'.

54 I have been told privately that Dacre performed poorly at interview.

55 The CPA 2021/2022 *Annual Report* states at p. 28: 'The original competition, launched in February 2021, was subject to pre-briefing in the media, which the Commissioner has consistently raised with the government as a destructive and cynical tool to distort the fair running of a competition and discourage applications... The Commissioner noted that a new competition must be, and seen to be, genuinely fresh, rather than an attempt to get a different answer from the outcome of the first competition.'

56 The 'Blob' was the term used by Michael Gove to describe the liberals in the education establishment who opposed his reforms when he was Secretary of State for Education. The use of this pejorative term was criticised by John Major in his speech to the Institute for Government in January 2022.

57 Grade's predecessor was a genuine independent, Lord Burns, a former senior civil servant.

58 Jane Martinson in the *Guardian* on 25 March 2022 said: 'His trenchant views could not have been more visible if he had lit them up on ticker tape – essentially big broadcasters and platforms are bad, free speech and Conservatives are good'. 'One more lapse' refers to the then recent revelations about how the BBC had secured the interview with Princess Diana through Martin Bashir. Alan Rusbridger also exposed an attempt by Robbie Gibb to gain the appointment of Lord Gilbert as Chair of the BBC; see *New European*, 20 November 2023.

59 *Guardian*, 11 February 2021.

60 Cabinet Office, *Better Public Appointments: A Review of the Public Appointments Process*, March 2016 (Grimstone report), para. 3.3.

61 CPA, *Annual Report*, 2020/2021, p. 23.

62 See Chapter 7 in relation to the House of Lords.

63 George Osborne is the odd one out as Chair of the British Museum; he was a Conservative Cabinet minister but not, so far as is known, a donor.

64 *Sunday Times*, 20 February 2022. See also Simon Heffer, *Daily Telegraph*, 22 January 2023.

65 Amersi was also a client of Elliot's concierge business Quintessentially.

66 Harding presided over the loss of 150,000 customers' details when in this role.

67   This was put in the court decision on the Good Law Project case at para. 82: 'The programme for this was initially led from within the Department for Health and Social Care, but the Secretary of State decided it would not be possible for the capacity required to be developed at speed either within his department or by Public Health England, the organisation which then had responsibility for diagnostic testing. He decided a new organisation was required with dedicated leadership. This organisation came to be known as NHS Test and Trace.'

68   Kate Bingham had been working for thirty years at SV Health Investors.

69   Pre-pandemic, Harding was appointed as Chair of NHS Improvement, a quango, through the normal process. Secondly, she was brought in to run COVID Test and Trace. She was also subsequently appointed to be the head of the National Institute of Public Health without open competition and then expressed publicly the wish to become leader of the whole NHS, from which competition she withdrew.

70   Jeremy Farrar and Anjana Ahuja, *Spiked* (Profile Books, 2021), p. 145.

71   A friend of mine who was a Labour Party member applied for this post. She had worked in the charity sector, run a charity, been a charity trustee and been on the bill committee for the reform of charity law. She had been instrumental in the setting up of the community fund. She was not even short-listed for the role.

72   *Guardian*, 8 November 2021.

73   Ironically, Nadine Dorries as Secretary of State said on his appointment on 10 December 2021: 'I look forward to working with Martin as he takes on this important post, ensuring public confidence in our charities is maintained'.

74   Thomas said: 'I was not sure whether a company that advertised using sexual content should be partnered with a charity which helped women escape sexual violence. I took a photo of an item for sale in a Victoria's Secret store which I felt was appropriate to illustrate my point. Instead of sending it to the charity CEO … I sent it in error to another colleague. I apologised immediately….'

75   See OCPA, *Report*, March 2022, para. 4.

76   Evidence to the House of Commons Digital, Culture, Media and Sport Committee.

77   *Guardian*, 12 January 2022. The Committee also lambasted William Shawcross, who had given evidence before it, for indicating that, as the CPA, he was already 'satisfied with the process', a judgement he made before he had been able fully to investigate it. Shawcross had told the Committee that the appointment process was difficult and controversial but 'not a tragedy'.

78   His father-in-law, Earl Peel, has close links with the Palace.

79   Dipesh Gadher and Gabriel Pogrund, 'Royal links of the watchdog that oversees prince's charities', *Sunday Times*, 31 July 2022.

80   For example, the Commission cleared the Prince of Wales Charitable Fund when it had accepted €3 million handed in a suitcase and Fortnum & Mason bags in cash, which is counter-intuitive.

81   Interviewed 10 May 2022.

82   Ruth Levitt calculated even in 2013 that more than 300 tsars had been appointed since 1997, more than 100 of them by coalition ministers alone. Gordon Brown holds the ministerial record, with forty-six appointments in all, twenty-three as Chancellor and twenty-three as Prime Minister. David Cameron appointed twenty-one, Michael Gove eleven. Levitt's research suggests that tsars come principally from business (40% of the total) and the public service (37%); several are serving or former politicians (18%) and the rest include academics and researchers, lawyers and media people. Some are specialists, others are generalists, or advocates with known views. Overall,

they are strikingly un-diverse: predominantly male (85%), white (98%), over fifty years old on appointment (83%), and indeed 38% were titled. Ruth Levitt, *Whitehall Watch*, 17 October 2013.

83 See for example Frank Vibert, *The Rise of the Unelected: Democracy and the New Separation of Powers* (Cambridge University Press, 2007), p. 80.

84 See Robert Hazell *et al.*, *Critical Friends? The Role of Non-Executives on Whitehall Boards* (Constitution Unit, 2018).

85 See Ruth Levitt and William Solesbury, *Evidence-Informed Policy: What Difference Do Outsiders in Whitehall Make?* (Economic and Social Research Council, 2016) and Jonathan McClory, Vanessa Quinlan and Zoe Gruhn, *All Aboard? Whitehall's New Governance Challenge* (Institute for Government, 2011).

86 Institute for Government, *Government Departments' Boards and Non-Executive Directors* (2021).

87 Interviewed 7 December 2022.

88 *Guardian*, 30 June 2021.

89 See Hazell *et al.*, *Critical Friends?*, p. 10.

90 Interviewed 18 October 2022.

91 *USPL*, recommendation 25.

92 Interviewed 30 May 2022.

93 Interviewed 15 February 2022.

94 Riddell pointed to 'misunderstandings about what is an inherently political process' so that politicisation is not the correct term (evidence to CSPL, in *USPL*). Para. 5.4 of the Appointments Code is encouraging: 'Ministers should feel free to put names forward to the Advisory Assessment Panel for interview'.

95 Interviewed 22 March 2022.

96 Interviewed 28 March 2022.

97 As another example, Tony Blair ennobled his flatmate Charles Falconer and made him Lord Chancellor, replacing Derry Irvine, Blair's former head of chambers.

98 OCPA, *Third Report*, 1997/1998, pp. 3–5; *Sixth Report*, 2000/2001, p. 4.

99 Someone who can bring a long perspective to the problem is Jackie Ashley, who used to write in the *Guardian*. She says: 'In terms of historic issues, I well remember Labour ministers offering their pals various roles, including Children's Commissioner at one point. But I don't think there was as much pressure in those days to ensure that no one of a different political persuasion was ever given anything.'

100 Tax Payers' Alliance, 'Nearly half of last year's political quangocrats supported the Labour Party', 30 January 2020, available at www.taxpayersalliance.com/nearly_half_of_last_year_s_political_quangocrats_supported_the_labour_party (accessed 26 July 2023).

101 Interviewed 28 July 2022. I was told much the same by David Bennett, who headed the Number 10 Policy Unit under Blair, and Lord Wood of Anfield, who served as an adviser to Ed Miliband. The latter added, 'that is very different to what is happening now, when there is a real link between donations to the Conservative Party and appointments. Appointments are handled centrally by a few people in Downing Street; control from the centre is extended to cultural bodies and there is much pre-briefing.'

102 Answers to written questions, 10 March 2023.

103 There is a converse allegation that in Wales it is necessary to be close to the Labour Party to gain public appointments.

104 Interviewed February 2022.

105 Interviewed 2 February 2022.

106 In this context, it is worth noting that the Prime Minister directly appoints the Interception of Communications Commissioner and the Intelligence Services Commissioner under the Regulation of Investigatory Powers Act 2000, sections 57 and 59.

107 See Robert Hazell, 'Improving Parliamentary scrutiny of public appointments', *Parliamentary Affairs*, 72:2 (2018), 223–244. In 2007 the second Commissioner for Public Appointments, Janet Gaymer, expressed a series of important reservations: that pre-appointment hearings might deter good candidates, politicise and lengthen the appointments process; that committees would ask inappropriate questions; that ministerial accountability for appointments would be changed (evidence to Public Administration Select Committee, 2007).

108 See *USPL*, recommendation 22.

109 Budget Responsibility and National Audit Act 2011, section 11. See Chapter 9 also.

110 PACAC, *Pre-Appointment Hearings: Promoting Best Practice*, Tenth Report of Session 2017–19, HC 909, 17 September 2018, para. 11.

111 *Ibid.*

112 PACAC, *Propriety of Governance in Light of Greensill: An Interim Report*, Third Report of Session 2021–22, HC 59, 20 July 2021, para. 66.

6. The Advisory Committee on Business Appointments

1 *Hansard*, vol. 667, 12 November 1962, col. 1000.

2 As related to Peter Kellner and Lord Crowther Hunt in *The Civil Servants* (MacDonald, 1980), p. 199.

3 Anthony Courtney, *Sailor in a Russian Frame* (Johnson Publications, 1968), p. 63.

4 Select Committee on Ministers' Interests, HC 44-viiii, p. 220.

5 See Chapter 2.

6 CSPL, *Strengthening Transparency Around Lobbying*, 13 November 2013, para. 6.2.

7 See Chapter 2.

8 Quoted in PACAC, *Propriety of Governance in Light of Greensill: An Interim Report*, Third Report of Session 2021–22, HC 59, 20 July 2021, 2 December 2022, para. 16.

9 See Chapter 14.

10 *USPL*, para. 4. Government submission to the Standards Matter 2 Review – see *USPL*, para. 50.

11 Interviewed 2 September 2022.

12 Occasionally also an outsider is parachuted into Parliament and straight into the Cabinet, as in the cases of Frank Cousins by Harold Wilson and John Davies by Ted Heath. Neither of these was conspicuously successful. More recently, we have seen a diplomat/civil servant, David Frost, promoted to the House of Lords and the Cabinet by Johnson.

13 Also brought in again by Boris Johnson in 2021 to advise on civil service reform. Under Tony Blair there was also Geoff Mulgan, Wendy Thompson (from local government) and Peter Gershon.

14 He made peers of Admiral West and Digby Jones.

15 As David Hine and Gillian Peele put it, 'the presence of neutral civil servants at the heart of policy making and their sensitive knowledge of individuals, issues and processes, means that some of them command a market price on departure from public service that can appear at odds and occasionally may actually be at odds with, the

254

public service values with which they have been socialised'. David Hine and Gillian Peele, *The Regulation of Standards in British Public Life: Doing the Right Thing* (Manchester University Press, 2016), p. 154.

16 First-Tier Tribunal, Information Rights, Appeal Reference: EA/2016/0055, Advisory Committee on Business Appointments, 7 December 2018.

17 Lord Pickles on the PoliticsHome website (https://www.politicshome.com) The House, 9 October 2022.

18 Unlike MPs, ministers cannot hold outside appointments under any circumstances.

19 The BARs apply to the Diplomatic Service, the intelligence agencies and the armed forces as well as the Senior Civil Service (SCS). Individuals in the SCS who consider taking up an outside appointment are required to fill out an application form specifying any previous connection with the company through their work. This information is checked by the counter-signing officer in the relevant department and passed on to the ACOBA Secretariat, which makes a recommendation on the basis of its own research and with the aim of ensuring consistency with previous decisions.

20 'On leaving office, Ministers will be prohibited from lobbying Government for two years. They must also seek advice from the independent ACOBA about any appointments or employment they wish to take up within two years of leaving office. Former Ministers must abide by the advice of the Committee' (Ministerial Code, section 7.25).

21 Elizabeth David-Barrett has listed the various conflicts that may arise as: abuse of power to ingratiate oneself with a potential future employer; abuse of office; potential bribery; influencing former associates to implement or shape policy to benefit a potential new employer; undue influence or state capture; profiting financially from stature or knowledge gained while in public office; profiteering; representing a policy position in direct opposition to the government position, having previously represented the government on the same issue; switching sides and using privileged information or using one's powers while in public office to favour a company or industry in which one was previously employed; and regulatory capture.

22 On 14 October 2012 the *Sunday Times* published details of an undercover investigation in which journalists posed as working for a South Korean arms firm. High-ranking retired military officers agreed to use their contacts with ministers and colleagues on behalf of the fictitious firm for large payments. Of the eight approached, only two refused.

23 See ACOBA's 2005 *Annual Report*.

24 A report by Transparency International EU published in January 2017 analysed the career paths of former EU officials and indicated that 30% of Members of the European Parliament went on to work for organisations on the EU lobby register after their mandate and approximately one-third of the Commissioners serving under José Manuel Barroso as President of the Commission later took jobs in the private sector. Transparency International EU, *Access All Areas: When EU Politicians Become Lobbyists*, 31 January 2017.

25 CSPL, *Strengthening Transparency Around Lobbying*, para. 6.19.

26 Civil Service Code, 16 March 2015, www.gov.uk/government/publications/civil-service-code/the-civil-service-code (accessed 18 September 2023).

27 *Standards in Public Life: First Report of the Committee on Standards in Public Life*, 1995, p. 52.

28 *Ibid.*, ch. 3, para. 29.

29 *Ibid.*, para. 34.

30 Interviewed 11 January 2023.

31 See p. 179.

32 *USPL*, para. 4.19.

33 Hine and Peele, *The Regulation of Standards*, p. 194.

34 Bernard Jenkin, *Civil Service World*, 10 December 2013.

35 Jenkin also said that 'The line between public service and private gain is shamefully blurred'.

36 ACOBA, *Annual Reports*. The Committee's advice is provided to the Foreign Secretary if the applicant is from the Diplomatic Service; to the Defence Secretary for most Ministry of Defence staff, both civilian and military; to the First Ministers of Scotland and Wales in the case of applications from the devolved administrations; to the relevant Permanent Secretary if the applicant is a Special Adviser; and to the Prime Minister for all other Crown servants. The Committee publishes its advice in all cases where it is aware that the appointment or employment has been taken up and of course there may be some where it is not told.

37 ACOBA, 'Advice letter: Lieutenant General Sir Tyrone Urch, Independent Consultancy', 6 December 2021, available at www.gov.uk/government/publications/urch-tyrone-commander-home-command-standing-joint-command-in-the-uk-ministry-of-defence-acoba-advice/advice-letter-lieutenant-general-sir-tyrone-urch-independent-consultancy (accessed 20 June 2023).

38 *Ibid*. See also *Guardian*, 2 January 2024.

39 At least twelve civil servants have gone to work for Facebook (now Meta) over the last few years, including Nicola Aiken, who led the Counter Online Manipulation Team at the Department for Culture, Media and Sport until February 2021. The extensive interchange of staff between government and Uber is covered in Chapter 10.

40 Douglas Carswell raised the issue in Parliament of a contract to buy sixty-two Lynx Wildcat helicopters from Agusta/Westland, a subsidiary of that firm.

41 *The Times*, 13 April 2021.

42 His career is forensically taken apart by Ian Dunt in his book *How Westminster Works: And What Happens When It Doesn't* (Orion Publishing, 2023), pp. 1–28.

43 He resigned in order to be free to vote against the government's policy on Brexit.

44 See House of Commons Public Administration and Constitutional Affairs Committee, *Managing Ministers' and Officials' Conflicts of Interest: Time for Clearer Values, Principles and Action*, 18 April 2017. They should be reported to the Cabinet Office.

45 Interviewed 7 July 2022.

46 *USPL*, para. 4.33.

47 Similar issues arose with the definition of public appointments. See Chapter 5.

48 Bill Crothers also started in this shadowy role before being appointed as Chief Procurement Officer for the Government.

49 ACOBA said: 'We disapprove of the announcement of Mr Osborne's appointment as Editor of the *Evening Standard* without waiting for ACOBA's advice. This demonstrates disrespect for ACOBA and for the Business Appointment Rules and sets an unhelpful example to others in public life who may be tempted to do the same' (para. 75). Osborne also became an investment manager at BlackRock and chair of the advisory committee at Expor, an investment firm.

50 He was also a partner at Buckthorn, a fund manager, and a non-executive director at Ardagh Group, a packaging company.

51 'I do not consider it was in keeping with the letter or the spirit of the government's rules for the former chancellor to contact HMT on behalf of a bank which pays for his advice', Pickles wrote to Michael Gove. See the *Guardian*, 26 November 2021.

52 John Bowers, *A Practical Approach to Employment Law*, 8th edition (Oxford University Press, 2019).

53 *Review of Business Appointment Rules*, 25 February 2005.

54 House of Commons Public Administration Select Committee, *Business Appointment Rules*, HC 404, 17 July 2012.

55 Public Administration and Constitutional Affairs Committee, *Managing Ministers' and Officials' Conflicts of Interest*, para. 145.

56 Committee on Standards in Public Life, *Reinforcing Standards*, 12 January 2000, para. 11.3.

57 *Ibid.*, para. 11.25.

58 See Chapter 14.

59 See below.

60 The Permanent Secretaries at each department were asked to check how many of their civil servants had other jobs in the private sector but in fact there were very few which occasioned any concern. Most such 'second jobs' which were combined with civil service roles were on the lines of being governors of schools, where there would be no conflict of interest.

61 See Chapter 14.

62 Interviewed 21 September 2022.

63 Interviewed 22 March 2022.

64 Liz Truss retained Mark Fullbrook as Chief of Staff on a consultancy basis, and instances like that would be covered by the system.

65 See PACAC, *Propriety of Governance*, para. 23.

66 CSPL, *Strengthening Transparency Around Lobbying*, recommendation 6.

67 *Ibid.*, recommendation 8.

68 PACAC, *Managing Ministers' and Officials' Conflicts of Interest*, para. 63. PACAC *Propriety of Governance*, para. 29.

69 Interviewed 7 July 2022.

70 See Chapter 14.

71 *USPL*, para. 4.31.

72 PACAC, *Propriety of Governance*, para. 35.

73 *The Times*, 4 July 2023.

7. Appointments to the House of Lords

1 It has twenty-five bishops, 666 life peers and ninety-one hereditary peers.

2 The Labour Party called for its abolition in the Commission presided over by Gordon Brown in December 2022. Commission on the UK's Future, *A New Britain: Renewing Our Democracy and Rebuilding Our Economy*, Labour Party, 5 December 2022.

3 This is inevitably impossible to verify.

4 *Daily Telegraph*, 13 July 2006.

5 In the aftermath of the poisoning of Alexander Litvinenko, Lebedev approvingly tweeted a *Daily Mail* article asking whether MI6 had some involvement, saying: 'Was Litvinenko murdered by MI6? … Certainly, more to it than the generally accepted Putin link.'

6 The Tortoise website reported that Lebedev had sought to set up an unmonitored phone line between Johnson, the then Foreign Secretary, and Lavrov, the Russian Foreign Minister, to discuss the Salisbury poisonings, which had happened nearly two

months earlier. But the call never took place because Johnson overslept. There was also a meeting at City Hall in London in 2015 with Lebedev and Mikhail Piotrovsky, Director of the Russian State Hermitage Museum, the latter being an associate of Putin.

7   *Hansard*, vol. 711, 29 March 2022, col. 743.
8   Letter to William Wragg as Chair of PACAC, 22 December 2020.
9   *Sunday Times*, 6 March 2022.
10 Parliamentary debate, 12 May 2022, on the Humble Address, available at https://questions-statements.parliament.uk/written-statements/detail/2022-05-12/hcws22 (accessed 18 September 2023).
11 *Guardian*, 13 May 2022.
12 Starmer wrote: 'The accusations made by Lord Lebedev that the British security services had any involvement in the murder of Alexander Litvinenko is insulting. I have seen first-hand the real impact of Russian interference in Britain and the difficulties prosecutors encounter when dealing with those who act on behalf of Putin. This is clearly a matter for national security.'
13 See 'How Boris Johnson's friendship with Evgeny Lebedev deepened despite MI6 concerns', *The Times*, 12 March 2022, available at www.thetimes.co.uk/article/how-boris-johnsons-friendship-with-evgeny-lebedev-deepened-despite-mi6-concerns-56bl5hklb (accessed 31 July 2023).
14 PACAC, Oral evidence: House of Lords Appointments Commission, HC 1238, 20 April 2022, available at https://committees.parliament.uk/oralevidence/10107/html (accessed 31 July 2023).
15 See also Chapter 2.
16 Information shared with the author by a confidential source.
17 *Ibid.*
18 He had to return £130,000 of the £180,000 in damages he had initially been awarded. Michael Spencer, Conservative Party Treasurer between 2007 and 2010 and founder of ICAP, had his nomination blocked by HoLAC at least three times. See Oliver Ralph and George Parker, 'Michael Spencer's allies decry unfairness in lack of peerage', *Financial Times*, 24 July 2016.
19 'Peter Cruddas: PM overrules watchdog with Tory donor peerage', BBC News website, 22 December 2020, at https://www.bbc.co.uk/news/uk-politics-55414981 (accessed 25 September 2023).
20 There was a vacancy on HoLAC after the resignation of Lord Moore in 2019. Just before he left office, Boris Johnson appointed Harry Mount, a journalist he worked with on the *Spectator*, as the new independent member from 11 September 2022, but he resigned within a month. See further in the Appendix.
21 Between 1925 and 2000 the Political Honours Scrutiny Committee was composed of a member from each of the three main parties and it scrutinised the list of appointees.
22 Lord Bew, evidence to PACAC, 20 April 2022.
23 Letter from Lord Bew to Sir Keir Starmer, 17 March 2022.
24 *Ibid.*
25 The Constitutional Reform and Governance Act 2010.
26 HoLAC, 'Guidance on political donations', December 2019, available at https://lordsappointments.independent.gov.uk/wp-content/uploads/2022/01/GUIDANCE-ON-POLITICAL-DONATIONS.docx-2.pdf (accessed 21 June 2023).
27 HoLAC, 'Vetting', available at https://lordsappointments.independent.gov.uk/vetting (accessed 31 July 2023).

28 Seth Thévoz, 'Want a seat in the House of Lords? Be Tory treasurer and donate £3m', *Open Democracy*, 6 November 2021, available at www.opendemocracy.net/en/dark-money-investigations/want-a-seat-in-the-house-of-lords-be-tory-treasurer-and-donate-3m (accessed 21 June 2023).

29 University of Oxford, Department of Economics Discussion Paper 744, March 2015.

30 Gwilym Gibbon Centre, Working Paper, 'Conservative Party Treasurers and peerages 1986–2016', undated work in progress.

31 HoLAC, 'Guidance on political donations'.

32 Gordon Brown, *Guardian*, 30 July 2022.

33 This included the appointment of Johnson's brother Jo, and Dominic Johnson, the founder with Jacob Rees-Mogg of Somerset Capital Company, became a Lord and Business Minister in October 2022. Boris Johnson also wanted his father to receive a knighthood.

34 *USPL*, para. 2.37.

35 House of Lords (Peerage Nominations) Bill, 7 June 2022, available at https://bills.parliament.uk/publications/46690/documents/1899 (accessed 22 June 2023).]

8. Party funding and the Electoral Commission

1 Lord Evans, Hugh Kay Lecture, the Institute of Business Ethics, 11 November 2020.

2 Prime Minister's Foreword to the Ministerial Code, Cabinet Office, May 2010.

3 See for example Matthew Bond, 'Elite social relations and corporate political donations in Britain', *Political Studies*, 55:1 (2007), 59–85.

4 Open Democracy, *Who Funds You?*, 2022.

5 *Scotsman*, 26 July 2022. He said that 'money talks and wealth whispers'.

6 Interviewed 8 January 2023.

7 See Chapter 13.

8 Speech delivered on 10 February 2022.

9 See Chapter 7. The exceptions are Sir Mick Davis and Sir Ehud Sheleg.

10 *The Times*, 2 June 2022.

11 Donors' funding of different political viewpoints at the same time suggests that they have no strong beliefs (unless they are even-handedly trying to reinforce democracy across the board, which we can probably discount). It is natural to wonder whether they have other motives. For example, Peter Virdee, a.k.a. Hardip Singh, backed both main horses in the political race, giving about £100,000 to the winning Conservatives and £2,000 to the Labour shadow minister Preet Gill. He was given a jail sentence of three years and three months by a Frankfurt court in December 2021 for his role in a £100 million international VAT fraud in Germany. He was also arrested by the National Crime Agency on suspicion of bribery of Commonwealth politicians in Antigua and St Kitts. See *The Times*, 23 March 2022. There is nothing to restrain him contributing more if he wishes.

12 *Guardian*, 27 February 2022.

13 Sascha Lavin, 'Major Russian donor funds Conservative member of Intelligence Committee', *Byline Times*, 29 June 2022.

14 *Guardian*, 18 November 2021.

15 *Spectator*, 25 June 2020.

16 Intelligence and Security Committee of Parliament, *Russia*, HC632, July 2020.

17 *The Times*, 13 May 2022.

18 The co-owner, Viktor Fedotov, was allegedly involved in a corruption scheme, which he denies.

19 The documents were disclosed after a freedom of information request. On 3 October 2019, Kwarteng said 'PS excellent to see you at the [Conservative] conference this year', which does tie the influence to the political giving. See *The Times*, 8 April 2021.

20 'The Tory donors with access to Boris Johnson's top team', *Sunday Times*, 19 February 2022.

21 Interviewed 22 March 2022.

22 Interviewed 21 February 2022.

23 Answers to written questions, 10 March 2023.

24 CSPL, *Fifth Report*, October 1998, Cm 4057-I, para. 11.7

25 Commissioners may be removed from office only by the King, on an Address from the Commons; but this must follow a report from the Speaker's Committee, stating its case that a statutory reason for removal is made out in respect of the Commissioner.

26 The Public Administration and Constitutional Affairs Committee published recommendations for reform on 20 October 2022. One of these is that the maximum penalty for rule breaches should be raised to £500,000, as the current maximum of £20,000 'may not act as an effective deterrent' for well-resourced parties and campaigners.

27 Stripping it of the power to bring prosecutions is also regressive.

28 PACAC, *The Elections Bill*, Fifth Report of Session 2021–22, 13 December 2021.

29 *Guardian*, 2 February 2022.

30 Interviewed 23 March 2022.

31 Interviewed 23 March 2022.

32 The offence charged was under s84 of the Representation of the People Act, where an election agent fails to deliver a true return of election expenses.

33 The judge said that 'she would be serving a prison sentence' had her husband not been 'gravely ill' (p. 7, lines 6–7 of the transcript of the judgement at www.judiciary.uk/wp-content/uploads/2019/01/marion-little-sentencing-remarks.pdf, accessed 3 August 2023).

34 *Ibid.*, p. 3, line 8 (my emphasis).

35 Interviewed 8 December 2022.

36 Interviewed 22 March 2022. Issues about whether extremist parties should be funded would need to be tackled.

37 Interviewed 8 December 2022.

38 See Chapter 4.

9. The CSPL and NAO

1 Interviewed 24 May 2022.

2 David Hine and Gillian Peele, *The Regulation of Standards in British Public Life* (Manchester University Press, 2016), p. 54.

3 Professor Peele was subsequently appointed in 2021 as a member of the CSPL.

4 *HC Deb.*, vol. 248, col. 758, 25 October 1994.

5 On 5 February 2013, the Committee's terms of reference were clarified following devolution so that 'in future the Committee should not inquire into matters relating to the devolved legislatures and governments except with the agreement of those bodies'.

6 See Chapter 5.

7 Interviewed 24 May 2022.

8 See Chapter 5.

9 Peter Riddell, *Report of the Triennial Review of the Committee on Standards in Public Life*, 19 December 2012.

10 See Public Administration Select Committee, Written evidence submitted by David Hine and Gillian Peele, 12 September 2013.

11 Public Administration Select Committee, *Ethics and Standards: The Regulation of Conduct in Public Life*, Fourth Report of Session 2006–07, HC 121-I, 19 April 2007, para. 100.

12 Interviewed 21 September 2022.

13 See Chapter 8.

14 Robert Hazell, Marcial Boo and Zachariah Pullar, *Parliament's Watchdogs: Independence and Accountability of Five Constitutional Regulators*, Constitution Unit, University College London, July 2022, para. 6.22.

15 The Committee's original terms of reference were: 'To examine current concerns about standards of conduct of all holders of public office, including arrangements relating to financial and commercial activities, and make recommendations as to any changes in present arrangements which might be required to ensure the highest standards of propriety in public life'. It does not investigate individual cases and says a flat no on the many occasions when opposition politicians call for it to do so. As an example, the Labour Party in March 2021 sought an investigation of David Cameron's involvement with Greensill Capital, which was not within the Committee's remit.

16 His intervention in the Owen Patterson case, for example, was when speaking to the IfG; this happened to be on the day the issue broke and was crucial in shaping the ethical conversation.

17 Interviewed 16 March 2022.

18 Interviewed 21 September 2022.

19 Riddell, *Report of the Triennial Review*.

20 Angela Rayner, the deputy leader of the Labour Party, told HuffPost UK: 'Out of 173 applicants, there must have been many candidates who were more representative of British society and eminently more qualified than the prime minister's chum'. The CSPL Code of Practice provides that 'Non MP Members must not hold any paid or high-profile unpaid office in a political party, and not engage in specific political activities on matters directly affecting the work of the Committee'.

21 Interviewed 24 May 2022.

22 Interviewed 21 September 2022.

23 Mark Philp told me: 'A really important question is how do you get the public to know what the rules are. There needs to be a better understanding of government among the public and this needs to start in schools.' Interviewed May 2022.

24 Tom Bower, *Boris Johnson: The Gambler* (W. H. Allen, 2020), p. 250. The Secretary of State for Transport formally directed his accounting officer to increase the Department's pre-construction exposure for a limited period, citing wider benefits to the government's agenda and the London economy.

25 HC 722, Session 2016–17, 11 October 2016. See also 'The Garden Bridge – executive summary', at www.london.gov.uk/sites/default/files/garden_bridge_review_1.pdf (accessed 23 September 2023).

26 See generally Margaret Hodge, *Called to Account* (Abacus, 2016).

27 The 2021–2022 *Annual Report* states: 'While our permanent staff numbers were 911 against a planned headcount of 940, we made up for this shortfall by the use of temporary staff to supplement our work during peak periods. Including these, staffing numbers for the year were the equivalent of 939 full-time employees' (p. 88).

28 The C&AG can be removed by the monarch only after an address has been passed against the office holder in both the House of Commons and the House of Lords. The Budget Responsibility and National Audit Act 2011 states: 'The Comptroller and Auditor General has complete discretion in the carrying out of the functions of that office, including in determining whether to carry out an examination … and as to the manner in which any such examination is carried out'. The C&AG must now 'have regard to any proposals made by the Committee of Public Accounts'.

29 See NAO, 'What is a value for money study?', available at www.nao.org.uk/about-us/wp-content/uploads/sites/12/2016/10/What-is-a-value-for-money-study.pdf (accessed 3 August 2023).

30 See Chapter 13. The NAO also studied MRSA infections, which led to increased public interest in the topic.

31 Oonagh Gay, 'The UK perspective: ad hocery at the centre', in *Parliament's Watchdogs: At the Crossroads*, ed. Oonagh Gay and Barry K. Winetrobe (Constitution Unit, 2008), pp. 17–31.

32 *Investigation into Government Procurement During the COVID-19 Pandemic*, HC 959, 26 November 2020.

33 This is based on the tool at www.bankofengland.co.uk/monetary-policy/inflation/inflation-calculator (accessed 3 August 2021).

34 For example, David Walker of the *Guardian* argues that the NAO does not and cannot examine major strategic issues such as the underlying principles of the Private Finance Initiative.

35 Simon D. Norton and L. Murphy Smith, 'Contrast and foundation of the public oversight roles of the U.S. Government Accountability Office and the U.K. National Audit Office', *Public Administration Review*, 68:5 (2008), 921–931.

36 Colin Talbot and Jay Wiggan, 'The public value of the National Audit Office', *International Journal of Public Sector Management*, 23:1 (2010), 54.

37 Interviewed 28 July 2022.

38 Marcial Boo, *The Rules of Democracy* (Policy Press, 2022), p. 94.

10. The Registrar of Consultant Lobbyists and the lobbying industry

1 Tamasin Cave and Andy Rowell, *Lobbying* (Bodley Head, 2014), p. 12.

2 *Reader's Digest*, January 1989.

3 *Guardian*, 11 July 2022.

4 Internal Uber documents stated that Johnson 'was basically on the side of the black taxis'. *Guardian*, 11 July 2022.

5 *Ibid.*

6 She also worked consecutively for Google, Facebook and Netflix.

7 See for example Patrick Radden Keefe, *Empires of Pain* (Picador, 2021) in relation to the Sackler family (involved in the pharmaceutical industry and epidemic in opioid use) and lobbying.

8 The Transparency International review showed the following bodies were the most common lobbyists for meetings with ministers since 2013: BAE Systems (aerospace), Local Government Association, the Confederation of British Industry, Airbus, BT, the Federation of Small Businesses, the National Farmers' Union, Rolls-Royce and the BBC.

9 *Guardian*, 7 July 2022.

10 Jonathan Gullis MP actually read word for word from a brief written by Bet365 during a Westminster Hall Parliamentary debate. He later apologised for forgetting to declare receipt of tickets to see Stoke City Football Club, which were worth £540. Philip Davies, the Shipley MP, earned almost £50,000 working for Entain and £6,788 of tickets to sporting events from the betting companies Entain, Gamesys, Star Sports, Flutter and BGC.

11 *Guardian*, 21 August 2022. This is not an All-Party Parliamentary Group, which is a separate topic covered later.

12 Rowena Mason and Patrick Wintour, 'No 10 chief of staff accompanied Libyan militiaman to Foreign Office meeting', *Guardian*, 17 October 2022.

13 *Financial Times*, 17 April 2021.

14 See Elizabeth David-Barrett (lead author), *Lifting the Lid on Lobbying: The Hidden Exercise of Power and Influence in the UK* (Transparency International, 2015).

15 Peter Hennessy, *Whitehall* (Fontana, 1989), p. 338.

16 Interviewed 7 September 2022.

17 John Smith as party leader said Labour should speak for the people without a voice.

18 Hansard Society poll, *Guardian*, 7 April 2019.

19 The survey was taken by YouGov in April 2022.The age group 18–24 was the least likely to say democracy serves them well: 19% said yes, 55% no. See P. Patel and H. Quilter-Pinner, *Road to Renewal: Elections, Parties and the Case for Renewing Democracy* (IPPR, 2022), available at www.ippr.org/publications/road-to-renewal (accessed October 2023).

20 Quoted in Grant Jordan, ed., *The Commercial Lobbyists* (Aberdeen University Press, 1991), p. 3.

21 'Rebuilding trust in politics', a speech delivered on 8 February 2010.

22 *USPL*, para. 6.1.

23 CSPL, *Strengthening Transparency Around Lobbying*, November 2013, p. 23.

24 Baroness Finn owned 35% of the company set up by Francis Maude called FMAP Ltd. She later served as Deputy Chief of Staff at Number 10. Oliver was named in documents submitted to the Leveson Inquiry into media standards as being one of eight Downing Street advisers to have had contact with News Corporation lobbyist Frédéric Michel in respect of the takeover of BSkyB by the Murdoch empire.

25 Interviewed July 2022.

26 Words like 'institute' or 'centre' give a respectability to what may be in fact be lobbying.

27 *USPL*, para. 6.6.

28 The IfG report *Government Transparency: Departmental Releases: Ministers and Officials* (2021) analysed selected government information published between July 2015 and March 2021. It also found that in measuring reliability, quality and accessibility, the transparency tests set by Theresa May as Prime Minister, departments vary in the speed at which they publish data and the level of detail they share. Further, between July and September 2018, special advisers at the Cabinet Office had sixteen meetings with media representatives. Eight were described as 'lunch' and another was described as 'breakfast'.

29 See *USPL*, para. 6.5.

30 Interviewed 1 June 2022. A good example of such breaches concerns the healthcare company Randox (detailed in Chapter 13). The report into that affair by the NAO described it as follows in the summary, para. 18: 'The Department did not disclose Randox's attendance at four ministerial meetings as it should have done in line with transparency requirements. We have reviewed documents on ministerial contacts

with Randox provided to Parliament on 3 February 2022, as well as additional departmental documents. From the information provided, we have identified four ministerial meetings for which the Department did not record Randox's attendance on its quarterly transparency releases. Meeting minutes were kept for two of eight meetings on testing involving ministers and Randox that took place in 2020 and 2021.' National Audit Office, 'Investigation into the management of PPE contracts', 30 March 2022, available at https://www.nao.org.uk/wp-content/uploads/2022/03/Investigation-into-the-governments-contracts-with-randox-laboratories-ltd-summary.pdf (accessed 24 July 2023).

31 See pp. 130.

32 Francis Ingham (Director General of the Public Relations and Communications Association) in evidence to PACAC. In the United States, the 1995 Lobbying Disclosure Act also exempts from the requirement to register those who spend less than 20% of their time on lobbying.

33 Interviewed 31 January 2022.

34 *USPL*, para. 6.21.

35 See Chapter 14.

36 Interviewed 1 June 2022.

37 Interviewed 7 February 2022.

38 Interviewed 28 July 2022.

39 I am not here looking at self-regulation by the trade bodies, the Chartered Institute of Public Relations, which has a Royal Charter, the Public Relations Consultants Association and the Association of Professional Political Consultants.

40 There had been resolutions on bribery in 1695, on fees for professional services in 1830 and on advocacy for reward in 1858.

41 Quoted in Lewis Baston, *Sleaze: The State of Britain* (Channel 4 Books, 2000), p. 131.

42 A House of Commons Resolution of 6 November 1995.

43 See Chapter 12.

44 *Guardian*, 9 May 2023.

45 *The Times* reported on 29 April 2023 that he said 'if you wait [in the lobby] for five minutes, the minister has to pass you. And then you've got 10 minutes while you walk around to the next vote to have his ear.' He also offered to ask Parliamentary questions.

46 House of Commons Committee on Standards, *All-Party Parliamentary Groups: Improving Governance and Regulation*, Seventh Report 2021–2022, HC 672, 26 April 2022. The social enterprise organisation Policy Connect largely works to support them.

47 There have been consistent reports of misbehaviour by MPs on overseas trips for APPGs; see for example Rowena Mason, *Guardian*, 28 December 2022.

48 House of Commons Committee on Standards, *All-Party Parliamentary Groups*, Sixth Report, 19 November 2013, para. 12. There is a whole separate issue of think tanks which are well funded but whose funding is opaque. Many are based in Tufton Street in Westminster. See for example www.theneweuropean.co.uk/55-tufton-street-sw1-taxpayers-alliance (accessed 18 September 2023), which contains the following excellent description: this is 'not a case of the banality of evil, but of the banality of influence'. In *Who Funds You*, November 2022, Open Democracy rates think tanks on the basis of how open they are about their funding, and many are not transparent at all, especially the Adam Smith Institute, the Centre for Policy Studies, Civitas, the Institute of Economic Affairs and the Tax Payers' Alliance. It concludes: 'opaque think tanks that seek to influence public policy must be treated with caution until they are prepared to

be honest and open about their funding'. 55 Tufton Street, Westminster, is or has been the home of at least a dozen lobbying groups, including BrexitCentral, Leave Means Leave and the Tax Payers' Alliance.

49 Commons Committee on Standards, *All-Party Parliamentary Groups*, 2022.
50 *Ibid.*, para. 55.
51 According to his website as of 31 July 2019, Martin Vickers, Conservative MP for Cleethorpes, was *very* busy as the Vice Chair of the APPGs for Albania, Azerbaijan, Central America, Faroe Islands, Iceland, Isle of Man, East Coast Main Line, Economic Development, Fair Fuel for UK Motorists and UK Hauliers, Fisheries, Football, Rail in the North, Transport Across the North, and Yorkshire and Northern Lincolnshire. He was the Secretary of the APPG for Australia and New Zealand and the Treasurer for the APPG for Heritage Rail. He is also the Chair of the APPG for Kosovo, North Macedonia, Freeports, the Oil Refining Sector and Rail. Vickers is co-Chair of the APPG for Montenegro and an officer for the APPGs for Serbia and the River Thames.
52 *Guardian*, 5 April 2023.
53 Guide to APPG rules, March 2015, revised May 2017, para. 4.
54 *Ibid.*, para. 5.
55 Committee on Standards, *All-Party Parliamentary Groups*, 2022, Oral evidence:.
56 Interviewed 20 March 2022.
57 Guide to APPG rules, para. 21.
58 *Ibid.*, para. 33.
59 See Committee on Standards, *All-Party Parliamentary Groups*, 2013, para. 18.
60 Committee on Standards, *All-Party Parliamentary Groups*, 2022, para. 28.
61 Interviewed 8 August 2022.
62 Interviewed 28 October 2022.
63 Interviewed 28 July 2022.
64 Interviewed 31 January 2022.
65 Committee on Standards, *All-Party Parliamentary Groups*, 2022, para. 38.
66 See for example www.bbc.co.uk/news/uk-politics-59984380 (accessed 18 September 2023).
67 Committee on Standards, *All-Party Parliamentary Groups*, 2022, para. 48.
68 *Ibid.*
69 *Ibid.*, para. 58e.
70 Nigel Boardman, *Review into the Development and Use of Supply Chain Finance (and Associated Schemes) in Government, Part 1: Report of the Facts*, Cabinet Office, July 2021, p. 16.
71 See Chapter 14.
72 Interviewed 21 September 2022.
73 He resigned as Tsar over partygate in June 2022.
74 See CSPL, *Strengthening Transparency Around Lobbying*, November 2013.
75 The Ministerial Code, para. 8.14, now requires departments to publish details of ministers' meetings with external organisations on a quarterly basis.
76 Even the industry bodies, the Chartered Institute of Public Relations (CIPR) and Public Relations and Communications Association (PRCA), have called for the Register to be expanded to cover 'all those engaged in lobbying', including in-house lobbyists in 'charities, campaigning groups, think tanks, trade unions, business, organisations, and private companies'. PRCA, *Open Letter to Government on Lobbying Reform*, 2021.
77 CSPL, Sixth Report, para. 7.28.
78 Interviewed 21 September 2022.
79 *USPL*, para. 6.3.

80 *Ibid.*, paras 6.10 and 6.31. Contributors to the CSPL review that produced *USPL* recommended that consultant lobbyists who contact special advisers and senior civil servants below Permanent Secretary level (including Directors General and Directors) should be required to register.

81 *Ibid.*, para. 4.17. In Australia, 'people who retire from office as a minister or a parliamentary secretary (assistant minister) are prohibited from engaging in lobbying activities relating to any matter that they had official dealings with in their last 18 months in office, for a period of 18 months after they cease to hold office'. See www.ag.gov.au/integrity/australian-government-register-lobbyists/information-lobbyists (accessed 18 September 2023).

82 *USPL*, p. 12.

83 PAC, *Tax Avoidance: The Role of the Big Accountancy Firms*, 26 April 2013.

84 *USPL*, para. 6.20.

85 *Ibid.*, para. 6.17.

86 Interviewed 1 June 2022.

87 Lucy Bannerman, 'Party-loving aide "showed off Johnson's mischievous texts"', *The Times*, 10 September 2018.

88 'MP leads campaign against "barbaric" electric shock dog collars', Conservative Animal Welfare Foundation, 9 February 2019.

89 Jennifer McKiernan, 'Boris backs Aberdeen MP's call for electric shock dog collar ban', *The Press and Journal*, 20 February 2018.

90 Harry Cole, 'Pets unleashed: electric shock pet collars to be banned for being "unnecessary and cruel"', *Sun*, 26 February 2018.

91 Department for Environment, Food and Rural Affairs, 'Animal welfare: banning the use of electronic training collars for cats and dogs', 12 March 2018.

92 *The Electronic Collar Manufacturers Association (An Unincorporated Association) Petsafe Limited* v. *Secretary of State for DEFRA*, [2019] EWHC 2813 (Admin) especially para. 41.

11. The Civil Service Commission

1 *Hansard*, 2 November 1995, col. 472.

2 Published by Palgrave Macmillan in 2012.

3 *Financial Times*, 10 September 2022.

4 In March 2023 a document over the signature of Suella Braverman said that 'we tried to stop the small boats crossings without changing our laws. But an activist blob of left-wing lawyers, *civil servants* and the Labour Party blocked us' (my emphasis).

5 Sir Stephen Lovegrove was also removed in the first week of the short-lived Truss government, as national security adviser in September 2022. Alice Thomson commented in *The Times* on 30 October 2022 that 'civil servants should not be shuffled around by ministers like mugs on a desk'.

6 Lord Agnew of Oulton, a minister, stated that Scholar had blocked policies and presided over 'groupthink'. Quoted in *The Times*, 15 September 2022.

7 These spats are not entirely new. Dick Crossman, Minister of Local Government under Harold Wilson, dismissed his Permanent Secretary (Dame Evelyn Sharp), and there was a falling out between Dame Helen Ghosh as Permanent Secretary and Theresa May as Home Secretary.

8 *The World This Weekend*, BBC Radio 4, 11 September 2022.

9 *Guardian*, 27 September 2022.

10 Interviewed 9 August 2022.

11 Interviewed 18 October 2022.

12 See Chapter 4.

13 Interviewed 11 January 2023.

14 There was also concern about the appointment without competition of Case's predecessor, Mark Sedwill, previously the National Security Adviser. More broadly, *The Times* reported on 9 August 2022 that more than a third of civil servants were looking for new jobs.

15 WhatsApp messages that he shared with Matt Hancock were published in the *Daily Telegraph* in March 2023. One showed him finding it 'hilarious' that travellers were being locked up in quarantine in Premier Inns during lockdown.

16 Another issue is the need to learn private-sector management techniques, which leads to management consultants being hired to oversee contracts or seconded to government departments. They can then influence public policy and benefit from winning public contracts. See Mariana Mazzucato and Rosie Collington, *The Big Con: How the Consulting Industry Works* (Allen Lane, 2023).

17 Tony Blair described in a speech on 26 April 2002 the 'scars on his back' from dealing with the civil service.

18 The relationship between minister and civil servants has been characterised by Lord Hennessy, the leading historian of Whitehall, as a 'marriage'. As such, it effectively places the interests of those working within it ahead of voters, taxpayers and service users. See IfG, *Annual Report*, 2018/2019.

19 Sky News interview, 3 June 2016.

20 This figure includes the Northern Ireland civil service (which has around 25,000 employees) and the Diplomatic Service (totalling around 14,000).

21 Section 1 of the Constitutional Reform and Governance Act 2010 (CRGA) provides that appointment to the civil service must be on merit, and on the basis of open and fair competition.

22 CRGA, section 10.

23 See Chapter 5.

24 See Benjamin Meggitt, 'Partnering with agents: how the Covid-19 pandemic changed relations between the UK government and public service contractors', *Political Quarterly*, 93:2 (2022), 244–252.

25 The CRGA sets out the principles on which the Civil Service Code must be based.

26 For more on the Civil Service Code, see IfG, 'Explainer: Civil Service Code', 21 January 2021. available at www.instituteforgovernment.org.uk/explainer/civil-service-code (accessed 27 June 2023).

27 Available at www.legislation.gov.uk/ukpga/2010/25/contents (accessed 27 June 2023).

28 CSPL, *Defining the Boundaries within the Executive: Ministers, Special Advisers and the permanent Civil Service*, Ninth Report, 1985. Lord Hennessy described the civil service as 'a piece of transferable human technology from one properly elected administration to another'. It was put in the following way in the leading case of *Carltona Ltd* v. *Commissioner of Works* [1943] 2 All ER 560: 'Civil servants, who are servants of the Crown, are seen by the courts as an extension of the minister and by the Civil Service Code as "owing their loyalty to the duly constituted Government"'.

29 Civil Service Code 2015; CRGA, section 5. There are similar codes for the Diplomatic Service and Northern Ireland.

30 *Guardian*, 11 February 2022. Michael Gove told me: 'When I used the word "blob" it was intended to refer to a group of people with a shared mindset on education,

who were resistant to change of any kind'. Suella Braverman treated civil servants as 'enemies' in an email to Conservative supporters in 2023.

31 Thomas Balogh, 'The apotheosis of the dilettante', in *The Establishment*, ed. Hugh Thomas (Anthony Blond, 1959), p. 99.

32 Bingham noted that: 'Across government there is a devastating lack of skills and experience in science, industry, commerce, and manufacturing…. Currently there are very few with science or operating backgrounds at all levels of government. If you lack scientific knowledge, then you cannot make decisions about science…. We need to embed science into policymaking, at every level of government.' Bingham, 'Another war is coming', Romanes Lecture, 23 November 2021.

33 Tom Bower, *Boris Johnson: The Gambler* (W. H. Allen, 2020), p. 424.

34 Interviewed 23 November 2022.

35 It went on: 'A single mindset bias, producing a workforce that is too cognitively homogeneous, prone to groupthink, and lacking in varied expertise, experience, specialism, and competence in the practical skills of innovation and delivery. This also results in an insularity, or defensiveness, when it comes to external scrutiny and input.' Simon Kaye, *Reimagining Whitehall: An Essay* (Reform, September 2022).

36 *Guardian*, 19 October 2023.

37 The House of Commons Foreign Affairs Committee issued a devastating report on the evacuation of Kabul, *Missing in Action: UK Leadership and the Withdrawal from Afghanistan*, 24 May 2022, which stated: 'One whistleblower, a senior FCDO official, told us that she had "never in my career seen anything within the civil service so badly managed. There was no induction for new staff on the team, no clear tasking, no system for recording decisions or actions and no system for handovers between shifts. The team was severely understaffed and the rostering system was ineffective…".' See also Ian Dunt, *How Westminster Works* (Weidenfeld & Nicholson, 2023).

38 See also pp. 49.

39 Anthony King and Ivor Crewe, *The Blunders of Our Governments* (OneWorld, 2013), p. ix.

40 Sam Friedman, Daniel Laurison and Lindsey Macmilla, *Social Mobility, the Class Pay Gap and Intergenerational Worklessness: New Insights from the Labour Force Survey*' (Social Mobility Commission, 26 January 2017).

41 Michael Gove, Ditchley Lecture, 27 June 2020.

42 They cannot engage in public canvassing such as for Parliamentary candidates in constituencies. Section 7(5) of the CRGA, however, says that special advisers need not 'carry out their duties with objectivity or impartiality'.

43 Suella Braverman was the first to introduce this into what had been seen previously as a purely legal role.

44 It was significant, for example, that SpAds were moved into a room next to hers by Liz Truss when she was appointed to the Foreign Office.

45 Civil Service (Amendment) Order 1997. Another informant, however, told me that too much was made of the Order because 'if SpAds know their minister's mind, and are able to convey that to officials, they're effectively giving them direction already; that's part of the job'.

46 An informant who had worked in the civil service, however, put it like this: 'SpAds take their leads from ministers – if ministers consider their SpAds to be more important than senior civil servants, their SpAds will behave accordingly'.

47 Interviewed 13 April 2022.

48 For the history of special advisers, see Andrew Blick, *People Who Live in the Dark: The History of Special Advisers in British Politics* (Politico's, 2004).

49 Interviewed 13 April 2022.

50 Hugh Dalton, a minister in the Attlee government, described them as the 'congenital snaghunter' or 'Mr Wait a Minute', as Jim Callaghan said to Peter Hennessy while at Number 10. See Hugh Dalton, *High Tide and After: Memoirs 1945–1960* (Muller, 1961), p. 16.

51 See Chapter 4.

52 Interviewed 7 July 2022. He suggests that new ministers should begin their period in office with a team-building exercise with their civil servants, such as an early away day.

53 Interviewed 25 November 2021.

54 See Chapter 15.

55 PACAC, *The Role and Status of the Prime Minister's Office*, First Report of Session 2021–22, para. 57.

56 *Ibid.*, para. 51.

57 See p. 45.

58 Edward Malnick, 'Top civil servants on Tories' "hit list"', *Daily Telegraph*, 22 February 2020.

59 He wreaked a revenge of sorts in that it was his condemnation of Boris Johnson's failure to recollect that he knew about Chris Pincher's past misdemeanours, which did for Johnson's premiership. By then McDonald was the head of a Cambridge College.

60 Beckie Smith, '"I didn't make it to cabinet secretary but I got close": Jonathan Slater on leading – and leaving – DfE', *Civil Service World*, 10 November 2020.

61 He had earlier been forced to resign from the May government because he leaked documents relating to a decision about the Chinese Huawei company and its involvement in infrastructure projects.

62 Interviewed 4 November 2022. The requirement is under section 92 of the Employment Rights Act 1992.

63 Antonia Romeo was apparently lined up to be the successor, and she was seen as an outsider in that she had never worked at the Treasury, but Number 10 pulled back when it gauged the very negative response from the markets to the Kwarteng mini-budget. A Treasury insider was appointed.

64 *The Times*, 20 July 2023. The newspaper calculated that Truss's brief period in Downing Street cost the taxpayer nearly £34,000 a day in compensation payments.

65 An informant told me that 'the skills you need when you get there are not the skills to get you there'.

66 See House of Commons Library Briefing Paper by Hazel Armstrong, 24 October 2018.

67 See Chapter 1.

68 Publication of the Direction to the PAC and to the public is a key feature, so that a further worrying fact about the Sonia Khan letter is the delay in the matter being made public. This took nine months, the Direction having been given to Sir John Manzoni on 3 March 2020. This was also the case with the Garden Bridge and British Steel indemnity Directions (although the delay was a mere five months).

69 This covers England. There are separate provisions for Scotland (Ministerial Code, February 2018, paras 6.6–6.7), Wales (Ministerial Code, November 2017, paras 3.9–10) and Northern Ireland (*Managing Public Money*, January 2013, para. 3.4).

70 Enshrined in the Exchequer and Audit Departments Act 1866.

71 *Civil Service World*, 6 December 2017.

72 HM Treasury, *Managing Public Money*, May 2023.

73 Directions must be formally notified to the Treasury and to the Comptroller and Auditor General, who tells Parliament's Public Accounts Committee.

74 Letter from Department of Transport, 26 February 2015.

75 National Audit Office, *Accountability to Parliament for Taxpayers' Money*, 23 February 2016, available at www.nao.org.uk/wp-content/uploads/2016/02/Accountability-for-Taxpayers-money.pdf (accessed 24 July 2023).

76 *The Accounting Officer's Survival Guide* (HM Treasury, December 2015), available at https://assets.publishing.service.gov.uk/government/uploads/system/uploads/attachment_data/file/486677/AOs_survival_guide__Dec_2015_.pdf (accessed 24 July 2023).

77 Interviewed 25 May 2022. The website is www.civilservant.org.uk (accessed 26 October 2023).

78 Thirty-nine of them were issued since the 2010 election but none between 2011 and 2014.

79 See Chapter 3.

80 The direction was issued on 22 July 2020.

81 See also Chapter 15.

82 A full list is available in National Audit Office, *Accountability to Parliament for Taxpayers' Money*, p. 29.

83 *Guardian*, 17 April 2022.

84 An unconvincing counternarrative holds that a virtue of the civil service is that knowledge and expertise resides not so much in the heads of individuals but within teams, and with the associated ability to research very quickly what has happened before.

85 It covered chief executives, chief financial officers and monitoring officers of councils.

12. MPs for hire

1 *International Herald Tribune*, 12 June 1989.

2 Committee on Standards, *Third Report – Mr Owen Paterson*, 26 October 2021, available at https://publications.parliament.uk/pa/cm5802/cmselect/cmstandards/797/79702.htm (accessed 24 July 2023).

3 See further in Chapter 13.

4 Committee on Standards, *Third Report*.

5 *Ibid.*

6 *Financial Times*, 26 October 2021.

7 The Conservative Father of the House, Peter Bottomley, said he could not in conscience vote for the measure. Fifteen of the fifty-nine MPs who put their names to the amendment had second jobs.

8 Lord Evans, speech to IfG, 4 November 2021. Mark Fletcher, a backbench Tory MP for Bolsover (a newbie Red Wall-conquering hero, as he unseated Dennis Skinner), pertinently noted, 'it has been suggested by some senior colleagues on the back benches on this side that as I have only been here for two years that we don't know how this place really works; I think that is sufficient time to know the difference between right and wrong'.

9 The Leader of the House, Jacob Rees-Mogg, would later say the government had made 'a mistake' in introducing the amendment, explaining that his own individual judgement had been coloured by sympathy for Paterson over the death of his wife the previous year.

10 Committee on Standards, *Oral Evidence: Code of Conduct Consultation*, HC 954, 25 January 2022, available at https://committees.parliament.uk/oralevidence/3345/pdf (accessed 24 July 2023).

11 In a sense, being a minister is a second job (in addition to being an MP), but constituents benefit as they can be more influential by reason of their position. MPs who are members of the government (ministers, ministers of state, parliamentary secretaries) are additionally subject to the Ministerial Code, which states that 'when they take up office, Ministers should give up any other public appointment they may hold'. Thus, government members are not permitted to earn money in the private sector.

12 Simon Weschle, 'Parliamentary positions and politicians' private sector earnings: evidence from the UK House of Commons', *Journal of Politics*, 83:2 (2021), 706–721.

13 *Guardian*, 8 January 2023. John Redwood, Andrew Mitchell and Chris Grayling (prominent Conservative MPs) received more than £200,000 additional income each during that period.

14 Interviewed 1 February 2022.

15 Interviewed 31 January 2022.

16 Daniel Martin, 'A fifth of MPs have a second job on the side', *Daily Mail*, 3 July 2018. In 2021, 114 Conservative MPs, twenty Labour MPs and twelve others (mainly SNP) had at least one second job.

17 Rachel Wearmouth, 'Shameless Tory MP has made £900,000 during Covid', *Daily Mirror*, 12 August 2021.

18 Rowena Mason, Dan Sabbagh, Heather Stewart, Aubrey Allegretti and Peter Walker, *Guardian*, 10 November 2021.

19 Andrew Bridgen committed a different sort of misconduct at about the same time. He was suspended from Parliament in 2023 for five days because of a 'cavalier' attitude over lobbying breaches for a timber company that paid him £5,000. He failed to declare this in the Parliamentary register. He also called into question the integrity of the Parliamentary Commissioner for Standards. His suspension was upheld by the Committee on Standards. *Guardian*, 9 January 2023. He later joined the Reclaim Party.

20 *The Times*, 10 November 2021.

13. Anatomy of a recent scandal

1 Interviewed 24 March 2022.

2 Thomas Pope, 'The government must bring an end to its risky Covid crisis procurement', speech at Institute for Government, 5 February 2021.

3 Leader, *The Times*, 23 April 2021.

4 National Audit Office, *Investigation into the Management of PPE Contracts*, 30 March 2022, available at www.nao.org.uk/reports/investigation-into-the-management-of-ppe-contracts (accessed 24 July 2023).

5 Interviewed July 2022.

6 See also Mark Mardell, 'The fixer' podcast (Tortoise Media), 21 January 2021.

7 The full story cannot yet be told because of ongoing legal actions.

8 *Guardian*, 22 June 2021.

9 NAO, *Investigation into the Management of PPE Contracts*.

10 See the Knox House Trust site, https://knoxhousetrust.com/about-knox-house-trust (accessed 24 July 2023).

11 *Guardian*, 23 November 2022.

12 See Matt Hancock, *Pandemic Diaries* (Biteback, 2022).

13 *Guardian*, 23 November 2022 and 17 December 2023.

14 David Rose, 'Will the £42 BILLION 'Operation Moonshot' test and trace plan actually work?', *Daily Mail*, 13 November 2020.

15 NAO, *Report: Investigation into Government Procurement During the COVID-19 Pandemic*, 26 November 2020.

16 The Good Law Project (GLP) succeeded in its judicial review and the VIP lane was ruled unlawful essentially for being anti-competitive. The GLP is discussed below.

17 Beyond PPE, the Johnson government generally had an even worse record on transparency than its recent predecessors: only 16% of departmental information releases on spending over £25,000 were published on time in 2020, down from to 38% in 2014.

18 *Guardian*, 18 December 2021. See also his book *Bringing Down Goliath* (W. H. Allen, 2023).

19 See Chapter 5.

20 *World Anti-corruption Day Newsletter*, 9 December 2020.

21 PAC, *Report: Management of PPE Contracts*, 20 July 2022.

22 19 July 2022.

23 Department of Health and Social Care, 'PPE procurement in the early pandemic', 17 November 2021.

24 House of Commons Public Accounts Committee (PAC), *Government's Contracts with Randox Laboratories Ltd*, 20 July 2022, p. 6.

25 *Guardian*, 22 April 2021.

26 The procurement problem is in fact broader than COVID: Public First, a public affairs company, gained some £500,000 of contracts with Number 10 on the recommendation of Cummings and people around him. An internal civil service memo suggested doubts on the grounds that this was use of public money to carry out opinion research in the interests of the Conservative Party. A High Court judge found that there was no breach of the procurement rules but the transaction was infringed by apparent bias, although this was overturned by the Court of Appeal.

27 The relevant official, a Mr Webb, 'candidly admitted that he was not even aware of the time limits [for publication of the notices] in the Transparency Policy', the judge hearing the case said.

28 The names discovered by GLP through disclosure requests include Dominic Cummings and Liam Fox.

29 *Good Law Project News*, 18 November 2021.

30 *Guardian*, 11 March 2021.

31 David Rose, 'Priti Patel's SECOND bid to help her friend win PPE deal worth millions', *Daily Mail*, 28 May 2021.

32 NAO, *Investigation into the Management of PPE Contracts*, para. 20.

33 David Rose, 'Embattled peer Lord Bethell is under renewed pressure amid mystery of the 33,000 emails linked to £90 million Covid deals in his private account', *Daily Mail*, 16 September 2021.

34 *The Queen on Application of Good Law Project Limited and Others* v. *Secretary of State for Health and Social Care* [2021] EWHC 346 (Admin) heard by Mr Justice Chamberlain. He found the Secretary of State acted unlawfully by failing to comply with the Transparency Policy. Contract award notices were published late for 217 (42%) of the 520 contracts awarded on or before 7 October 2020 to which that obligation applied. At para. 140, the judge said: 'The public were entitled to see who this money was going to, what it was being spent on and how the relevant contracts were awarded. This was important not only so

that competitors of those awarded contracts could understand whether the obligations owed to them under the PCR 2015 had been breached, but also so that oversight bodies such as the NAO, as well as Parliament and the public, could scrutinise and ask questions about this expenditure.' At para. 149, he concluded: 'the overall picture shows the Secretary of State moving close to complete compliance. The evidence as a whole suggests that the backlog arose largely in the first few months of the pandemic and that officials began to bear down on it during the autumn of 2020. I have no doubt that this claim has speeded up compliance.' No mandatory relief was justified.

35 PAC, *Government's Contracts with Randox Laboratories Ltd.*
36 *Ibid.*, Conclusions.
37 Chapter 12.
38 PAC, *Government's Contracts with Randox Laboratories Ltd.*
39 *Ibid.*, p. 10.
40 *Ibid.*, Summary.
41 David Rose, 'A cynical and brazen cronyism: as new report reveals £18bn coronavirus PPE farce', *Daily Mail*, 18 November 2020.
42 Meller was also involved in the controversy over the Presidents Club, at whose events sexual harassment was alleged to have taken place. See Rupert Neate, 'Presidents Club scandal: hostess agent promises "never again"', *Guardian*, 31 July 2018.
43 As well as its Chair, Lord Chadlington was a paid director of Sumner Group Holdings, with an estimated £5 million in shares.
44 NAO, *Investigation into the Management of PPE Contracts*, p. 6.

14. Greensill

1 Rachel Reeves, the Shadow Chancellor, said: 'There is a real risk that the government are attempting to brush under the carpet or cover up this scandal of cronyism, of contracts and of involvement of the former prime minister in lobbying current ministers'. BBC News, 12 April 2021.
2 I consider overlapping jurisdictions in the final chapter.
3 The firm gained £7 million of government contracts in the year of his appointment.
4 National Audit Office, *Investigation into the British Business Bank's Accreditation of Greensill Capital*, Session 2021–22, HC 301, July 2021, para. 7. Nigel Boardman, *Review into the Development and Use of Supply Chain Finance (and Associated Schemes) in Government, Part 1: Report of the Facts*, Cabinet Office, July 2021; *Part 2: Recommendations and Suggestions*, August 2021. House of Commons Treasury Committee, *Lessons from Greensill Capital*, Sixth Report of Session 2021–22, HC 151, July 2021.
5 See Chapter 6.
6 Duncan Mavin described him thus: 'Lex rules the room like a mandarin, surrounded by his courtiers'. *The Pyramid of Lies* (Macmillan, 2022), p. 3.
7 Boardman (*Review, Part 1*) described two types of arrangement previously known as 'factoring' in his review:
a. the payment to a supplier at a discount of its invoice by a third-party financier before the due date of the contract where the invoice has been accepted as valid by the buyer and
b. purchase order or pre-purchase order finance where the buyer undertakes to make purchases from a supplier and a financier pays the supplier on the strength of that undertaking.

8   *Sunday Times*, 11 April 2021.

9   Boardman in his *Review, Part 1*, found that 'Based on advice provided by Lex Greensill, the Department [of Health] assumed that the NHS could achieve savings of £100 million per year in pharmaceutical supplies through supply chain finance. The Department is unable to provide evidence of realised benefits.'

10 PACAC, *Propriety of Governance in Light of Greensill: An Interim Report*, Third Report of Session 2021–22, HC 59, 20 July 2021, para. 34: 'The role of Crown Representative was created to oversee and coordinate the Government's procurement activity and manage its relationships with suppliers. Initially, these were mostly held by officials with significant procurement expertise, but Lex Greensill became one of an increasing number drawn from the commercial sector, working part time as Crown Reps whilst simultaneously continuing their business careers.' This category was introduced in 2011 to deal with key strategic suppliers and to act as focal points for particular groups of providers looking to supply to the public sectors (Boardman, *Review, Part 1*, p. 19). Crown Representatives work with strategic suppliers in support of policy in areas such as modern slavery, prompt payment, net zero, value and outsourcing. Further, 'they have worked on activity in support of Covid-19 programmes to assess financial risk and to engage the market as part of the ventilator challenge' (*ibid.*, p. 21).

11 *Ibid.*, p. 30.

12 Interviewed 18 October 2022.

13 Held on 23 October 2012.

14 Boardman, *Review, Part 1*, p. 45.

15 *Ibid.*, p. 86.

16 *Ibid.*, p. 9.

17 PACAC, *Propriety of Governance*, para. 41.

18 Boardman, *Review, Part 1*, p. 24.

19 Cameron in a statement admitted that he gained generous amounts but refused to give precise figures.

20 In his statement Cameron said that he 'was neither a director of the company nor involved in any lending decisions, he has no special insight into what ultimately happened'.

21 The former Prime Minister has emphasised that 'the idea of my working for Greensill was never raised or considered by me until well after I left office'.

22 The Ministerial Code says a private secretary or official should be present for all discussions relating to government business. This type of activity was not confined to Westminster: Greensill took the SNP Rural Economy Secretary to one of Glasgow's finest restaurants and there were no notes kept of the meeting.

23 He was also a NED at the Cabinet Office. He lobbied for the Greensill product Earnd to be rolled out in other public services, including the police.

24 Greensill was an approved lender for both the Coronavirus Large Business Interruption Scheme and the Coronavirus Business Interruption Scheme but not for the other schemes and he wanted to be one; indeed, he wanted it very badly, as the viability of his operation apparently depended on it.

25 See also Chapter 5.

26 See *The Times*, 14 April 2021.

27 See Mavin, *The Pyramid of Lies*. This in turn put at risk some 5,000 jobs at Liberty Steel, which depended on various Greensill schemes.

28 Some also pointed to the fact that it was released on the day that the Duke of Edinburgh died.

29 See Chapter 10.

30 See Chapter 6.

31 Here I consider only the recommendations which do not fall within other chapters.

32 Sadly, of course, Heywood could not speak for himself for the purposes of this *Review*, but unlike other inquiries, where the family of those who have died since the incidents under review were interviewed during the course of the inquiry, Lady Heywood was afforded this facility only at the very end of the process. She says that Boardman agreed to meet her only a few days before his *Report* was published and that he merely read it out to her. This was after he had been threatened with an application to the High Court for judicial review. She told me Boardman made clear in several emails to her that he was not interested in reviewing her written submissions. This is markedly different from the approach taken by Lord Dyson when investigating the Bashir interview of Princess Diana. He allowed the widow of Steve Hewlett (the producer of *Panorama* at the time of the interview) to make representations throughout the process. In the Bloody Sunday Inquiry the families of victims and soldiers were allowed to make representations, as also happened in the Hillsborough Inquest.

33 At present, conflicts between the private and the public may be approved at the highest level. In one email Heywood wrote: 'Lex is giving huge amounts of his personal time to HMG and needs occasional use of No 10 to host senior business people'.

34 See Chapter 5.

35 Interviewed 30 May 2022.

36 *Strengthening Ethics and Integrity in Central Government*, 20 July 2023.

37 The Committee in its *Interim Report* said: 'It is unacceptable for Ministers to hide behind the Osmotherly Rules to prevent Select Committees from carrying out legitimate inquiries. We will be writing to the Chair of the Liaison Committee to consider ways in which we can clarify the responsibility of officials to appear before Select Committees' (PACAC, *Propriety of Governance*, para. 23).

15. Conventions

1 Lord Hailsham, *The Government Machine: The Dilemma of Democracy* (Collins, 1978), p. 155.

2 George Orwell, *The Lion and the Unicorn* (Read, 2020 reprint), p. 32.

3 Evidence to PACAC, Q74, 24 April 2022.

4 See Chapter 3.

5 Interviewed 15 September 2022. The system of fixed penalty notices (FPNs) for COVID restrictions had no administrative appeal process (as some other FPNs have) to challenge the legitimacy of their issuance. The only 'appeal' available was to decline the FPN and let the matter to be taken forward as a prosecution, but that risked a criminal conviction if the defence failed.

6 The 'Haldane convention' encapsulates the notion that civil servants have an indivisible relationship with their departmental ministers, quite different to many other models of government around the world, many of which are based on separation of powers. See the Armstrong memorandum covered in Chapter 11.

7 [2019] UKSC 41.

8 *Hansard*, vol. 814, 9 September 2021. This has echoes in the law of trusts. In a legal context, a trustee as a fiduciary must advance and protect the interests entrusted and hold all benefits on behalf of the entrustor, save for any openly negotiated payment that the terms of the entrusting agreement may provide. To *account* to another is to

narrate what happened to the assets or affairs entrusted to you: to give an account of what you did with your trust. On the other side of the relationship, to take an *audit* is to *hear* what your are told of the assets. Joshua Getzler, 'An interdisciplinary view of fiduciary law: "as if". Accountability and counterfactual trust', *Boston University Law Review*, 91:3 (2011), 973. This is taken up in the Lockean model of the fiduciary government official who must serve the public. The legal term 'fiduciary' today connotes high standards of loyalty and good faith in the performance of discrete obligations, the management of assets or the conduct of relationships. This is the spirit which should inform public officials, albeit they are not trustees in a strict legal sense.

9 Chapter 12.

10 The Lord Chancellor used to be the Speaker in the House of Lords and a judge in the House of Lords Judicial Committee, the forerunner of the Supreme Court, as well as the head of a government department and Cabinet member. Lord Irvine was between 1997 and 2003 the last person to be this 'three-in-one Holy Trinity'. This anomalous role was separated out by the Constitutional Reform Act 2005. Some think the abolition of the role of Lord Chancellor had a major detrimental impact on respect within government for the rule of law. The doctrine of separation of powers itself derives ultimately from John Locke's *Second Treatise of Civil Government* (1690) and Montesquieu's *The Spirit of the Laws* (1748). As to Britain, see Donoughmore Committee, *Report of the Committee on Ministers' Powers*, Cmnd 4060, 1932, p. 4.

11 Constitution Unit, *Parliament's Watchdogs*, July 2022.

12 [1995] 2 AC 513 at 567.

13 Since at least the political settlement reached in 1688, the sovereign cannot act alone and, as between the monarch and Parliament, the latter is supreme over the former.

14 For example the Act of Settlement 1701 and the Acts of Union 1800.

15 As Professor Lauterpacht said, 'the reality of that sovereignty [of Crown in Parliament] ends where Britain's international obligations begin'. Eli Lauterpact, 'Sovereignty – myth or reality?', *International Affairs*, 73:1 (1997), 137–150, p. 149. The Human Rights Act gave the European Convention on Human Rights direct effect in the UK, instead of the indirect effect it previously had by virtue of the citizen's right to enforce the state's duties by means of a complaint to the European Court of Human Rights.

16 It is also arguable that there is a convention for Parliament not to legislate contrary to basic principles of constitutionalism, although this has not been the subject of any legal ruling. Nick Barber, *The UK Constitution: An Introduction* (Oxford University Press, 2021), p. 98.

17 Vernon Bogdanor, *The New British Constitution* (Hart Publishing, 2010), p. 285. The counter-argument is that that there is no separation of the legislature and the executive in the UK (as there is in the US). Parliament is the legislature. The sovereign's governing ministers are chosen from the ranks of that legislature, usually from the party with an overall majority. The ministers act either under statutory powers set by Parliament or under royal prerogative. The latter is subject to restriction by Parliamentary legislation and ministers are answerable to the House of Commons in that their acts can be subject to a vote and voted down.

18 Barber, *The UK Constitution*, p. 10.

19 Keith Dowding, *The Civil Service* (Routledge, 1995), p. 153.

20 Cited in Peter Hennessy, *Whitehall* (Fontana, 1989), p. 306.

21 A speech delivered in Cambridge on 21 January 2019 titled 'Parliament, government, judiciary: is there any hope for the rule of law?'

22 Frank Vibert, *The Rise of the Unelected: Democracy and the New Separation of Powers*

(Cambridge University Press, 2007), p. 61. One convention is known as the Lascelles Principles and relates to when a monarch may refuse a dissolution of Parliament sought by a Prime Minister. Strangely enough (and in a very British way) these were formulated in a letter to *The Times* by the Queen's private secretary, Alan Lascelles, using the pseudonym Senex, on 2 May 1950.

23 The overall decision was that the government had to secure Parliamentary authorisation by primary legislation before using prerogative powers to trigger the process under article 50 of the EU Treaty to withdraw from the EU.

24 [2017] UKSC 5.

25 Para. 40.

26 A. V. Dicey, *The Law of the Constitution* (Macmillan, 1885). See K. C. Wheare, *Modern Constitutions* (Opus Books, 1966), p. 179. Jennings subsequently referred to conventions as allowing 'a rigid legal framework … to be kept up with changing social needs and changing political ideas', making it possible for 'the men who govern to work the machines'.

27 Relevant cases include *Re Resolution to Amend the Constitution* [1981] 1 SCR 753; *Madzimbamuto* v. *Lardner-Burke* [1969] 1 AC 645.

28 [2017] UKSC 5, para. 146. The case concerned whether the government had prerogative power it could use to inform the EU of the UK's intention to withdraw from EU treaties.

29 Lord Sewel was the Minister of State in the Scotland Office who was responsible for the progress of the Scotland Bill in the House of Lords in 1998. It was actually embodied in a memorandum of understanding between the UK government and the devolved governments originally in December 2001 (Cm 5240). The Supreme Court at para. 151 said: 'The Sewel Convention has an important role in facilitating harmonious relationships between the UK Parliament and the devolved legislatures. But the policing of its scope and the manner of its operation does not lie within the constitutional remit of the judiciary, which is to protect the rule of law.'

30 At para. 136.

31 Sometimes what were conventions are put into legislation. For example, Parliament's role with regard to treaties signed by ministers was formerly governed by a convention known as the Ponsonby Rule and is now found in the Constitutional Reform and Governance Act 2010 (sections 20–25).

32 Another way of putting this is that 'doing the decent thing' is an unwritten convention of the constitution. In her speech to the IfG on 29 November 2021, Angela Rayner said: 'Our democracy cannot hinge on gentlemen's agreements, it needs independent and robust protection'.

33 IfG, written evidence, January 2021, Standards 2, p. 16.

34 Professor S. E. Finer in *The Individual Responsibility of Ministers* (1956) 34 Pub Admin 377 at 394 said that 'a rule does not mean merely an observed uniformity in the past; the notion includes the expectation that the uniformity will continue in the future. It is not simply a description; it is a prescription. It has compulsive force.'

35 See also Chapters 2 and 11. Boris Johnson's introduction to the 2022 edition includes this: 'Thirty years after it was first published, the Ministerial Code continues to fulfil its purpose, guiding my Ministers on how they should act and arrange their affairs. As the Leader of Her Majesty's Government, my accountability is to Parliament and, via the ballot box, to the British people. We must show every day that we are worthy of this privilege by keeping our promises and delivering on the priorities of the British people.'

36 Cabinet Office, *Ministerial Code*, August 2019, para. 1.3c.

37 Herbert Morrison, *Government and Parliament: A Survey from the Inside*, 3rd edition (Oxford University Press, 1964), p. 332.

38 Two resignations which appear odd at least to modern eyes were those of Hugh Dalton, who casually spoke to a journalist about his budget, on the way to the Commons, and Nick Ridley, for saying what he really thought about the Germans. An example of Cabinet ministers who voluntarily resigned because of departmental failings (the Foreign Office) is the case of Lord Carrington and Humphrey Atkins (together with a junior minister, Richard Luce), who all went after the Falklands conflict erupted. Estelle Morris resigned in October 2002 when some ministerial targets were not met. She later said that she did not feel up to the job.

39 This involved land in Dorset purchased in 1938 for use as a bombing range and run as a model farm by the Ministry of Agriculture after 1945. In 1950 the land was sold for private use as one large farm rather than splitting it into its three former farms.

40 A-levels had to be re-marked. Williamson is a strong example of the system not ending a minister's career, as he had to resign over leaking information under Theresa May yet was brought back into Sunak's government, only to have to resign again a few days later over his alleged bullying of another Conservative MP.

41 This culture has been also reflected by many scandals in business life, which are outside the scope of this book. There was also Dominic Cummings and his various explanations of his trip during lockdown to Barnard Castle, although he was not a minister.

42 *Report of the Inquiry into the Export of Defence Equipment and Dual-Use Goods to Iraq and Related Prosecutions*, February 1996, p. 289.

43 If misconduct takes place in Parliament, the adjudicator is the Committee on Standards of whichever House is relevant.

44 Public Service Committee, *Ministerial Accountability and Responsibility*, Second Report of Session 1995–96, HC 313-I, 1996. There is the less likely route open for MPs to table a substantive motion (one that can be debated and voted on by the Commons) setting out the accusation. Erskine May, the definitive guide to parliamentary procedure, states: 'The Commons may treat the making of a deliberately misleading statement as a contempt.' This mechanism was used for example in 1963, when John Profumo was the subject of a motion accusing him of a 'grave contempt' for having made a statement in the Commons 'containing words which he later admitted not to be true'. He resigned before it could be debated. It is not a matter for the Speaker either. The current Speaker, Sir Lindsay Hoyle, has stated that 'the Speaker cannot be dragged into arguments about whether a statement is accurate or not. This is a matter of political debate.' More generally Sir Alex Allan told me: 'The Ministerial Code needs updating; for example it says nothing about text messages and emails from private accounts'.

45 Interviewed 25 May 2022.

46 'Not fit for purpose' was the description adopted by John Reid, who held the post between 2006 and 2007.

47 The Lessons Learned Review on Windrush generally found that 'a range of warning signs from inside and outside the Home Office were simply not heeded by officials and ministers'. See Wendy Williams, *Windrush Lessons Learned Review*, HC 93 2020–21, 19 March 2020.

48 There is an issue as to why Theresa May did not require Amber Rudd to resign as Home Secretary when she misled Parliament, leaving it to Rudd to make the decision herself a couple of days later.

49 A general principle extrapolated from something said by Alastair Campbell is that if a story about a minister continues for more than a week, the minister will have to go. The September 2021 reshuffle by Boris Johnson was interesting in that some of those who were most involved in the recent scandals were eventually moved on, in particular Robert Jenrick and Lord Bethell, as a delayed reaction against perceived misdeeds, but some who were affected by multiple scandals resolutely hung on to their positions because of crude political calculations.

50 Written evidence to the *Standards Matter 2* review.

51 *The Times*, 2 February 2022.

52 William Gladstone, *Gleanings of Past Years* (John Murray, 1879), vol. 1, p. 243.

53 *World This Weekend*, BBC Radio 4, 17 April 2022.

54 Lord Sedwill, former Cabinet Secretary, online evidence session, March 2021, recorded in *USPL*.

55 Interviewed 7 October 2022.

56 See the chapter 'Rule of law and its virtues' in Joseph Raz, *The Authority of Law* (Oxford University Press, 2009). Other issues identified by Raz are that laws should be relatively stable; the judiciary should be independent; natural justice should prevail; and discretion should be limited.

57 Brian Tamanaha, *On the Rule of Law* (Cambridge University Press, 2004).

58 Lord Steyn, *Democracy Through Law*, 2002 EHRLR 723, at 727.

59 Lord Diplock, in the House of Lords in *R* v. *Rimmington* [2005] UKHL 63, said, 'The acceptance of the rule of law as a constitutional principle requires that a citizen, before committing himself to any course of action should be able to know in advance what are the legal principles which flow from it'.

60 Cited in Tom Bingham, *The Rule of Law* (Penguin, 2020), p. 3.

61 In September 2005 the Council of International Bar Association said: 'the rule of law is the foundation of a civilised society. It enables a transparent process accessible and equal to all. It ensures adherence to principles that both liberate and protect.'

62 See Bingham, *The Rule of Law*. It is described as 'the backbone of our civilisation' in Geert Corstens, *Understanding the Rule of Law* (Bloomsbury, 2017), p. 13.

63 Lord Bingham [2007] CLJ 67 at p. 78.

64 [2017] ICR 1037, para. 66.

65 Quoted in Bingham, *The Rule of Law*, p. 62.

66 Vibert, *The Rise of the Unelected*, p. 60.

67 12 February 2022, in the midst of the partygate scandal.

68 See Chapter 1. In a sense, the Nolan Report operated as a codification of some conventions.

69 Cited in Bingham, *The Rule of Law*, p. 4.

70 A. V. Dicey, *Introduction to the Study of the Law of the Constitution* (Macmillan, 1959 edition), p. 194.

71 *Ibid.*, p. 193.

72 A. V. Dicey, *The Law of the Constitution* (Macmillan, 1885), p. 202.

73 'Northern Ireland Secretary admits new bill will "break international law"', BBC News, 8 September 2020.

74 *Guardian*, 11 February 2022.

75 See Chapter 4.

76 See also David Hine and Gillian Peele, *The Regulation of Standards in Public Life: Doing the Right Thing* (Manchester University Press, 2016), p. 18.

77 Jonathan Freedland, 'The Paterson fiasco confirms the threat Boris Johnson poses to British democracy', *Guardian*, 5 November 2021.
78 Steven Levitsky and Daniel Ziblatt, *How Democracies Die* (Random House, 2018), p. 33.
79 Quentin Letts said of Lady Hale: 'the beady eyed nanny goat who read yesterday's verdict in the court. Brenda Hale has long been a quintessential liberal blue stocking. If she's a leaver I'm a Martian'. Quentin Letts, 'Judges blew their hallowed status with the Supreme Court ruling', *Sun*, 25 September 2019.
80 The Lord Chancellor is required (along with other ministers) by section 3(1) of the Constitutional Reform Act 2005 to 'uphold the continued independence of the judiciary', but the Act does not specify precisely how this should be done.
81 This narrative revived when the Johnson government's policy of sending refugees to Rwanda was interdicted by the European Court of Human Rights in June 2022. See also Jack Doyle, 'Jacob Rees-Mogg accuses the Supreme Court of a "constitutional coup" over its stunning ruling', *Daily Mail*, 24 September 2019.
82 *Guardian*, 10 February 2022.
83 Harry Woolf *et al.* (eds), *De Smith's Judicial Review* (Sweet and Maxwell, 8th edition, 2018), para. 1-014.
84 25 October 2021.

16. Conclusion

1 Will Dunn, 'Boris Johnson promised to "fuck business", and that's exactly what he did', *New Statesman*, 7 July 2022.
2 See *USPL*, para. 2.39.
3 I have had to leave out, save tangentially, IPSA and the Parliamentary Commissioner for Standards.
4 Interviewed 28 June 2022.
5 Sir John Robert Seeley, *The Expansion of England* (1883).
6 There are other views. In an entertaining article, Dominic Lawson said that 'Tory sleaze just ain't what it used to be'. He contended that 'cash for curtains doesn't come close to Alan Clark, Archer and Aitken'. *Sunday Times*, 2 May 2021.
7 *Bolton* v. *Law Society* [1993] EWCA Civ 32.
8 Interviewed 27 July 2022.
9 'Sue Gray delivers a first report on those Downing Street parties', *Economist*, 5 February 2022.
10 See Chapter 9.
11 For a definition of culture in this context I turned to the social anthropologist Emma Crewe (interviewed 21 September 2022), who told me: 'Culture is what people do rather than something they have. Almost no one wants to be seen as unethical; people's ethics are influenced by the avoidance of anticipated shame. Once a government has been in office for a long period, their backbenchers get disgruntled and the constraints to behave well become weaker. This is amplified if their leaders take standards less seriously too. Standards are essentially about relationships.' Johnson did not appear to be capable of experiencing shame.
12 Interviewed 24 November 2022.
13 Peter Hennessy, '"Harvesting the cupboards": why Britain has produced no administrative theory or ideology in the twentieth century', *Transactions of the Royal Historical Society*, 4 (1994), 203–219, p. 205.

14 Interviewed 7 October 2022.

15 Interviewed 20 March 2022.

16 Interviewed 21 September 2022.

17 *USPL*, para. 1.28.

18 Interviewed 7 October 2022.

19 Interviewed 7 October 2022.

20 See Chapter 2.

21 Here the definition of corruption adopted is: 'the perversion of public interest decisions for private gain or the prospect of private gain'.

22 Isabel Hardman, in *Why We Get the Wrong Politicians* (Atlantic Books, 2018), draws attention to the need for considerable resources even to be in a position to be a candidate on the list of party possibles as well as the lifestyle once elected, and the loyalty bonds, whether to the whip or a sponsoring union, that ties them once elected.

23 Interviewed 27 July 2022.

24 Committee on Standards in Public Life, *First Report: Members of Parliament, Ministers, Civil Servants and Quangos*, Cm 2850, May 1995.

25 See Chapter 2.

26 Aditya Chakrabortty, *Guardian*, 26 May 2022.

27 The only areas touching on Parliament in this book are in respect of second jobs and lobbying.

28 Interviewed 2 February 2022.

29 Interviewed 21 September 2022.

30 Interviewed 7 December 2022.

31 Interviewed May 2022. See also Andrew Blick and Peter Hennessy, *Good Chaps No More? Safeguarding the Constitution in Stressful Times* (Constitution Society, 2019).

32 Constitution Unit, University College London, *Report of the Citizens' Assembly on Democracy in the UK: Second Report of the Democracy in the UK after Brexit Project*, April 2022.

33 *Ibid.*

34 A poll taken in July 2021, for example, asked respondents to imagine a future PM having to choose in a binary way between the importance of integrity and delivery: 49% favoured integrity against 35% for delivery. See Constitution Unit, University College London, *What Kind of Democracy Do People Want? First Report of the Democracy in the UK after Brexit Project*, January 2022.

35 Interviewed 2 February 2022.

36 Interviewed 28 June 2022.

37 Interviewed 7 December 2022.

38 See Hannah White, *Held in Contempt* (Manchester University Press, 2022).

39 It has been a recurring theme that the system reasserted itself over, for example, Paterson and partygate, but that this cannot be trusted always to happen.

40 Harold Wilson's Cabinets could go on for several hours.

41 Interviewed 27 July 2022.

42 Interviewed 28 July 2022.

43 Interviewed 21 March 2022.

44 Interviewed 24 March 2022. It is of course true that even statutory bodies can be abolished, as happened with the Audit Commission and the Standards Board for England, which regulated ethics in local government, but this is a more difficult and visible process, and in those cases proved controversial. The government would have to expend political capital, and it would need more than the nod of a head at the Privy Council as would happen with an Order in Council.

45 Interviewed 7 December 2022.

46 Matthew Parris, *The Spectator*, 8 May 2021.

47 Interviewed 21 September 2022.

48 [2019] UKSC 41.

49 See for example Oliver Bullough, *Butler to the World* (Profile Books, 2021) and Frank Vogl, *The Enablers: How the West Supports Kleptocrats and Corruption – Endangering Our Democracy* (Rowman and Littlefield, 2021).

50 He left in September 2023. See also https://www.theguardian.com/uk-news/2023/sep/26/are-hs2-bosses-really-kids-with-the-golden-credit-card (accessed 17 October 2023).

51 They are the real beneficiaries of the privatisation of the railways!

52 Under the Former Presidents Act 1958, US Presidents are given: lifetime protection by the Secret Service, as are their children until aged sixteen; transition funding for seven months; if necessary, medical treatment in military hospitals; a pension equal to the salary of a Cabinet Secretary; and a private office. In Britain they receive a pension based on half their annual salary at the time of leaving office. There needs to be a minimum service requirement as PM so that Liz Truss should not receive it (£115,000 per year) for serving just a few weeks in Number 10.

53 See Chapter 14.

54 There is an issue about those who suspend their membership of the House of Lords because they do not wish to disclose their earnings. They should be given a choice of whether to resign or maintain their membership with its transparency obligations.

55 If such a list had existed at the time, Cameron's role as a lobbyist employed by Greensill would have been picked up. Ironically, it was Cameron who defined it beautifully in his public statement (see Chapter 14): 'We all know how it works. The lunches, the hospitality, the quiet word in your ear. The ex-ministers and ex-advisers for hire, helping big business to find the right way to get its way.'

56 Interviewed 24 March 2022.

57 Brian Tamanaha, *On the Rule of Law* (Cambridge University Press, 2004).

58 Interviewed 28 July 2022.

59 Transparency International, *Corruption Laws: A Non-lawyers' Guide to Laws and Offences in the UK Relating to Corruption Behaviour* (2016).

60 *USPL*, p. 7. The IfG in *Improving Ethical Standards in Government*, April 2021, said that a 'patchwork of enforcement bodies oversee a range of rules on standards, ethics and access'. The Transparency International evidence to *Standards Matter 2* review included this: 'There should be a holistic review of the powers and sanctions available to those involved with upholding ethical standards in public life. This is particularly important with regard to codes and bodies that regulate the Executive.'

61 Interviewed 14 February 2023.

62 Interviewed 21 September 2022.

63 Interviewed 21 September 2022.

64 Interviewed 22 March 2022.

65 Interviewed 15 September 2022.

66 Interviewed 7 February 2022. Marcial Boo, former Director of Strategy and Communications at the NAO, pointed out the difference between regulators when interviewed on 28 July 2022:

> 'Some ethical regulators have relatively strong regulatory tools. But many ethics watchdogs are in comparison rather toothless. It is in the interest of those regulated (i.e. MPs and others in positions of power and influence) for their regulators to

be weak and divided. But, in theory, there could be a stronger, unified Ethics Regulator to oversee standards of behaviour and ethics, accountable to Parliament, with parallel powers to those of economic or utility regulators.'

67 Interviewed 18 October 2022.

68 Interviewed 12 January 2023.

69 *USPL*, para. 2.46.

70 Answers to written questions, 10 March 2023.

71 *USPL*, para. 2.47.

72 See Chapter 14.

73 David Hine and Gillian Peele, *The Regulation of Standards in British Public Life: Doing the Right Thing* (Manchester University Press, 2016), p. 292.

74 *Prospect*, June 2021, p. 8. It could even be known as Ofethics, to match Ofcom and Ofgem.

75 The various allegations in respect of Johnson's relationship with Jennifer Arcuri provide another example of multiple investigations:
a. The Independent Office for Police Conduct inquiry established no connection between Johnson's friendship with Arcuri and her gaining grants from the Greater London Authority (GLA).
b. The GLA launched a long running inquiry.
c. In 2019 the Department for Culture, Media and Sport decided that there was no impropriety in the award of a grant of £100,000 to a company owned by Arcuri.

76 See Chapter 5.

77 This has been described as competitive institutional pluralism.

78 The Registrar of Consultant Lobbyists' powers are minimal, as we have seen (Chapter 10).

79 A version of this was referred to in para. 2.8 of the executive summary of the Tenth Report of the CSPL: 'A Board of Public Appointments Commissioners would create a forum for strategic thinking about public appointments. It would also enable individual commissioners to be linked to one or more department to assist in some high-profile appointments and in the creation of annual Public Appointments Plans.' CSPL, *Getting the Balance Right: Implementing Standards of Conduct in Public Life*, Tenth Report, January 2005.

80 'We are attracted by the long-term potential of this proposal which removes Ministers from the selection process.' *Ibid.*, para. 2.56.

81 It is provided for in the Constitutional Reform Act 2005, sections 63–107.

82 IfG, *Reforming Public Appointments*, 2022, p. 34.

83 Peter Oborne has said: 'The Nolan Committee has become a pale powerless spectre'. *The Assault on Truth* (Simon & Schuster, 2021), p. 112. It is the restoring of a virtuous circle that is so important. There is in fact a precedent across the Irish Sea. Enforcement of the Northern Ireland Standards Code is by an independent standards commissioner. This arose after the scandal over a renewable heat incentive in the province.

84 OCPA, *Annual Report*, 2019/2020, p. 8.

85 *The Government's Response to the 10th Report of the Committee on Standards in Public Life*, Cm 6723, 15 December 2005, p. 2.

86 Interviewed 23 March 2022.

87 See CSPL, *Getting the Balance Right*, executive summary, para. 2.10. While the Commissioner cannot halt a process, he or she can and does inform select committees when there are concerns over a competition— Sir Peter Riddell (Public Appointments Commissioner from April 2016 to September 2021) told me that 'I

worked in cooperation with select committees on potentially contentious appointments'. Interviewed 15 February 2022.

88 Commission on the UK's Future, *A New Britain: Renewing Our Democracy and Rebuilding Our Economy*, Labour Party, 5 December 2022, p. 128.

89 *USPL*, p. 10.

90 Interviewed 7 February 2022.

91 Max Weber, 'Suffrage and democracy in Germany', in *Weber: Political Writings*, ed. P. Lassman and R. Spiers (Cambridge University Press, 1994), p. 83.

Appendix

1 She resigned in December 2022 during a live radio broadcast (after Boris Johnson had left office) without any obvious progress having been made, saying she was 'on a completely different planet' to the Home Secretary, Suella Braverman. *Guardian*, 17 December 2022.

2 See *Guardian*, 30 December 2022. She claimed that Dominic Raab as Justice Secretary expected her to be a 'puppet on a string'.

3 *Guardian*, 14 April 2021.

4 In 2016, the then Culture Secretary, Karen Bradley, initially blocked Althea Efunshile's appointment to the Channel 4 board and appointed four white men instead; she had been deputy chief executive of Arts Council England.

5 CSPL, *Getting the Balance Right: Implementing Standards of Conduct in Public Life*, Tenth Report, January 2005, para. 2.114.

6 See Alan Rusbridger, 'The real plot that's hidden in Nadine Dorries' potboiler', *New European*, 20 November 2023.

7 Ministers may dismiss chairs of public bodies save that of the Office for Budgetary Responsibility, where consent of the Treasury Select Committee is needed.

8 Interviewed 12 December 2022.

9 *R (Wakenshaw)* v. *Secretary of State for Justice*, 2018, EWHC Admin 2089, para. 31.

10 Letter to Rt Hon. Chris Grayling, MP, Secretary of State for Justice, from Rt Hon. Sir Alan Beith, MP, Chair of the Justice Select Committee, 5 March 2015.

11 *Independent*, 1 May 2021.

12 Interviewed 28 March 2022.

13 This was a controversial measure designed to reduce immigration.

14 Sir Vernon made clear in a letter to the *Guardian* published on 22 December 2022 that he did not intend to criticise the late Lord Heywood: 'I never felt that Lord Heywood committed any wrong. He was simply trying to flag that there were strong interests promoting this candidate.'

Select bibliography

Ahmed, Farrah, Richard Albert and Adam Perry, 'Judging constitutional conventions', *International Journal of Constitutional Law*, 17:3 (2019), 787–806.

Applebaum, Anne, *Twilight of Democracy: The Failure of Politics and the Parting of Friends* (Allen Lane, 2020).

Bacon, Richard and Christopher Hope, *Conundrum: Why Every Government Gets Things Wrong and What We Can Do About It* (Biteback, 2013).

Barwick, Steve, *Impartiality Matters: Perspectives on the Importance of Impartiality in the Civil Service in a 'Post Truth' World* (Smith Institute, 2019).

Baston, Lewis, *Sleaze: The State of Britain* (Channel 4 Books, 2000).

Baxendale, Catherine, *How to Best Attract, Induct and Retain Talent Recruited into the Senior Civil Service* (HM Government, 2015).

Bew, John, *Citizen Clem* (Riverrun, 2016).

Bingham, Tom, *The Rule of Law* (Penguin, 2010).

Blick, Andrew, *People Who Live in the Dark: The History of Special Advisers in British Politics* (Politico's/Methuen, 2004).

Bond, Matthew, 'Elite social relations and corporate political donations in Britain', *Political Studies*, 55:1 (2007), 59–85.

Boo, Marcial, *The Rules of Democracy* (Policy Press, 2022).

Bower, Tom, *Boris Johnson: The Gambler* (W. H. Allen, 2020).

Bryant, Chris, *Code of Conduct: Why We Need to Fix Parliament – And How To Do It* (Bloomsbury, 2023).

Cave, Tamasin and Andy Rowell, *A Quiet Word: Lobbying* (Bodley Head, 2014).

Christophers, Brett, *Rentier Capitalism* (Verso 2020).

Clark, Tom, 'Where have all the good chaps gone?', *Prospect*, March 2022.

Constitution Unit, University College London, *Parliament's Watchdogs*, July 2022.

Corstens, Geert, *Understanding the Rule of Law* (Bloomsbury, 2017).

Craig, Paul, 'Formal and substantive conceptions of the rule of law', *Public Law* (1997), 467–487.

Crewe, Emma and Andrew Walker, *An Extraordinary Scandal* (Haus Publishing, 2019).

Crick, Michael, *One Party After Another* (Simon and Schuster, 2022).

Cullen, Tom, *Maundy Gregory Purveyor of Honours* (Bodley Head, 1974).

David-Barrett, Elizabeth, 'Shirking Self-Regulation? Parliamentary standards in the UK', *Public Integrity* (2022), DOI: 10.1080/10999922.2022.2075632.

Davis, Aeron, *Reckless Opportunists* (Manchester University Press, 2018).

Dicey, A. V., *Introduction to the Study of the Law of the Constitution* (Macmillan, 1959 edition).

Donaldson, Frances, *The Marconi Scandal* (Bloomsbury, 2013).

Dowding, Keith, *The Civil Service* (Routledge, 1995).

Eggers, Andrew C. and Jens Hainmueller, *MPs for Sale? Returns to Office in Postwar British Politics* (Cambridge University Press, 2009).

Elliott, Mark and Robert Thomas, *Public Law: The Fundamentals* (Oxford University Press, 2020).

Ford, Rob *et al.*, *The British General Election of 2019* (Palgrave Macmillan, 2021).

Fukuyama, Francis, *The Origins of Political Order* (Profile Books, 2011).

Fukuyama, Francis, *Political Order and Political Decay* (Profile Books, 2014).

Gay, Oonagh and Barry Winetrobe, 'Watchdogs of the constitution: the biters bit?', in *Constitution Futures Revisited: Britain's Constitution to 2020*, ed. Robert Hazell (Palgrave, 2008), pp. 197–214.

Geoghegan, Peter, *Democracy for Sale: Dark Money and Dirty Politics* (Head of Zeus, 2020).

Gimson, Andrew, *Boris Johnson: The Rise and Fall of a Troublemaker at Number 10* (Simon and Schuster, 2022).

Guinote, Ana, 'How power affects people: activating, wanting, and goal seeking', *Annual Review of Psychology*, 68:1 (2017), 353–381.

Hacker, Jacob S. and Paul Pierson, *Winner-Take-All Politics: How Washington Made the Rich Richer and Turned Its Back on the Middle Class* (Simon and Schuster, 2010).

Hailsham, Lord ,*The Government Machine: The Dilemma of Democracy* (Collins, 1978).

Hardman, Isabel, *Why We Get the Wrong Politicians* (Atlantic, 2018).

Hazell, Robert, 'Improving Parliamentary scrutiny of public appointments', *Parliamentary Affairs*, 72:2 (2018), 223–244.

Hennessy, Peter, *Whitehall* (Fontana, 1989).

Hine, David and Gillian Peele, *The Regulation of Standards in British Public Life: Doing the Right Thing* (Manchester University Press, 2016).

Hodge, Margaret, *Called to Account* (Abacus, 2016).

Jaconelli, Joseph, 'The nature of constitutional convention', *Legal Studies*, 19:1 (1999), 24–46.

King, Anthony and Ivor Crewe, *The Blunders of Our Governments* (Oneworld, 2013).

Kuper, Simon, *Chums: How a Tiny Caste of Oxford Tories Took Over the UK* (Profile, 2022).

Leigh, David and Ed Vulliamy, *Sleaze* (Fourth Estate, 1997).

Lester, Anthony, *Five Ideas to Fight For* (Oneworld, 2016).

Levy, Lord, *A Question of Honour: Inside New Labour and the True Story of the Cash for Peerages Scandal* (Simon and Schuster, 2008).

Mavin, Duncan, *The Pyramid of Lies* (Macmillan, 2022).

Mell, A., S. Radford and S. Thévoz, 'Is there a market for peerages?', University of Oxford Working Paper 744, 2015.

Norton, Philip, *Governing Britain* (Manchester University Press, 2020).

O'Toole, Fintan, *Heroic Failure* (Head of Zeus, 2018).

Oborne, Peter, *The Assault on Truth* (Simon and Schuster, 2021).

Orwell, George, *The Lion and the Unicorn* (Read, 2020 reprint).

Owen, Jones, *The Establishment: And How They Get Away With It* (Allen Lane, 2014).

Paxman, Jeremy, *The Political Animal* (Penguin, 2002).

Payne, Sebastian, *Broken Heartlands* (Macmillan, 2021).

Payne, Sebastian, *The Fall of Boris Johnson* (Macmillan, 2022).

Perry, Adam and Adam Tucker, 'Top-down constitutional conventions', *Modern Law Review*, 81:5 (2018), 765–789.

Philip, Mark, 'The corruption of politics', *Social Philosophy and Policy*, 35:2 (2018), 73–93.

Purnell, Sonia, *Just Boris: A Tale of Blond Ambition* (Aurum Press, 2012).

Putnam, Robert D. and Shaylyn Romney Garrett, *The Upswing* (Simon and Schuster, 2020).

Raz, Joseph, *The Authority of Law* (Oxford University Press, 2009).

Riddell, Peter, *15 Minutes of Power: The Uncertain Life of British Ministers* (Profile Books, 2019).

Rose, Jonathan and Paul Heywood, 'Political science approaches to integrity and corruption', *Human Affairs*, 23:2 (2013), 148–159.

Rozenberg, Joshua, *Enemies of the People* (Bristol University Press, 2020).

Runciman, David, *How Democracy Ends* (Profile, 2019).

Searle, G. R., *Corruption in British Politics 1895–1930* (Oxford University Press, 1987).

Sumption, Jonathan, *Trials of the State* (Profile, 2019.

Thomas-Symonds, Nick, *Harold Wilson the Winner* (Weidenfeld and Nicholson, 2022).

Vibert, Frank, *The Rise of the Unelected: Democracy and the New Separation of Powers* (Cambridge University Press, 2007).

Wagner, Adam, *Emergency State: How We Lost Our Freedoms in the Pandemic and Why It Matters* (Bodley Head, 2022).

Waldron, Jeremy, 'The rule of law and the importance of procedure', *Nomos*, 50 (2011), 3–31.

Walzer, Michael, *Thinking Politically* (Yale University Press, 2007).

Weschle, Simon, 'Parliamentary positions and politicians' private sector earnings: evidence from the UK House of Commons', *Journal of Politics*, 83:2 (2020), 706–721.

White, Hannah, *Held in Contempt* (Manchester University Press, 2022).

Young, Alison, *Turpin & Tomkins' British Government and the Constitution Text and Materials*, 8th edition (Oxford University Press, 2021).

Index